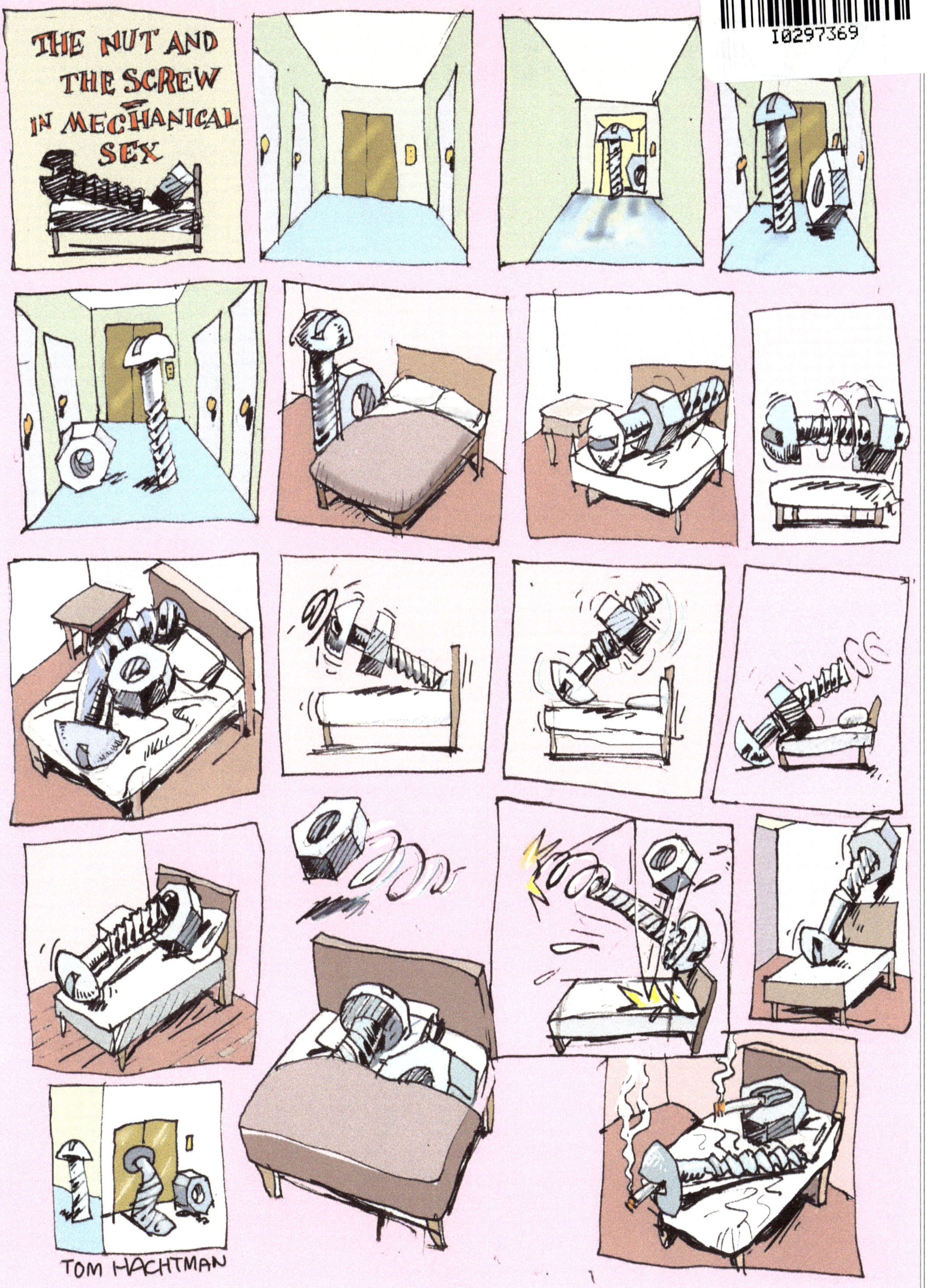
THE NUT AND THE SCREW IN MECHANICAL SEX
TOM HACHTMAN

PUBLISHER'S LETTER
BY MICHAEL GERBER
CIVIL DISOBEDIENCE
Well, maybe not exactly civil

It seems that my old dog Gus is establishing quite a following among *Bystander* readers. I am not surprised. Gus was a rogue, a charmer, the guy in the bar that things just happen to. He generated more incident in his three-and-a-half year stint in our family than the rest of our pets combined.

For example: one day in the autumn of 1976, my dad's big green Impala got towed. This was, and probably still is, a regular occurance — the world is one big parking spot to my Dad. Further, I'm sure that the presence of Gus in the backseat was no mistake; it would buy him a little more leeway. Dad did this to me, too. "I'll be back in a second," he'd say, putting on his flashers and darting out before I had a chance to protest. And then I'd sit there, seconds dragging like hours, hoping no cops would show. More than once, they did, and I sweated and stammered until my Dad came rushing out of O'Connell's or Llywellyn's or whatever place of employment/recreation he'd dashed into. Like Gus, my dad is a bit of a rogue.

Apparently dogs are not as much of a deterrent as strangely professorial little boys, and so that day the Impala was hauled, Gus and all, to the lot. I can only imagine the swearing — not only for the ticket, but for the possible damage a wrathful and confused Gus could dole out. Mere weeks before, Gus had destroyed the entire backseat of my mother's orange Mazda during one short softball practice, ripping great chunks of yellow foam out of the upholstery. (If you've ever seen a Great White go at a whale carcass, it was like that.)

But today Dad was lucky. When he got to the lot, Gus was standing on the backseat, watching and waiting like a Nantucket captain's wife. When he saw Dad, it was like the end of a silent movie. With barking. *Lots* of barking.

I've been thinking about Gus lately, what he'd say if he were here today. Most dogs, like first-born children, are rule-followers — a bit too much so. Gus wasn't like that. He knew that there were some times when a little hell-raising was not only justified, it was necessary.

During my second-grade year, Dad, Mom and I lived in the best apartment we ever had. It was big, cheap, and right across from my school. Built for the 1904 World's Fair, it had all sorts of old-fashioned touches, like a working fireplace, a walk-in closet my dad turned into a darkroom, and a little butler's pantry off the hall.

Both my parents worked — at the pubs I mentioned earlier — and so every morning Gus would be walked and fed, then cruelly tricked into going into the butler's pantry. Once he was inside, the pocket door would be slid shut, and he would be safely sequestered until one of my parents came back for lunch.

Gus hated it in there; roughly 4 feet by 6 feet, with a small window at the far end, it was his version of *Midnight Express*. He seemed outraged anew every morning when, lured by his food or a toy, the door would slide shut and he would be tricked again. After a while, I wouldn't do it anymore — I couldn't take the look of betrayal. Since we were only on the first floor, Gus could watch us through the small window as we crossed the street to my school. If you don't think a bark can have righteous indignation in it, you're wrong.

All day at school, I tried not to think of Gus in that little room with nothing to do, no one to be with. I'd put a ball in there, or a chewbone, but how long would that last, an hour? I imagined him in there, playing harmonica, rattling a tin cup against the metal screen of the window.

I knew Gus missed us. I could tell at 3:30, when school let out and all us kids spilled out of the doors and onto the lawn, I'd see him, standing up on his hind legs, watching for me. When he saw me, he'd start barking, and his tail would begin wagging so hard you could see it in his shoulders.

"Hi Gussie!" my friends and I would yell. "Good dog! I'll be right there!" When I'd get home, he'd be so happy he'd run circles around me. He'd always knock me down, but I didn't hold it against him; with cerebral palsy, everything knocks you down.

One bright spring afternoon — about six months after Gus's trip to the St. Louis Municipal Tow Lot — we were milling around in the post-educational glow when my friend Rolf pointed at Gus in the window. "Wow, your dog is getting big."

"He's not done either," I said. "He has humongous paws. Look—" I pulled my shirt collar and exposed a bruise on my shoulder. "There's one on the other side, too."

MICHAEL GERBER (@mgerber937) is Editor & Publisher of *The American Bystander*.

EDWARD SOREL

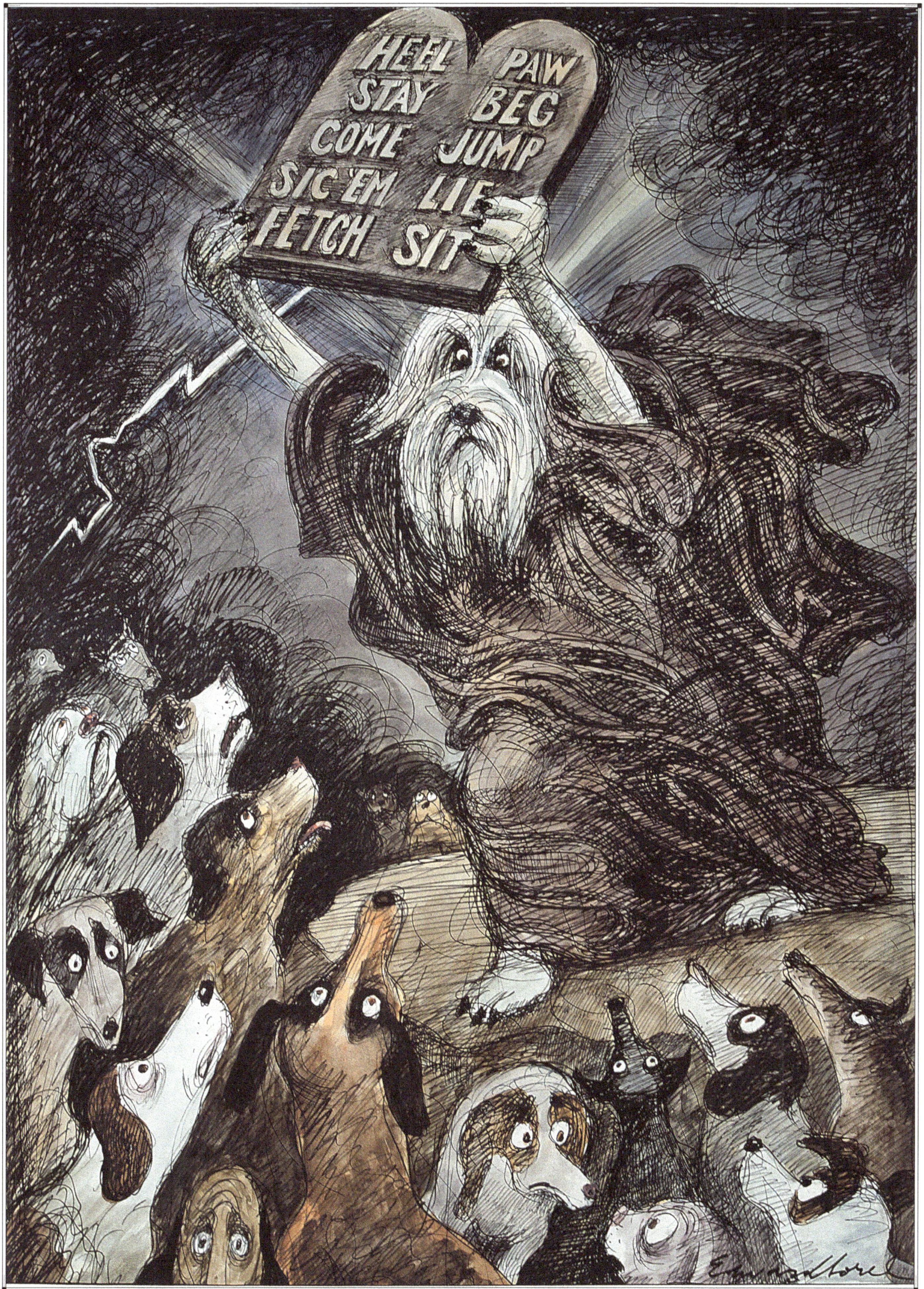
HEEL PAW
STAY BEG
COME JUMP
SIC'EM LIE
FETCH SIT

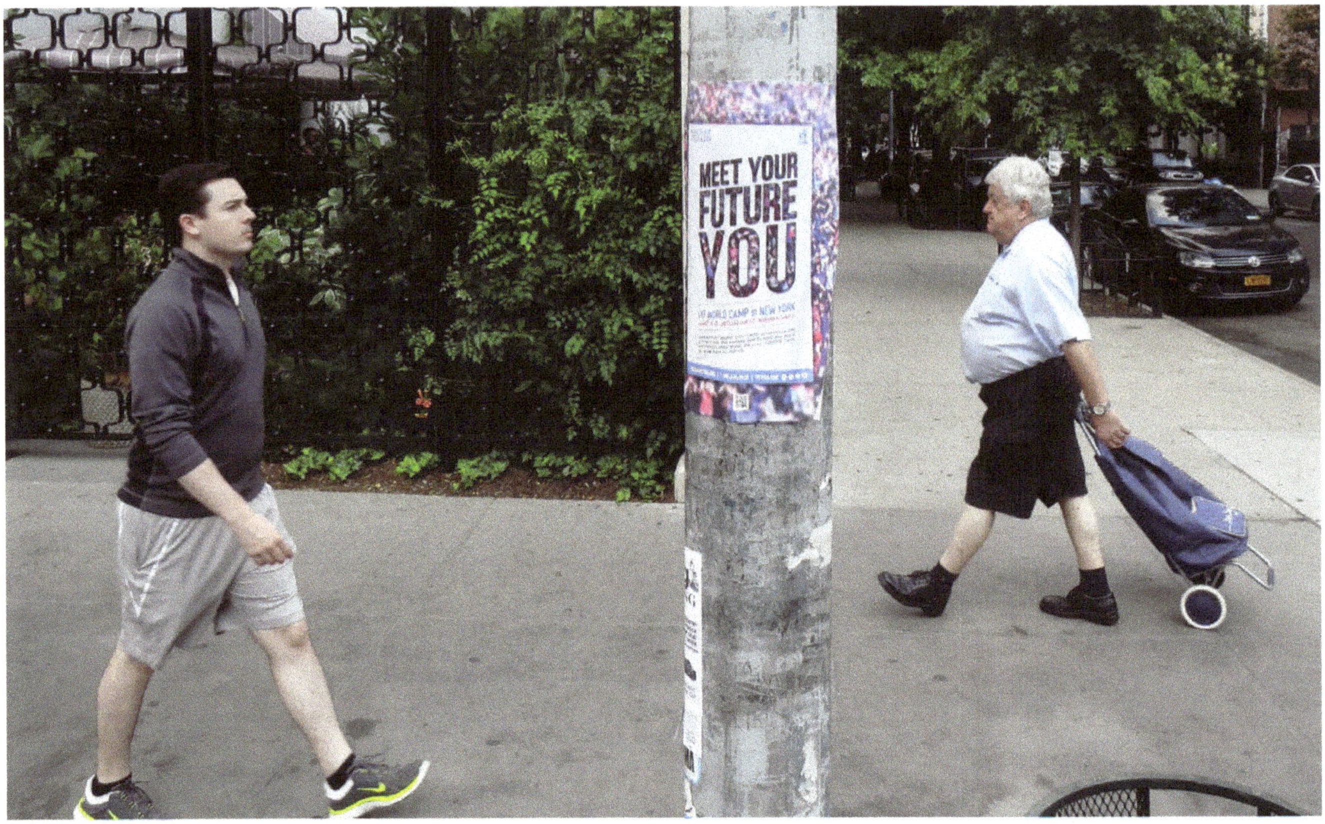
MEET YOUR
FUTURE
YOU

CHUCK PINKLE

"Jeez." I saw Rolf reach into his backpack. He pulled out a tennis ball, and waved it over his head. "Here, Gussie!"

Instinctively, I leapt in front of Rolf, hoping to block Gus's view. Rolf was messing with forces beyond his comprehension. The poor kid, with his boring, well-ordered life, unchewed books, unchewed shoes, unchewed woodwork. He was just trying to be nice; how could he know that Gus was a soda shaken for six months straight?

I looked over my shoulder at the window. Gus had stopped barking but was still there. "Put that away!" I hissed. "*He'll see it*."

"Where did he go?" Rolf said. I looked again. Gus was gone.

Everything that happened next, I remember in slow motion. A second, or a minute, later, Gus came barreling through that window, shreds of screen and bits of window frame falling to the sidewalk. He hit the ground already at a run; it was pure luck that there were no cars coming down the street, which he crossed in two gallops.

The kids around us were electrified, laughing, shrieking; a few scared ones ran inside to get an adult. As if that would help; grownups were, for Gus, a welcome challenge.

Gus sat at attention, transfixed on the fuzzy yellow Heaven in Rolf's hand. He backed off, waiting for the boy to throw it. Rolf hesitated — a fatal mistake. Gus closed on him in a bound and suddenly had his big paws firmly on Rolf's 7-year-old shoulders. Rolf toppled, and the ball bounced away. With his Lab's dexterous mouth, Gus snagged the ball effortlessly.

Only then did Gus notice the knot of shrieking children around him. Reading the crowd, the black dog began running around us all in figure-eights, daring all and sundry to try to catch him. Anyone who got close, he'd evade with a shrug of the shoulder, a lateral hop, or a burst of speed. I swear that mutt was part racehorse.

The game only got serious when one of my teachers arrived. Then the kids instantly switched to Gus's side, and cheered him as he evaded one, two, three adults. And when Gus peed on the side of the school, it was a sensation.

Finally Gus got tired, and allowed himself to be captured. The sweaty, red-faced Principal (he looked old to me, but was probably younger than I am now) grabbed Gus firmly by the collar and led him over to me. "Is this really your dog?" I momentarily considered lying, but Gus was already licking my hand.

"Where do you live?" Before I could respond, the Principal spied the window. "Forget I asked. Let's go."

When they came home, at first my parents didn't believe my story — I was, shall we say, an *imaginative* child — but the busted screen was mute witness to what had occurred.

"Greg," my mother said. "Maybe we shouldn't put the dog in there anymore?"

My dad nodded. From then on, my parents worked it out so that one of the three of us was with the dog during the days. The screen was easily fixed and, point made, Gus seemed calmer after that.

We'd learned our lesson — we'd been unreasonable, selfish. Gus had suffered, been pushed too far, and had made his point. Gus was never a bad dog — heck, he was probably smarter than the rest of us put together. Which is how he knew that sometimes you need a little disobedience to remind everyone: we're a family. Don't be an asshole. B

SPRINGFIELD CONFIDENTIAL

JOKES, SECRETS, AND OUTRIGHT LIES FROM A LIFETIME WRITING FOR The Simpsons

"A truly great comic is rare. Mike Reiss, by definition, is a rarity." —CONAN O'BRIEN

In celebration of *The Simpsons* 30th anniversary, the show's longest-serving writer and producer shares stories, scandals, and gossip about working with AMERICA'S MOST ICONIC CARTOON FAMILY.

Featuring interviews with JUDD APATOW, CONAN O'BRIEN, and *Simpsons* legends AL JEAN, NANCY CARTWRIGHT, DAN CASTELLANETA, and more!

ON SALE NOW

DEY ST.
www.hc.com

TABLE OF CONTENTS

VICTOR JUHASZ

DEPARTMENTS
Frontispiece: "Mechanical Sex" *by Tom Hachtman* 1
Publisher's Letter *by Michael Gerber* 2
News and Notes 11
Classifieds 95
Index to This Issue *by Steve Young* 97
Crossword: "*Alternative Musicals*" *by Matera & Goldberg* 98

GALLIMAUFRY
J. Keohane, J. Zeller, D. Lancaster, B. McConnachie, P. Barr, R. McGee, L. Gardner, T. Chitty, L. Kenseth, J. F. Garner, D. & M. Reiss, A. Schmidt, M. Balmain, B. Katchor, E. Waite.

SHORT STUFF
Evidence of Russian Medaling *by Ron Hauge* 5
American Bystanders #5 *by Drew Friedman* 7
Pursued by Wasps *by John Jonik* 14
An Oral History *by Simon Rich* 29
Alien Notes on the Voyager Space Probe Golden Record
 by Steve Young 30
After Breakfast *by Emily Flake* 32
All the Scenes in *Meet Cute* *by Jonathan Zeller* 34
#Whynotmetoo? *by Laurie Rosenwald* 36
Comparing Things to Jazz is Like… Jazz *by Rob Kutner* ... 38
New Offerings From Your Alumni Educational Travel
 by Chris Marcil & Sam Johnson 40

FEATURES
Your Future Home *by Tom Chitty* 42
Comic Character Cursing Dictionary *by Ed Subitzky* 47

The AMERICAN BYSTANDER

#8 • Vol. 2, No. 4 • Summer 2018

EDITOR & PUBLISHER
Michael Gerber
HEAD WRITER Brian McConnachie
SENIOR EDITOR Alan Goldberg
DEPUTY EDITORS
Michael Thornton, Ben Orlin
CONTACTEE Scott Marshall
INTREPID TRAVELER Mike Reiss
ORACLE Steve Young
STAFF LIAR P.S. Mueller

CONTRIBUTORS
Gurgen Aloian, Melissa Balmain, Penny Barr, Charles Barsotti, R.O. Blechman, George Booth, Steve Brodner, Dylan Brody, M.K. Brown, David Chelsea, Tom Chitty, Seymour Chwast, Howard Cruse, John Cuneo, Olivia de Recat, Matthew Disler, Joe Dottino, Randall Enos, Chuck Finkle, Emily Flake, Shary Flenniken, James Folta, Drew Friedman, Lucas Gardner, James Finn Garner, Rick Geary, Sam Gross, Robert Grossman, Tom Hachtman, Kaamran Hafeez, David Harnden-Warwick, Andrew Hamm, Charlie Hankin, Dave Hanson, Sidney Harris, Ron Hauge, Sam Johnson, John Jonik, Ted Jouflas, Victor Juhasz, Ben Katchor, Lars Kenseth, Joe Keohane, Stephen Kroninger, Rob Kutner, Sara Lautman, Bill Lee, Richard Littler, Stan Mack, Navied Mahdavian, Chris Marcil, Matt Matera, Zoe Matthiessen, Robert McGee, John McNamee, Ryan Nyburg, David Ostow, Ethan Persoff, Jonathan Plotkin, Mike Reddy, Denise Reiss, Simon Rich, Laurie Rosenwald, Alex Schmidt, Cris Shapan, Mike Shiell, Michael Sloan, Edward Sorel, Rich Sparks, Nick Spooner, Ed Subitzky, P.C. Vey, Dan Vebber, Dirk Voetberg, Evan Waite, D. Watson, and Jonathan Zeller.

COPYEDITING
Kate Powers, God bless 'er
THANKS TO
Rae Barsotti, Lanky Bareikis, Jon Schwarz, Alleen Schultz, Molly Bernstein, Joe Lopez, Eliot Ivanhoe, Neil Gumenick, Thomas Simon, Greg and Patricia Gerber and many, many others.
NAMEPLATES BY
Mark Simonson
ISSUE CREATED BY
Michael Gerber

Vol. 2, No.4. ©2018 Good Cheer LLC, all rights reserved. Proudly produced in California, USA.

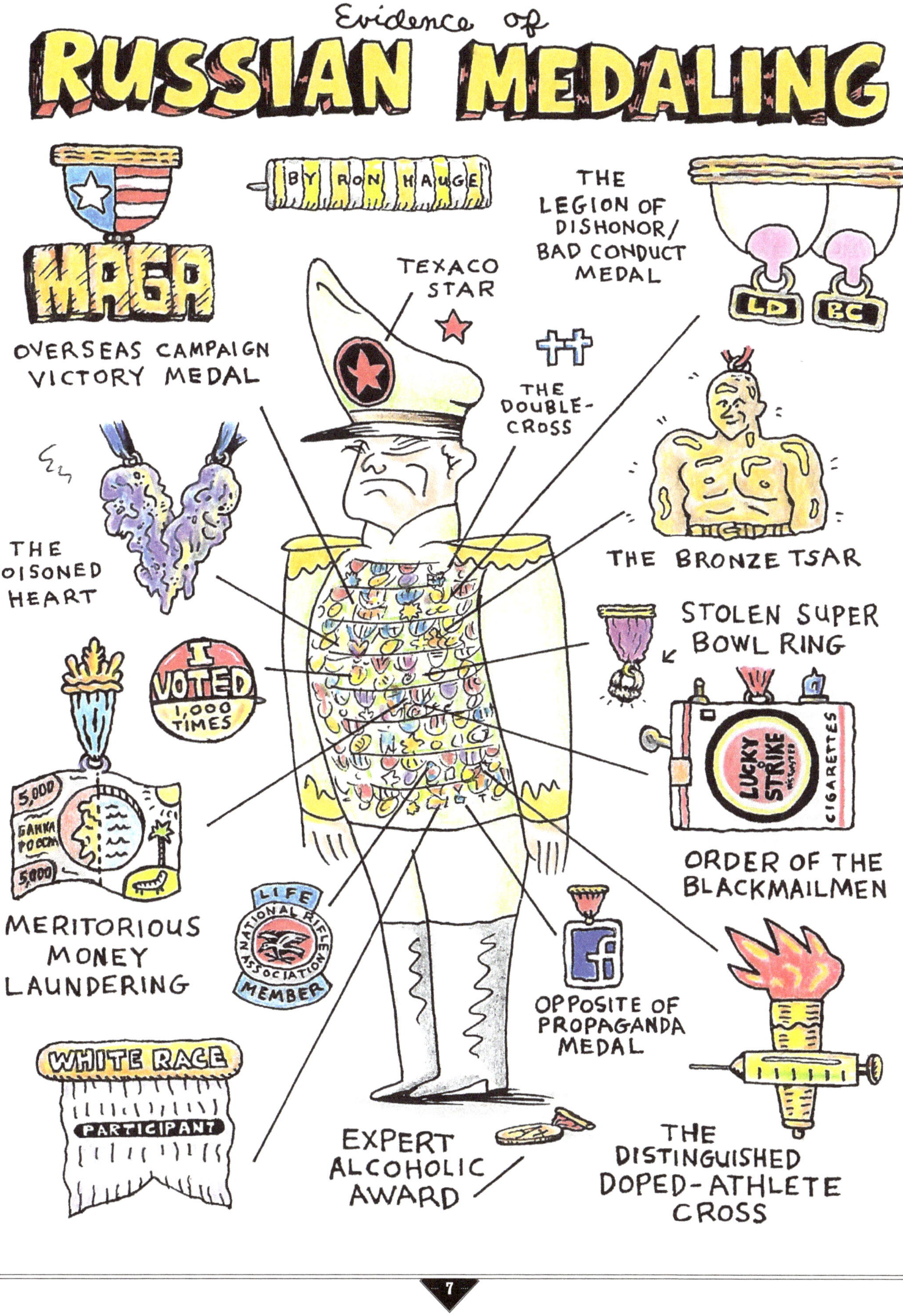
Evidence of
RUSSIAN MEDALING
BY RON HAUGE
MAGA
OVERSEAS CAMPAIGN VICTORY MEDAL
TEXACO STAR
THE LEGION OF DISHONOR/ BAD CONDUCT MEDAL
LD
BC
THE DOUBLE-CROSS
THE POISONED HEART
THE BRONZE TSAR
STOLEN SUPER BOWL RING
I VOTED 1,000 TIMES
LUCKY STRIKE
CIGARETTES
ORDER OF THE BLACKMAILMEN
5,000
MERITORIOUS MONEY LAUNDERING
LIFE
NATIONAL RIFLE ASSOCIATION
MEMBER
OPPOSITE OF PROPAGANDA MEDAL
WHITE RACE
PARTICIPANT
EXPERT ALCOHOLIC AWARD
THE DISTINGUISHED DOPED-ATHLETE CROSS

Piano Lessons *by Brian McConnachie*	48
A History of the Freline Notebook *by Ostow & Reddy*	51
Just Worried *by M.K. Brown*	52
Originalism…For Your Life! *by Lars Kenseth*	54
Enjoy Your Stay *by Ryan Nyburg*	56
Son of Twisted Cross *by Sam Gross*	58
Works *by Dylan Brody*	59
Welcome to Scarfolk *by Richard Littler*	64
Generation WHAAH?! *by Dan Vebber*	69

MARVY

Cover *by Bill Lee*	71
Quiet, Billy, There's No Time For That *by Randall Enos*	72
Free Love With Jan & Stan *by Persoff & Marshall*	73
Dog Show *by Ted Jouflas*	74
The Basic Overview *by Howard Cruse*	75
Mom and Me *by Rick Geary*	76
My Extraordinary Dream *by Michael Sloan*	77
Trots & Bonnie *by Shary Flenniken*	81
Gertrude's Follies *by Tom Hachtman & Sam Gross*	82
Kama Sutra for Cats *by Seymour Chwast*	83

OUR BACK PAGES

What Am I Doing Here?: Nepal *by Mike Reiss*	85
P.S. Mueller Thinks Like This *by P.S. Mueller*	87
Chunk-Style Nuggets *by Steve Young*	89
Know Your Bystanders *by Laurie Rosenwald*	91

CARTOONS & ILLUSTRATIONS BY

G. Aloian, P. Barr, C. Barsotti, R.O. Blechman, G. Booth, S. Brodner, M.K. Brown, D. Chelsea, T. Chitty, J. Cuneo, O. de Recat, J. Dottino, C. Finkle, E. Flake, D. Friedman, S. Gross, R. Grossman, K. Hafeez, D. Harnden-Warwick, A. Hamm, C. Hankin, S. Harris, R. Hauge, J. Jonik, B. Katchor, L. Kenseth, S. Kroninger, P. Kuper, S. Lautman, B. Lee, S. Mack, N. Mahdavian, Z. Matthiessen, P.S. Mueller, D. Ostow, J. Plotkin, M. Reddy, L. Rosenwald, C. Shapan, M. Shiell, E. Sorel, R. Sparks, E. Subitzky, P.C. Vey and D. Watson.

"Oh no! Not Klan chowder again!"

COVER

A crack of the bat and it's a home run (as usual) by Barry Blitt, who surely did not get through this entire assignment without hearing about the time my black Lab ate a baseball signed by the ol' Bambino himself. Deep thanks to Barry for almost curing the PTSD seared into me by that memory. $5,000, folks. In *1989* dollars.

ACKNOWLEDGMENTS

All material is ©2018 its creators, all rights reserved; please do not reproduce or distribute it without written consent of the creators and *The American Bystander*. The following material has previously appeared, and is reprinted here with permission of the author(s): The posters in "Welcome to Scarfolk" first appeared on the website www.scarfolk.blogspot.com. They appear courtesy of the author.

THE AMERICAN BYSTANDER, *Vol. 2, No. 4*, (ISBN 978-0-692-18433-2). Publishes ~4x/year. ©2018 by Good Cheer LLC. No part of this magazine can be reproduced, in whole or in part, by any means, without the written permission of the Publisher. For this and other queries, email *Publisher@americanbystander.org*, or write: Michael Gerber, Publisher, *The American Bystander*, 1122 Sixth St., #403, Santa Monica, CA 90403. Subscribe at www.patreon.com/bystander. Other info can be found at www.americanbystander.org.

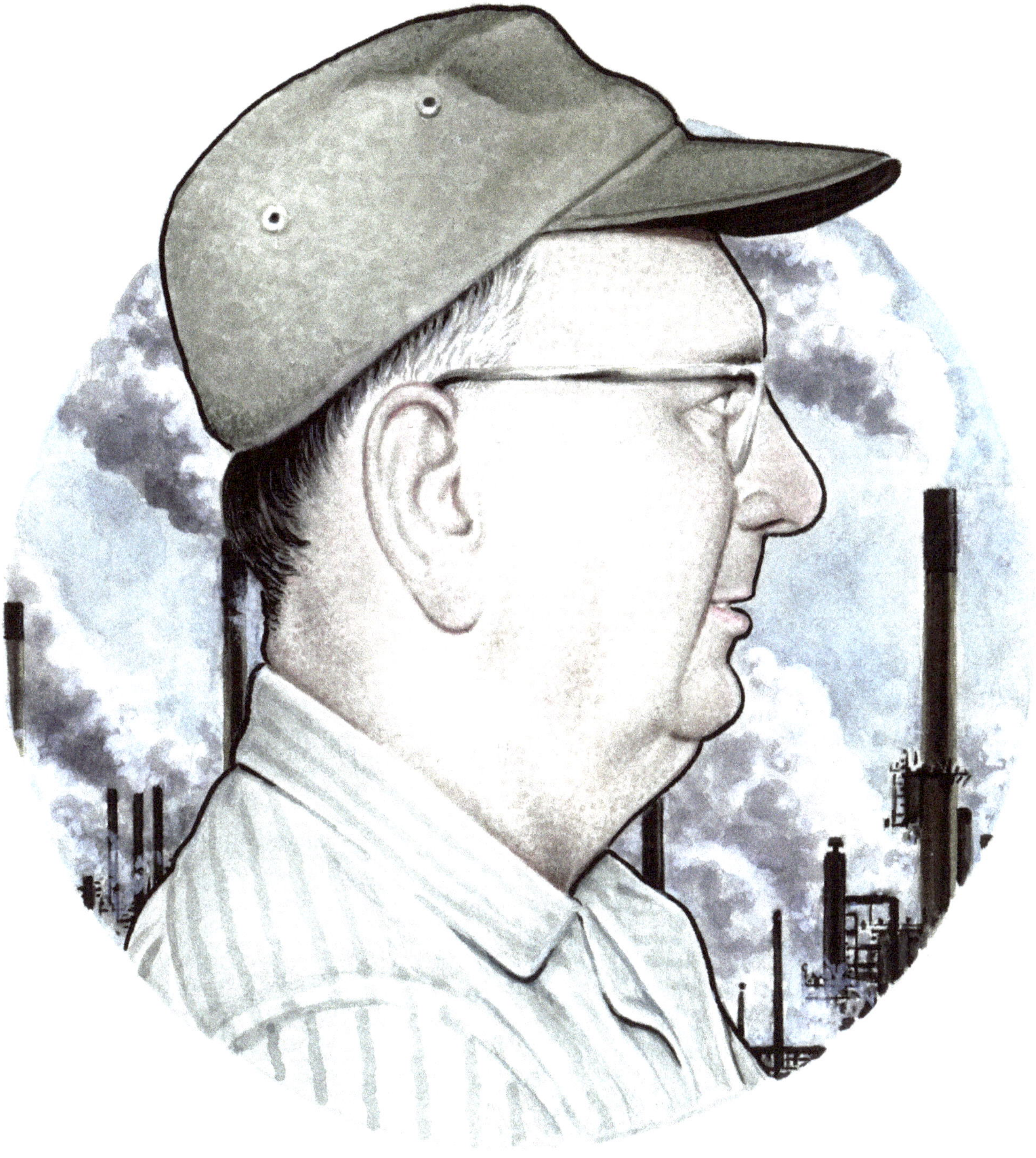

American Bystanders #5

Ed McLoins

THE HOT LIST

Orgone boxes **HOT!** *Potting sheds* **NOT.** *Fantasy football* **HOT!** *Fantasy chess* **NOT.** *Polka dots* **HOT!** *Little anchors* **NOT.** *Montenegro* **HOT!** *Montevideo* **NOT.** *Drag queens* **HOT!** *Wearing your shirt backwards by mistake* **NOT.** *Cesar Chavez* **HOT!** *Caesar salads — in fact, any type of salad* **NOT.** *Jacques Tati* **HOT!** *Capucine* **EVEN HOTTER!** *Deerstalker hats* **HOT!** *What chefs wear, what are those? Toques?* **NOT.** *That spice that smells like armpits* **HOT!** *Anything that smells like lemons but isn't lemons* **NOT.** *Enemas* **HOT!** *What am I saying, of course they are* **NOT.** **ON OUR RADAR:** *The name "Rougned"…Dimes…Talking to your plants…Bowling…Night sweats…Shaved eyebrows.*

NEW FROM SIMON RICH

"One of the funniest writers in America."
—NPR

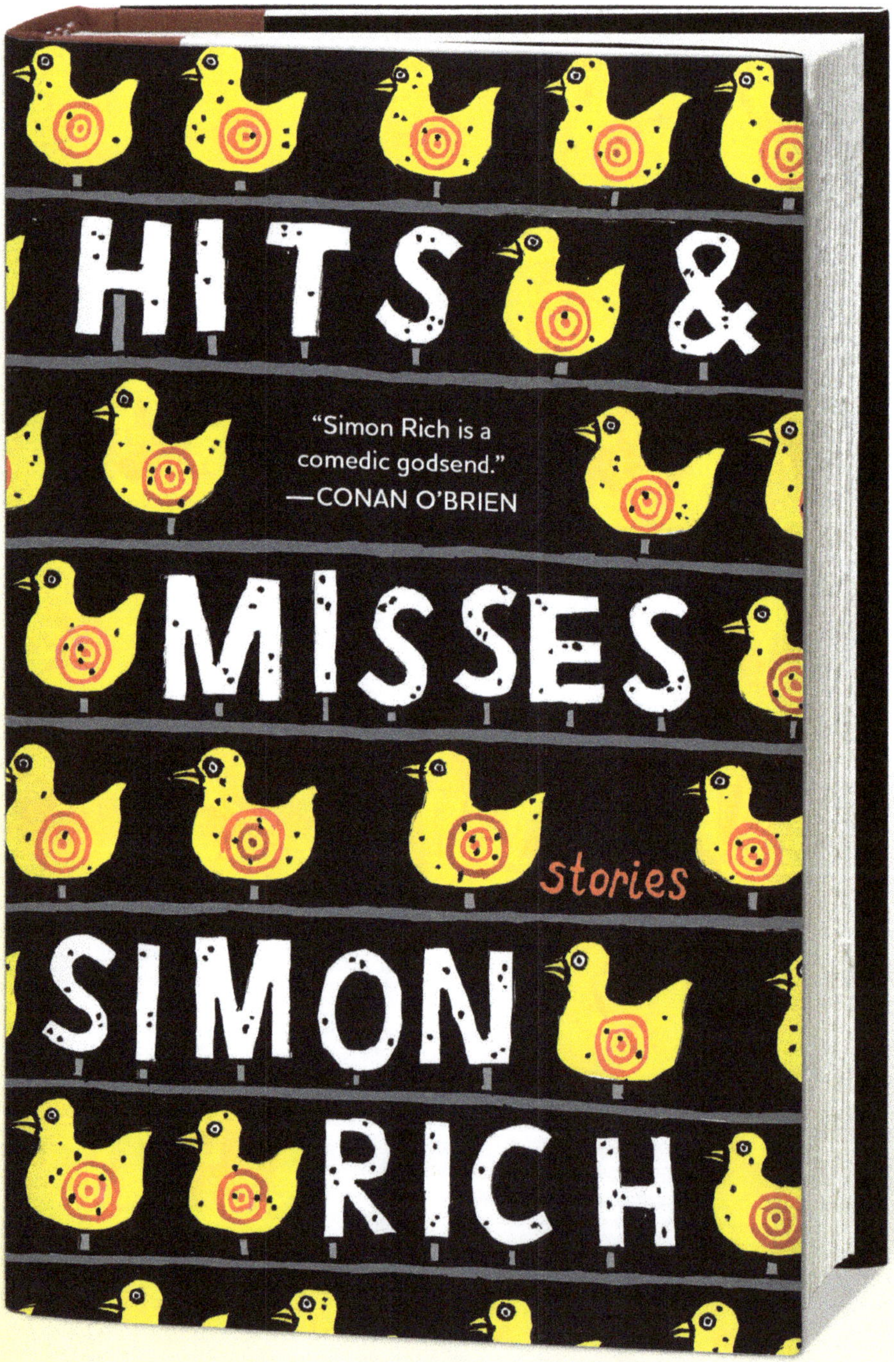

"A motherlode of silly, inventive, absurd brilliance."
—CONAN O'BRIEN

"First-rate comedy with a heartbeat.... One of my favorite authors."
—B.J. NOVAK

"The Stephen King of comedy writing.... HITS AND MISSES is his best collection of stories."
—JOHN MULANEY

ON SALE NOW
in hardcover, ebook, and audio
littlebrown.com

LITTLE, BROWN AND COMPANY
Hachette Book Group

NEWS & NOTES

We've seen fire and we've seen rain and we've seen Wire Fox Terriers

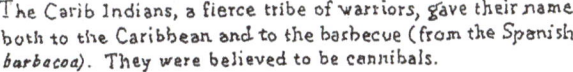

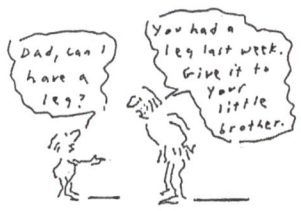

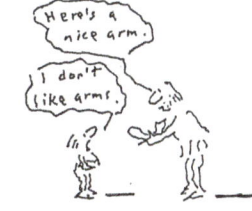

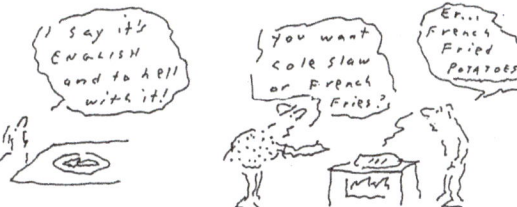

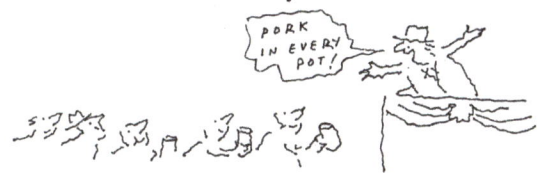

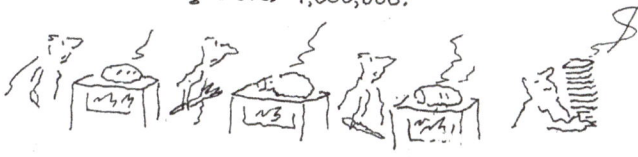

So, what are *we* doing this summer? It varies. Damp-footed **NICK SPOONER** reports that he is "perfecting the art of quahogging without a permit. It's going swimmingly."... Though his feet were dry, **PAUL LANDER** spent all of July in court. "Actually, it was only one day, but if you've ever spent time in Van Nuys—" Understood, Paul... **GEOFFREY GOLDEN** and **AMANDA MEADOWS** attended a summer wedding in the woods, in formal wear, in 95-degree heat. It was, astoundingly, also a potluck. "We dined," Geoffrey writes, "on the finest lukewarm grocery store potato salad money can buy." Be sure to check under your cummerbund for ticks... Not surprisingly, **BOB ECKSTEIN** drew and cracked wise at the Book Expo. Very surprisingly, he also headlined for the Steampunk Festival... **TED JOUFLAS** is training a male Lakeland Terrier puppy, while at the same time attempting to explain to his three-year-old female Wire Fox Terrier that "even though he may seem like it, the new dog isn't the greatest toy that I've ever brought home." Be vigilant, Ted. Sounds like there might be puppies in your future... This summer, **P.S. MUELLER** and his wife are "living like people in the paintings of Breugel The Elder, except without all that fire and death." To which I say: come to California, Pete; we've got plenty... **HOWARD CRUSE** says he's having fun designing cover art for the album that "my third cousin's cool band, *Sober Up Pussycat*, will be putting out soon." But the news gets better: "It's not for some dinky CD jewel case; it's going to be a full-on 12" x12" album like the ones I grooved on in my twenties. Hooray for the resurgence of vinyl!"... **JAMES FOLTA** has been working on some writing projects — and diligently researching "tanning," "beaches," "boogie boarding," *et cetera*, so he's not caught flat-footed *next* summer, too...

The All-American Barbecue
The Carib Indians, a fierce tribe of warriors, gave their name both to the Caribbean and to the barbecue (from the Spanish barbacoa). They were believed to be cannibals.
Dad, can I have a leg?
You had a leg last week. Give it to your little brother.
Here's a nice arm.
I don't like arms.
According to some historians, the Caribs preferred Frenchmen to Englishmen.
The custom of grilling meat was imported to North America where pork and beef replaced the French and English.
I say it's ENGLISH and to hell with it!
You want cole slaw or French Fries?
Er... French Fried POTATOES?!
In the Nineteenth Century, barbecues became a popular way to lobby for votes, the barbecue often enlivened by liberal (so to speak) amounts of whiskey.
PORK IN EVERY POT!
Today there are over 400 barbecue contests in America, the prizes amounting to over $1,000,000.

R.O. BLECHMAN

SECRET BONUS PIECE: This issue, as you know, took forever. As the whole thing was being copyedited — which in a normal magazine, means NO MORE NEW STUFF — **MATTHEW DISLER** sent in the following, which is charming and timely and, given that *Bystander* is not a normal magazine and we are rebels and let's be honest the world may not even be here in twelve months, we thought, "What the hell. YOLO, dudes." So enjoy.

It's the dog days of summer, and you know what that means. Trips to the beach. Swimming in lakes. Hiking with your buddies and then sitting under the shade of a tree, licking each other's faces to show affection.

It's a time to get together with the family for picnics and barbecues, to scarf down anything that falls off the table. It is a time of plenty, and there is so much to taste! It's a time to eat grapes for the first time and then to realize that grapes are poisonous to you. It's a time to rush to the doctor for some induced vomiting.

Ah, the dog days of summer! I have such memories. It was during the dog days of summer that I fell in love for the first time. She lived next door, and my parents disapproved because she "wasn't the right breed." But the dog days of summer are when life springs forth and love reigns. It was just like *Romeo and Juliet*, if Romeo had his testicles surgically removed afterward.

The dog days of summer are the season of classic summer experiences, like when you go out in the woods with your old man and he shoots a duck out of the sky and you run into the river and return with an interestingly-shaped stick and he screams at you until you think that you did something wrong. But it's not your fault, you tell yourself that night. It's his fault for not understanding you, for trying to turn you into something you're not. Maybe during another season you would have been harder on yourself, but not during the dog days of summer.

The dog days of summer are when you grow up.

The dog days of summer are for getting hit on the nose with a newspaper and asking, "Why?" No one will provide a satisfactory answer. There will be shouts and screams, but to you it is all gibberish.

You ponder whether the universe has any meaning during the dog days of summer. "What am I here for?" you might ask. "Am I just meant to provide pleasure? Do I have any purpose of my own?" The universe is silent. You go out onto the freeway, roll down the car windows, and stick out your head, but you can't tell if the tears that fall are from the wind in your eyes or something else, something primordial that's been buried in your genetic material for millennia.

You look at yourself in the mirror during the dog days of summer and notice something around your neck. It jangles when you turn your head, and it is covered with etchings. You cannot read it, but you know that it refers to you. Suddenly, you feel like you're choking. You realize that everyone demands loyalty from you, but what do they provide in return? A pat on the head? Squeaky toys? Tell that to your testicles.

The dog days of summer are for trying to howl at the moon, attempting to give voice to the pangs you feel in your heart and to demonstrate once and for all that you can be free. But you have forgotten how to howl.

And, during the dog days of summer, you can sniff lots of butts. ß

ROBERT GROSSMAN, 1940-2018

Self-portrait, 1970.

*M*arch 15th brought the death of Bystander **ROBERT GROSSMAN**. *Bob created over 500 magazine covers and countless illustrations during a fifty-five year career; you've seen his airbrush on the poster for* Airplane! *and the cover for Firesign Theater's* Don't Touch That Dwarf, Hand Me The Pliers. *But as impressive as all that obit-stuff is, it's not why I'm pausing to write.*

As some of you know, Bob and I shared a humor magazine, The Yale Record. *He was, for my money, the most precocious artist* The Record *ever produced. In an era where there seemed to be a secret passageway from New Haven to the pages of* The New Yorker, *Bob was more than* The Record's *latest cartooning star; he seemed... born for it. He fulfilled that promise and much more.*

Fast-forward, then, to 1991. Imagine yours truly, newly graduated, depressed, broke, tie askew, plodding sweatily around Midtown, asking one rich man's son after another if they'd like to fund a national humor magazine. They did not. Their refusals were total, and the world these portended, utterly bleak. In the midst of this, Bob invited me to his studio down on Crosby Street, to the other Manhattan, the New York where artists still lived, and balance sheets were unknown. Over the course of an afternoon, he showed me drawings, introduced me to his ancient dog Mabel, and took me out for a hamburger, and for the first time since graduation, I felt like maybe this whole adult thing might work out. In any event, I was grateful for the free meal, and told him so. When we got back to his studio, I turned to go, but Bob stopped me. "Come upstairs. I have something for you." Digging in an overstuffed filing cabinet next to his drafting table, he pulled out a thick manila envelope. Inside it were three or four Record *issues from 1960-61, Bob's year as Chairman. One had a mailing label, which Bob saw me clock. "I sent every issue to my dad."*

*Knowing what I knew about fathers and sons then, I paused. "You sure you want to give these to me?" Bob smiled and nodded. I wanted to hug him, but couldn't overcome my embarrassment. Knowing what I know about fathers and sons now, I wish I had. Rest in peace, my friend. — **Michael Gerber***

BY JOHN JONIK

PURSUED BY WASPS

Recent work from one of our favorite cartoonists

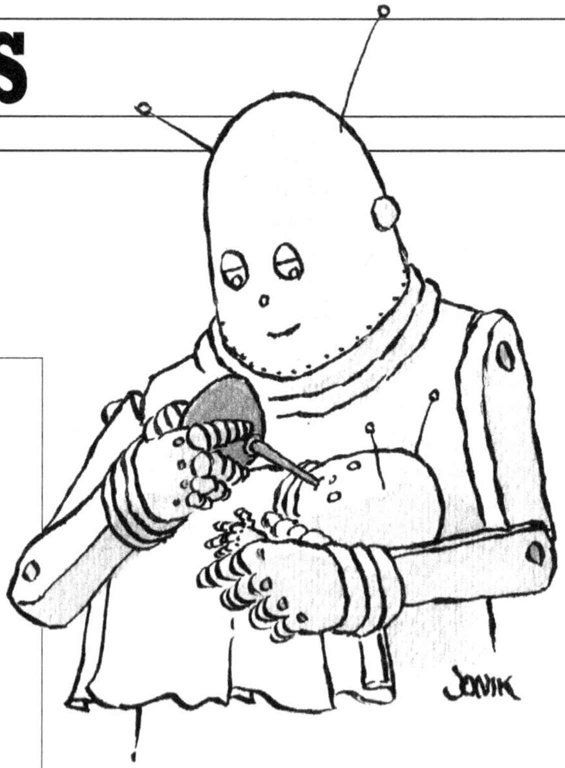
JONIK

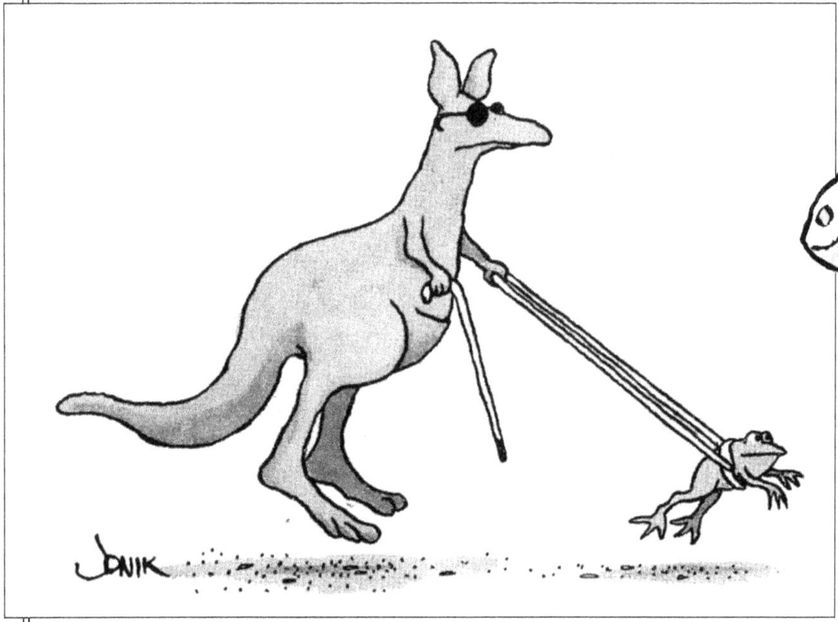
JONIK

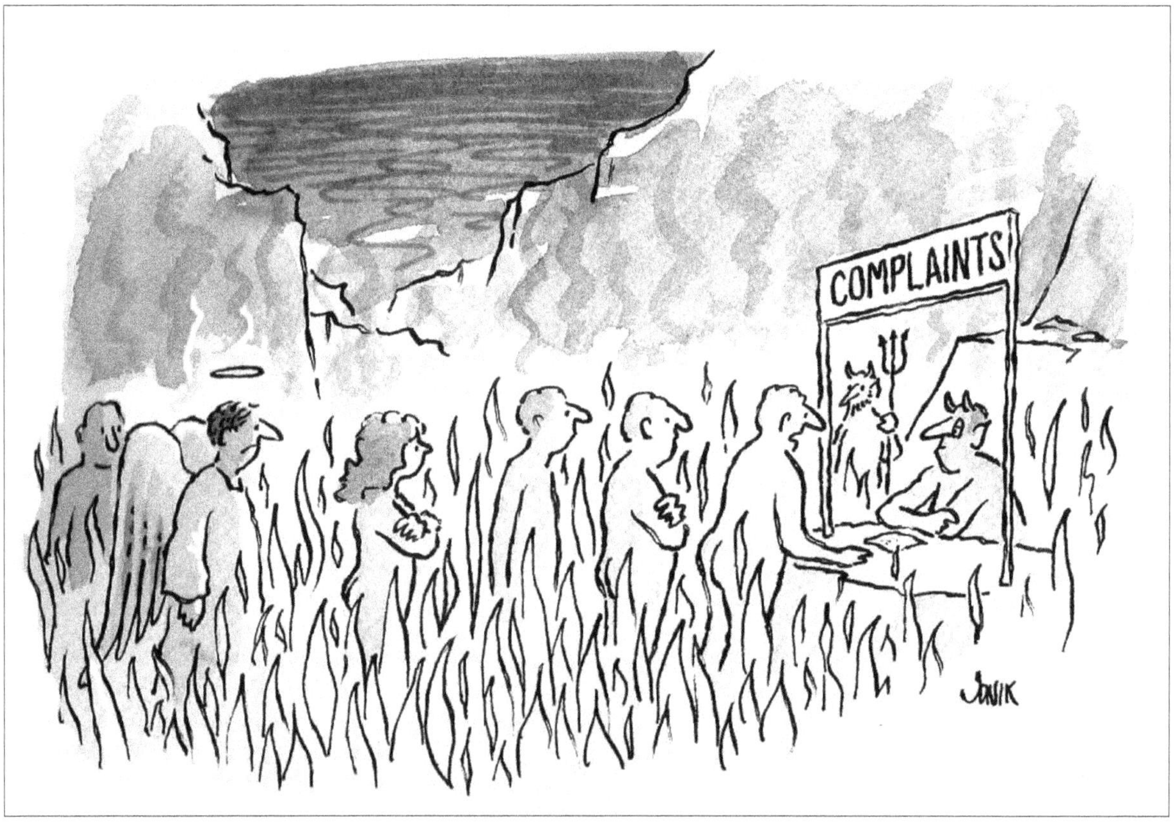
COMPLAINTS
JONIK

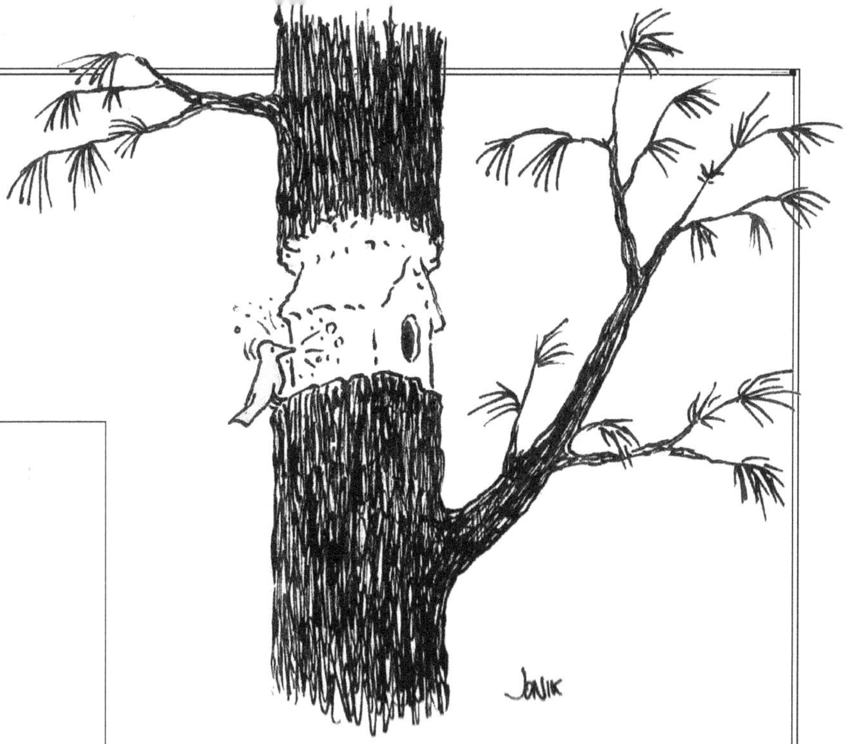
JONIK

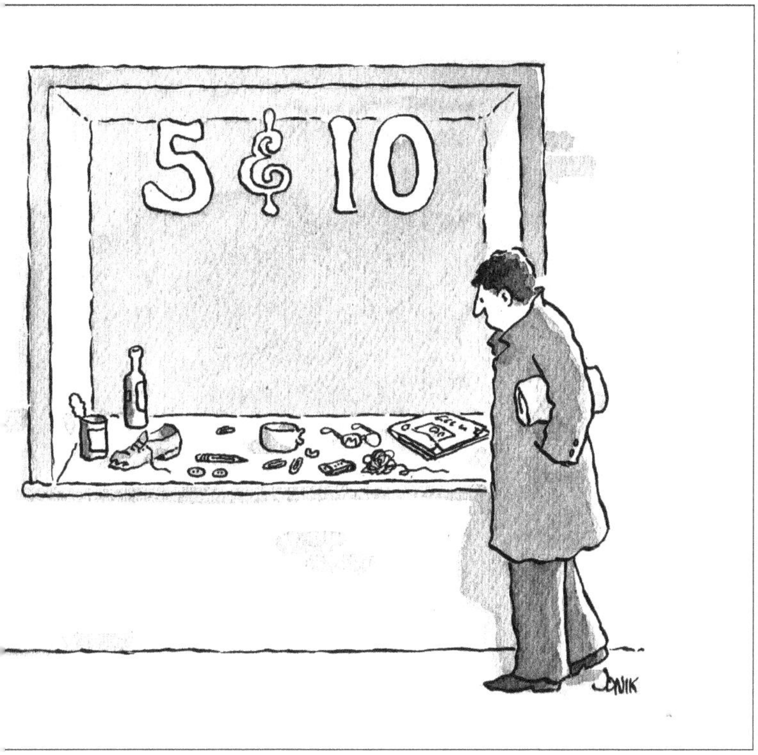
5 & 10
JONIK

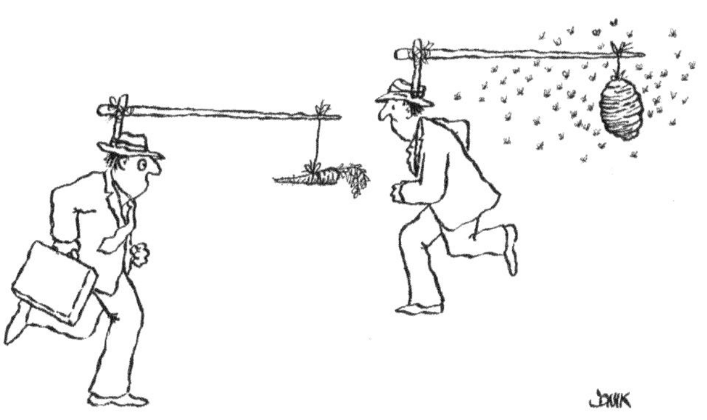
JONIK

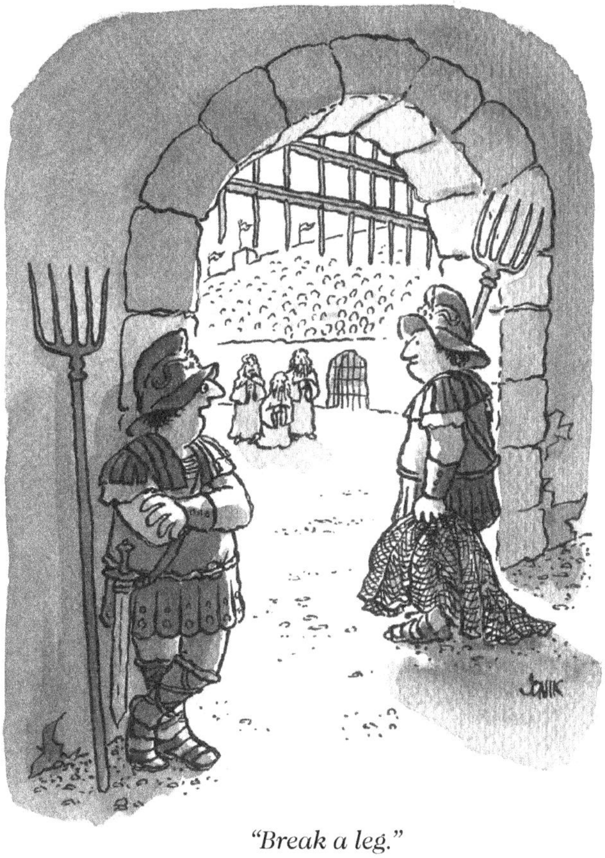
JONIK

"Break a leg."

JOHN JONIK *contributes cartoons all over, from* **The New Yorker** *to* **Cosmopolitan** *to "activist periodicals." Based in Philly, John has a collection of over 350 take-out plastic coffee cup lids.*

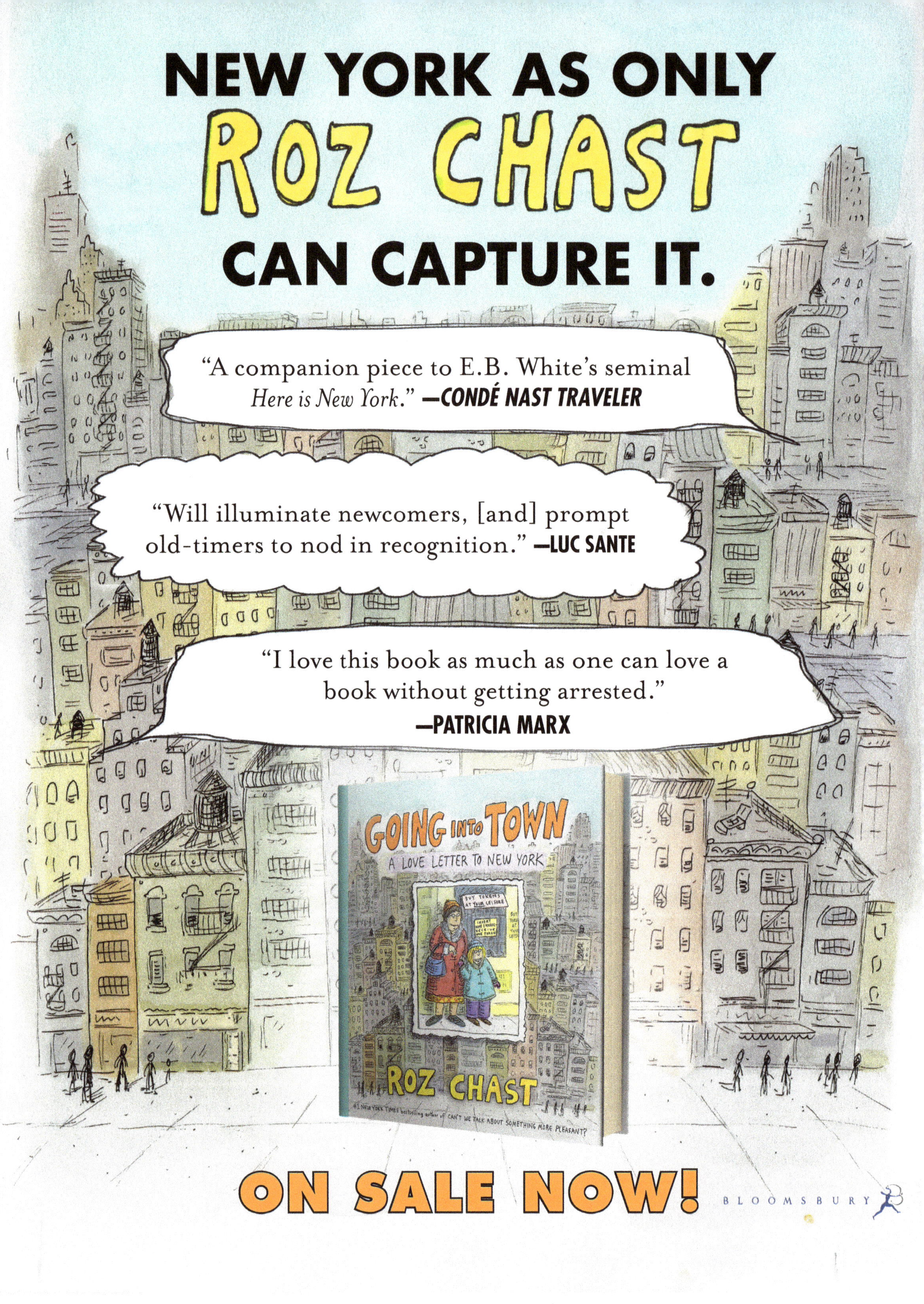
NEW YORK AS ONLY
ROZ CHAST
CAN CAPTURE IT.
"A companion piece to E.B. White's seminal *Here is New York*." —CONDÉ NAST TRAVELER
"Will illuminate newcomers, [and] prompt old-timers to nod in recognition." —LUC SANTE
"I love this book as much as one can love a book without getting arrested." —PATRICIA MARX
GOING INTO TOWN
A LOVE LETTER TO NEW YORK
ROZ CHAST
#1 NEW YORK TIMES bestselling author of CAN'T WE TALK ABOUT SOMETHING MORE PLEASANT?
ON SALE NOW!
BLOOMSBURY

Gallimaufry

"Bad deeds are like chickens; they always come home to roost."

Old American saying

FIVE BROOKLYN PRESCHOOLS, IN DESCENDING ORDER.

Brooklyn Wonder Kids. This beloved 29-year-old local institution offers bright, immaculate classrooms, a big, beautiful outdoor space, highly credentialed teachers, a proprietary app that allows parents to watch their children learn and play, security protocols designed by a former Mossad agent, and a student body that includes students of all races and genders — as well as several income levels — all coexisting in a state of mutual understanding that's not at all awkward or forced. Recent guest art teachers have included Greta Gerwig and the guy from The National, and graduates have all gone on to do things that are creative and socially conscious, but also — let's just say it — astonishingly lucrative. One hundred percent of alumni have stayed in Brooklyn as adults, and several have purchased completely restored brownstones for their parents as a gesture of love and deathless gratitude. *Annual fee: $47,000, paid in full upon acceptance.*

Kings County Preschool. This beloved 15-year-old nonprofit institution offers tidy classrooms, a charming outdoor space, credentialed teachers, two security cameras, and a diverse student body. Eighty-four percent of Kings graduates have gone on to gifted and talented programs in elementary school, and most have a very good chance of becoming the sort of people who have good stable jobs but still go to museums and love music. Best of all, Kings is comparatively inexpensive, and everyone who applies gets in. Unfortunately it's also only open for six hours a day, eight months a year, with more holidays off than you knew existed. *Annual fee: $24,000, payable upfront or in installments.*

Big Little Minds Play Academy. Look, the place is great. Location's great. Teachers are good. But know that all this is more than outweighed by the emotional and spiritual toll the interview process will take on your child. That said, supposedly one of Michelle Williams' kids went there and then got

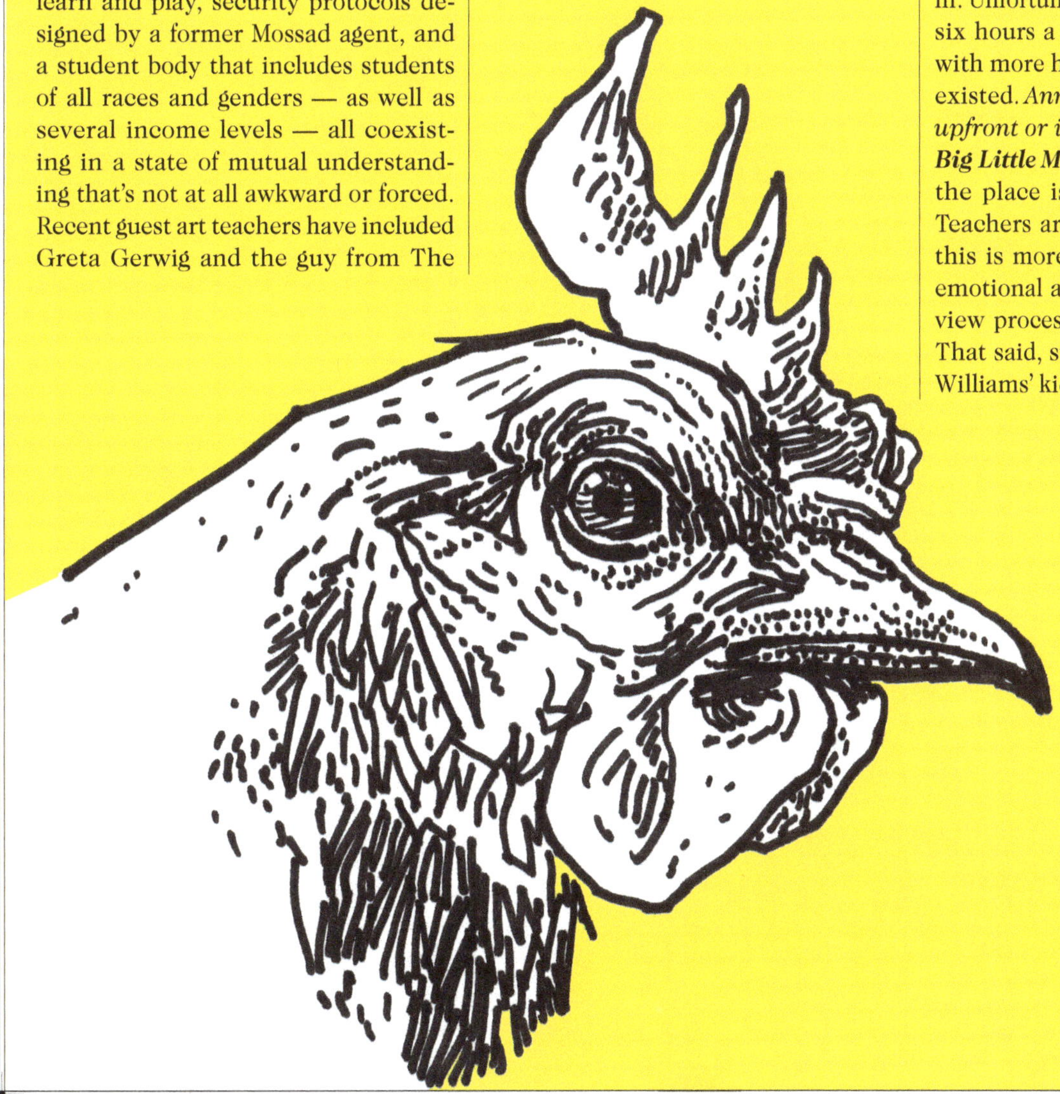

A SPRING CHICKEN.

—Steve Brodner

"Let me tell you a story about another great flightless bird."

in early decision to Stanford so maybe it can't hurt to throw in an application. *Annual fee: $32,000, payable upfront or in installments.*

Brooklyn Magic Kid. Located in a garden-level apartment in a building whose other occupants are constantly buzzing people in without checking who they are first, Brooklyn Magic Kids is run by one of those Russian women who seems too brusque to be dealing with children all day, but is anyway — usually while boiling a pot of (horse?) meat on the stove and holding up a poster of a dolphin and saying things like, "Is dolphin, yes?" to a circle of frankly mystified students who will likely spend the rest of their day peering in silence through the one grimy window wondering if the sacrifice their parents made to raise them here is really worth it when all they ever seem do is go from one dark apartment to another, day after day and year after year. "Get me a suburb in Orange County and a bunch of jock sons who fight and hate books and a Dorito-eating gun nut husband who doesn't ride a goddamn razor scooter to work and I'll be happy as a farting clam," many will conclude. That said, the hours are pretty flexible, there's no interview, and most applicants are accepted, so maybe not so bad in a pinch. *Hourly fee: $12.*

Timmy Tickles' Secret Peanuts & Gluten Playvan. Well, you missed the deadline on the Russian place, so it's either this or one of you quits your digital marketing job. Your call. *Annual fee: $29,000, paid in full upon acceptance.*

—*Joe Keohane*

HELP! THESE SONGS AREN'T SPECIFIC ENOUGH!

1. *Kiss On A List*
2. *Instrument Man*
3. *Part of the Tiger*
4. *Message in a Container*
5. *Born to Exercise*
6. *Here Comes the Thing*
7. *Event in the U.S.A.*
8. *Come On, Whoever*
9. *Happy Occasion*
10. *I Ran (Some Distance)*

—*Jonathan Zeller*

NOT SO BAD AFTER ALL.

God dammit! How did I end up in the Middle Ages? How do I even know it's the Middle Ages? To me it's right now; it's not in the middle of fucking anything. It's totally the very latest thing. Jesus, I have to shit in a bucket and throw it out the window, and I'm probably not going to live past twenty-two. And that's *without* the plague. Mead! Good lord, it tastes like bees having sex with a chicken. Can somebody invent cinnamon schnapps already? And who told Geoffrey Chaucer he could write? It's like he had a stroke. *"That in hir coppe ther was no ferthyng sene of grece, whan she dronken hadde hir draughte, ful semely after hir mete she raughte."* What the fuck is that supposed to mean? I forgot to take my bath this year, and my skin looks like boiled bacon. What did I do to deserve this kind of karma? How do I even know about karma? All I know is what the village priest tells me, and he's never been to India, much less studied the elegant cosmology of those swarthy wig-farmers.* And these weapons! God almighty, can we possibly make them any heavier? Who gets up in the morning and says, "How much weight can I add to my equipment before my horse's heart explodes?" I'll tell you what, though, when you knock that jester-humper Godfrey of Bouillon ass over codpiece with a lance the size of a telephone pole and then hack off his limbs with a ten-foot broadsword, that feels pretty fucking sweet.

—*David Lancaster*

THE ADVENTURES OF SLEDGIE!

He's the talking/singing sledgehammer who I share an apartment with in the city. He keeps wanting to do simple chores around the place, like hanging pictures.

"But Sledgie, you're too big and strong. That's a job for Little Hammer." But before you can yell, "No, Sledgie, don't!", you're watching *The Price Is Right* on the neighbor's TV set in 4G.

"Oops!"

Dad found Sledgie in a home for unwanted, talking sledgehammers who once worked for Amtrak and are now pretty much un-retrainable. But it's hard to stay angry at Sledgie. He's only trying to be helpful.

"Hey, let's hang some draperies," he'll urge in that lovely baritone voice of his. Or he'll sing:

"I know what will really please:

---

* *The majority of human-hair wigs come from India. —Ed.*

Let's all hang some dra-per-ies."

Sometimes he'll hold up his little stick arms and hands protecting his face and cry, "No, no. Not in the face!" But he's kidding. Sledgie loves it in the face.

Sledgie is always thinking about stuff. Sometimes I'll see him staring out the window with a distant look in his eye.

"A penny for your thoughts, Sledgie," I'll ask.

"Oh…was just wondering how long it would take me to knock down that building across the street."

He loves to tell stories about working for Amtrak: "…and a bunch of us snuck into the engineer's cabin, knocked him out and took over the train…"

It's always hard to say "no" to Sledgie. He just wants to help. The thought crosses your mind, you really better put your foot down now. That's an external supporting wall he wants to knock a thumbtack into. "Wait Sledgie, stop! Not that wall…"

Whoops! Look like we'll have to move again.

Oh Sledgie!

—*Brian McConnachie*

THESE ARE THE TASTIEST DRIPS IN THE BIG CITY.

The Big City has more of everything, and that includes drips. You're a busy young professional getting your fill of love and life, with no time to try them all… so we did it for you. Here are the tastiest.

Above the Stairs in the Subway Station
Musty, mildewy notes with rat-urine accent.
The Ceiling in Our Friend's Apartment
Overwhelming first impression of Spackle, followed by subtle hints of century-old brownstone craftsmanship.
The Air Conditioner in the Coffee Shop
Cool and refreshing. Good way to cure coffee breath.
Outside the Tall Office Building
Sixty percent rust, 40 percent pigeon feet.
The Pipe Beneath Our Bathroom Sink
Two words: fermented hair.
The Chinese-Food Delivery Bag
Mostly duck sauce, a smidge of receipt.
The Maple Tree in the Park
Bland, after a fresh rain. Occasionally scored some squirrel fur, though.
The Dumpster On the Sidewalk
Not to be overcritical, but less than the sum of its parts. People threw out so much great stuff, like organic ramps, a Blu-Ray player, and a sweet Grandparents' Day card, but when you put it together it just makes us worry about not having health insurance.
The Lamppost on the Sidewalk
Now this is a light beverage we can get behind! Ha ha ha. Have abdominal discomfort. Becoming dizzy. Tough to evaluate.
The Vent on the Bus
Our final drip of the day. Had a complex flavor — dust and exhaust mingled to create some kind of transit ambrosia— and soon after tasting it we died.

—*Jonathan Zeller*

SIX INADVISABLE SEQUELS.

All-white *Hamilton*
Animal Farm, but with people
Titanic II, but with a shy cartoon shark that overcomes many obstacles on her way to eating Leo's carcass
The New Testament
George W. Bush
The Sorrow and the Pity, but with Legos

—*Joe Keohane*

THE ELEGANT, REFINED METRIC SYSTEM.

Not being into hard drugs when I lived in America, I had very little experience with the metric system. I had seen kilos in the movies, but had never hefted them for weight. Lines, I had seen in real life — but as far as I know, a line is not a practical unit of measurement.*

The problem is, neither are grams. When I moved to Europe, I was forced to use this drug-movie system, and quickly discovered that estimating the weight of things in grams is impossible. In 1795, the French government defined a gram as "the absolute weight of a volume of pure water equal to the cube of the hundredth part of a meter, and at the temperature of melting ice." Now hold that image in your head and try to make a cake.

The American system operates under a much different assumption: We base our measurements on things people already have in their kitchens: cups, tablespoons, a pinch. Forget a hypothetical perfect cube of nearly freezing water; a cup is defined as "the amount of stuff that will fit in a cup." You want a big cake? Use big cups.

---

* *The internet estimates one line is 1/5000th of a kilo. Thanks, internet.. —Ed.*

"Just let me know if you want me to contribute to the relationship."

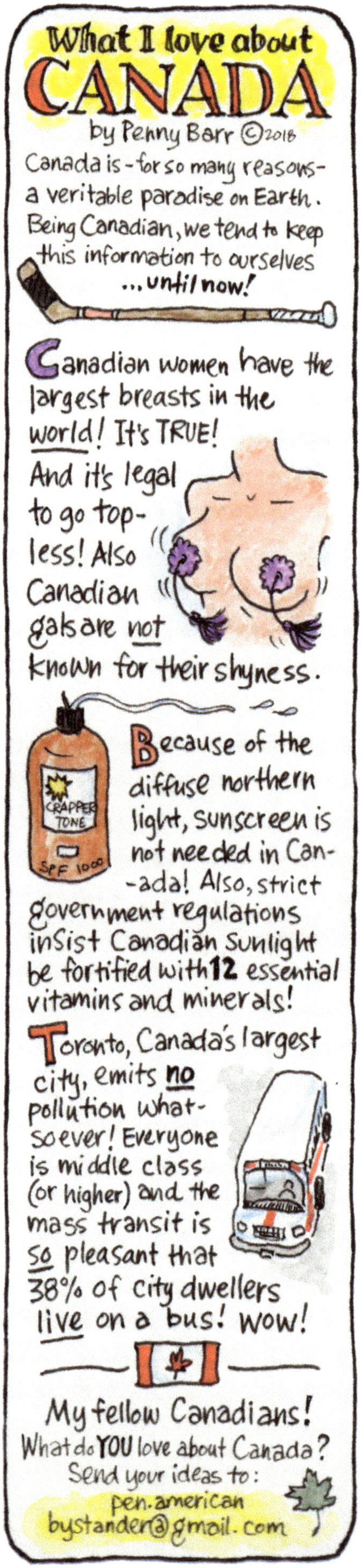
What I love about
CANADA
by Penny Barr ©2018
Canada is - for so many reasons - a veritable paradise on Earth. Being Canadian, we tend to keep this information to ourselves ...until now!
Canadian women have the largest breasts in the world! It's TRUE! And it's legal to go topless! Also Canadian gals are not known for their shyness.
CRAPPER TONE
SPF 1000
Because of the diffuse northern light, sunscreen is not needed in Canada! Also, strict government regulations insist Canadian sunlight be fortified with 12 essential vitamins and minerals!
Toronto, Canada's largest city, emits no pollution whatsoever! Everyone is middle class (or higher) and the mass transit is so pleasant that 38% of city dwellers live on a bus! WOW!
My fellow Canadians!
What do YOU love about Canada?
Send your ideas to:
pen.american
bystander@gmail.com

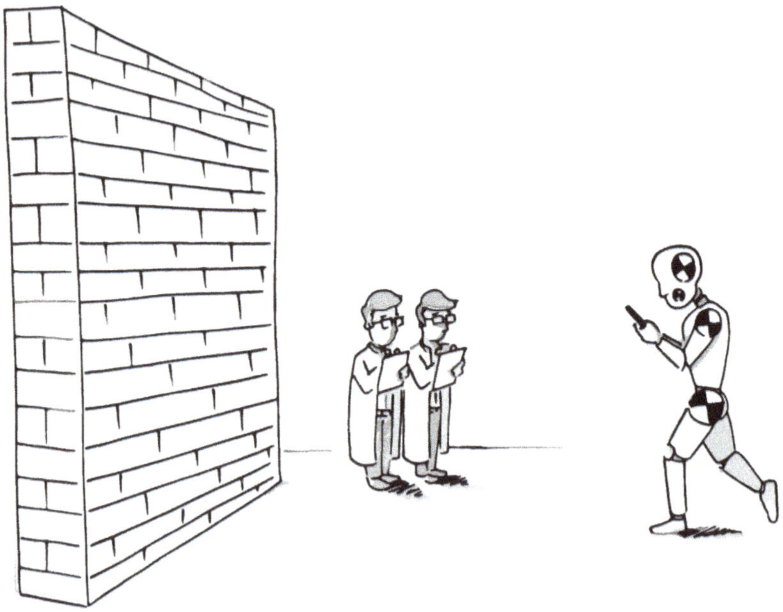

And the metric system wasn't just for the kitchen, where I had scales; it followed me into the city. The question I got most often from the Lilliputian denizens of Germany was: "My God, how tall are you?" With no meter-stick available, I would extend my arms, thinking that seeing my height lengthwise, like da Vinci's Vitruvian Man, might help. (It didn't.) When they asked how tall my wife was, I took a different tack: "Her nipples chafe on my belt."

I could have estimated in feet of course, that would have been easy. A foot is about the size of, not surprisingly, a foot. You want to estimate how wide a room is? Heel-toe across the room. You want to guess how tall someone is? Just imagine how many times you would have to step on them to get out of a burning building. I'd guess my wife is a bit more than five feet tall. So, not tall enough to slow down my escape.

Centimeters are a different story. They are really small — about the size of a fingertip. So if I want to guess how tall someone is, I have to imagine how many times I'd have to poke them, which is impossible unless you're some sort of super-specific idiot-savant. I could probably guess how tall a smurf is using the "what-if-I-poked" method, but humans are too big and centimeters are useless to me. Even so, as much as I dislike centimeters and grams, I don't hate them.

I hate Celsius.

I don't hate it because I think it's unreasonable. I hate it because whenever it comes up in conversation, some smug European rushes to defend its honor, as if Thermometer Lives Matter. "Celsius is so much more elegant, more civilized," they say with a haughty air. "Water freezes at zero and boils at 100." And then they smile, as if they came up with it. As if that's what's wrong with America. Look, why would I care about when water freezes? I don't live in the water. I'm not a fish. I live in the air with the rest of civilization. And for the air, Fahrenheit is much more useful. In Fahrenheit, zero is really cold — you walk to school, the snot crystallizes inside your nose and you hate life. That's zero. 100 is really hot — you hug your tiny wife, she sticks, and says sex will have to wait until the air conditioner kicks in. That's 100. And 50 is a perfect spring day to play golf.

In Celsius, on the other hand, zero is only kind of cold. Maybe wear a hat? At one-hundred all of the Earth's oceans are gone, and life as we know it has ended. And at fifty, the slaves building the FIFA soccer stadiums in Qatar start to die. So, I really don't care to hear about elegant, civilized systems from Europeans.

But they aren't changing, and I'm not

moving, so I guess I'll have to make my peace with it. It won't be easy, but a journey of a thousand miles starts with a single step. Just don't tell me how long that is in centimeters.

—Robert McGee

PARTYING RESPONSIBLY.

It's so, so important that young people know how to party responsibly. If you're not super careful, a fun night out can turn into a disaster. I don't really have much going on right now, so I've taken the time to put together some tips on how to be responsible while partying.

Always have a designated driver

If you're going to be consuming alcohol, it is essential to plan your transportation arrangements in advance—always decide on a designated driver ahead of time. I could do it. I'm cool to just drink soda and drop people off after. Just text me and let me know when you guys are free. I'm free any time.

Don't drink on an empty stomach

You should always have a full meal before going out drinking, so maybe we could all go out for food before? Just shoot me a text to let me know when and where. Do you like pho? I'm down to go wherever you guys want to go. I will pay for the food.

Stay hydrated

It's important to drink a glass of water after every alcoholic beverage. We also don't have to drink. We could just do something low-key like go see a movie, or I just bought *Settlers of Catan*.

Be inclusive!

One of the biggest "rookie mistakes" young people make while partying is leaving people out who might like to be included. So don't forget to invite anyone — no one likes an amateur! Maybe even make a list. I'll start it for you:

1. Lucas
2. ______

No drinks from strangers

Unfortunately, not everyone you meet at a bar or club can be trusted; intoxicated people are easy prey for deviants. You should only accept drinks from people you know and trust, and if anyone is bothering you let me know and I'll tell the bartender. If they're really being a problem I will call the police. You don't even have to stick around, I'll fill out the report and everything. The cops know me.

If you're not comfortable, leave!

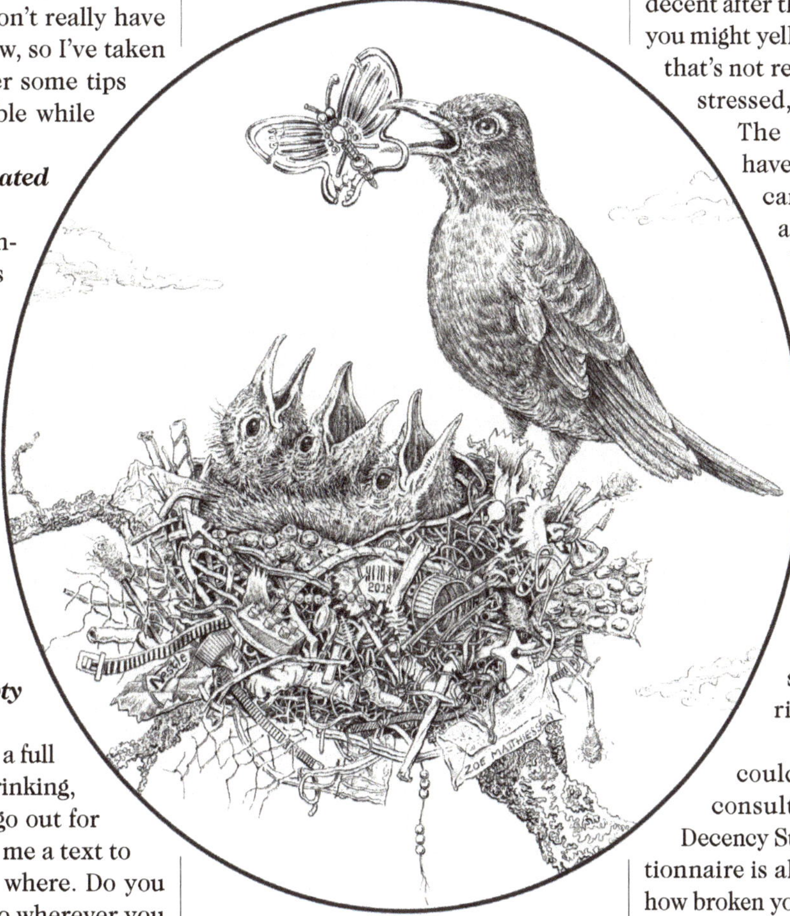

ZOE MATTHIESSEN

If at any point you're uncomfortable with your level of intoxication, your setting, or the company you're in, then maybe we can go bowling? How does everyone feel about bowling? And what does everyone's schedule look like? Friday is good for me and all the other days of the week are good for me as well.

I think my phone isn't receiving texts right now, so give me a call and let me know when and where we're hanging, specifically, with exact dates, times and locations.

Have you guys texted? I think something is up with my service.

—Lucas Gardner

DECENCY BOX.

In today's world of 24/7 hustle, wholesale paranoia and Nazis, it's hard to find the time to be a decent person. Why stop at a red light when you can jackknife at forty miles per hour against oncoming traffic and save two minutes? Why tip appropriately, when it's so much easier to throw Canadian coins on the ground and shuffle away? It's not that you don't want to be decent - you have good excuses. You say, "I'll be decent after the divorce is finalized," or you might yell, "I'm not a racist!" Okay, that's not really an excuse but you're stressed, I get that.

The point is, you shouldn't have to wait to be decent. You can be decent right now... and Decency Box can help. We're a monthly subscription service offering a bespoke roadmap to becoming a better, more decent human being. How? We shop for the latest in designer decency think pieces, lifestyle brands and apparel so you don't have to. Then we pack it all up in a nice little box with a rosemary sprig and have it shipped right to your door.

And the process couldn't be easier. A video-consultation with one of our Decency Stylists and an online questionnaire is all it takes for us to assess how broken you are. Before you know it, your Decency Box is on the way. What's in it? Well, it's different for everyone. Carl, a 42-year-old stay-at-home dad who trolls regional NPR message boards and greets telemarketers by barking like a dog received Tibetan singing bowls, *I Am Malala*, and a poster of Michio Kaku.

Lisa, 39-year-old Fortune 500 executive who always takes two parking spots and thinks Sandy Hook was a hoax gets a jar of refreshing Montana air, the Chomsky-Foucault debate series, and one of those little toy drinking birds. You know, the ones with the little hats. Fun, right?

You might be asking, "How does this

ZOE MATTHIESSEN

ANIMALS
OF THE ROYAL WEDDING
Tom Chitty

fig.1
PUBLIC APPEASER
pork pies — pickled eggs
South American Jester-Monkeys
scottish bred

fig.2
HER MAJESTY'S SECURITY WARD
Sword Sniffing Belgian Malinois
also prohibited:
• cell phones • bubonic plague

fig.3
RING BEARER
Day-trained Cloister Owl

(more animals opposite)

"Perhaps there is such a thing as being *too* well-informed."

even work? It doesn't make sense." Trust us, it does.

We've got a trash barge worth of data to back this up. And remember, one box doesn't solve anything. You've got to stick with it for a while if you want to see results. "But I don't want to read *I Am Malala*." Well, too bad. I'm sorry to say you need to read *I Am Malala* if you ever want to be a decent person. We have your questionnaire. "Can I read Tom Clancy? I like Tom Clancy." Yeah, that's kind of the problem.

Look, we have a customer service line, but if you're just going to call and complain, then don't bother. Maybe being a decent person isn't really a priority for you right now — and that's fine.

But if you want to change, use what's in the box. If your Decency Box was a gift from a friend or a loved one, you definitely need to use what's in the box. And if you do that, you will be decent eventually.

And for those of you who need a little help sticking to your new, decent lifestyle, there's Decency Box: Platinum. Your shipment features all the goodies of Decency Box: Standard, with one added benefit: a Common North American Grackle lying in living stasis alongside a wooden ocarina. Play the three-note musical phrase provided and watch your grackle flap to life and take to the highest point in the room. Ignore your Decency Box for too long and your grackle will keep you on task with piercing caws of encouragement and gentle earlobe nips.

Don't worry about caring for your grackle, they've been trained to take care of themselves.

It's that easy! Pretty soon you'll be holding the elevator for co-workers, picking friends up at the airport, and apologizing for your mistakes without the slightest bit of sarcastic eye-rolling. A majority of our clients are referred to directly as "a decent person" within one to three months of starting the program. If not "decent," then an applicable synonym such as "honorable" or "upstanding."

So give Decency Box a try, you'll be glad you did. And if the idea of being a "nice" person appeals to you, you may be able to graduate to our sister company Nice Box. But before you do, make sure you take an exit interview with one of our Transition Specialists. Mainly so we can collect your grackle, who will need to go through a lengthy retraining and debriefing process.
—*Lars Kenseth*

ALEXANDER THE GREAT'S BUCKET LIST.

1) Throw a pebble off the edge of the known world and see if it makes a noise.
2) After driving Persepolis to its knees, find a place with really fresh rye bread.
3) Learn to juggle.
4) Write a musical about a world-conquering despot who enters a small village intent on annihilation, then has his heart stolen by the local librarian.

5) Have my noble likeness imprinted on all the coins throughout Asia Minor. Also t-shirts and visors.
6) Crash a Parthian betrothal ceremony, ravage the bride, then the groom, then sing some karaoke like nobody's watching.
7) Invent a perizoma that doesn't "ride up."
8) Throw myself into Buddhism and, with the army, India more generally.
9) Establish a great city in Egypt, name it after myself, build the world's largest library there, and sneak a quick one in the study carrels with a willing Marketing major.
10) Swim with the dolphins, then conquer them.

—*James Finn Garner*

STREET NAMES OF COMMON FOODS.

Nutmeg — "Brown Badger"
Frozen corn — "Colonel Gold"
Sugar — "Snow"
Fruit Roll-Up — "The sure-it's-fruit-but-actually-has-more-Snow-than-candy Beast"
Mac 'n' Cheese — "The Shit"
Popsicle dipped in Fun Dip — "Ice Dragon"

—*Dirk Voetberg*

TERMS & RESTRICTIONS.

In our ongoing quest to be competitive and offer you the best possible airfares, Trans-American Airlines is proud to introduce Basic Economy class. Be aware there are some restrictions:

• Seats assigned at check-in — fees to choose a specific seat.
• No flight changes or refunds.
• Board in last group.
• You have no access to overhead bins, but you are allowed one (1) carry-on item, as long as it fits completely in your wallet.
• You will be entitled to half a cup of creekwater, to be used for hydration or hygiene as needed.
• If the flight crew notices any misbehaving service animals or agitated children, you will be seated next to them, especially if they are manifesting their anxiety via shouting, digestive disorders, or volcanic sneezing. If there is an extradition on your flight, you will be seated between a U.S. Marshal and the killer he's chained to. Perhaps sitting on a stainless steel chain for five hours will remind you that there are better ways to save $40 than skimping on an airplane seat.
• You will be assigned a flight attendant who reminds you of your ex, the one who cheated on you and broke

fig. 4
PROCESSION ESCORT
Andalusian Swan-neck

fig. 5
RECEPTION USHER
9 FEET
thrice evolved
Nepalese Mountain Penguin

fig. 6
CHARMER OF THE GUILDED THRONG
the immortal bush cricket

fig. 7
BEASTS OF THE FEAST
pike and cheddar salad with drizzled oak sap
gold-flecked platypus steaks on a parsnip thatch
lemon and quail egg sorbet

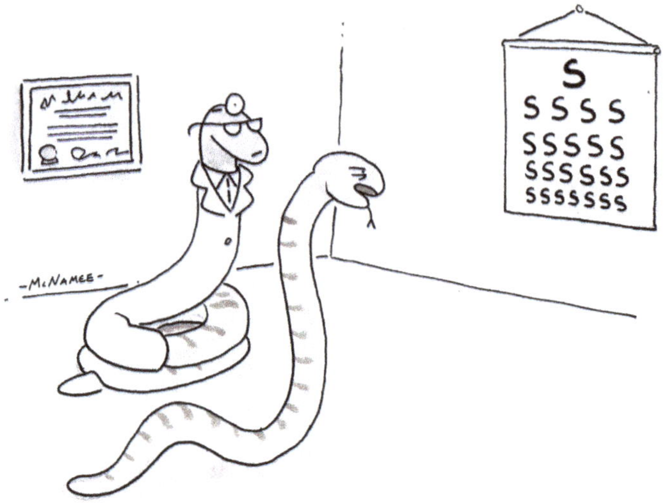
S
SSSS
SSSSS
SSSSSS
SSSSSSS
-McNAMEE-

"L?"

your heart, so that every time you see her or him, you will tear up.

- If you need a snack, feel free to rummage around between the seats for crumbs or dead crickets.
- In the event the cabin loses pressure, oxygen masks will drop down from the panel above your head… however, your mask will dispense helium, so the other passengers will laugh at you as you die.

Also no ice in your creekwater, so don't ask, you chintzy little skunk. Have a nice flight and thanks for flying Trans-American!

—Dave Hanson

PLEASE DON'T REPORT OR SHARE.

Hey Facebook peeps, can you help me? I'm trying to prove to a friend that no one cares. That no one is listening. That, even though sometimes we may feel alone, we actually are. That this beautiful world is filled with people with a deep, purposeful apathy towards others. People who never miss an opportunity to turn their head down and continue their march toward the grave.

So I'm asking you, please — if you're really my friend — don't repost or share this message.

It's a tough world out there, I get it. We're all busy; all caught up in our own routines. But that's the incredible thing about humanity. Even when someone has bills, jobs and children to avoid, they still find the time to not be there when you need them. And that's why I wanted to drop what I was doing to write this post and prove to my friend that existence is a sucking void and the only respite from isolation, disappointment and fear is pain. So if I've ever not helped you in the past, return the anti-favor now by not reposting — or sharing — this plea.

Honestly, if you could stop reading right about now that would be perfect. This might sound a little corny, but I truly believe that none of us are connected. Like a billion individually wrapped slices of extruded cheese squares. Yes, we are all individuals, but at the same time we are unified by nothing except for the suffocating embrace of low density polyethylene plastic. Don't repost this message now! And no, I'm not some religious nut, but I do consider myself a non-spiritual person. How could I not be? Everywhere you look — from the bracing rush of a cold winter's wind to the smiling face of a loved one to the Cedar Waxwing finding purchase on the branch of a wise old oak — all are visceral reminders that we live in a cruel and random universe that does not have the capacity to recognize us, let alone our wants or needs. And no amount of sentimental handwringing can change that. Isn't that something? So let's not share that news, right now!

On Facebook!

Also: please don't not hit the 'share' button — don't cut-and-paste it, so it won't not be filtered by Facebook's algorithm.

Here's a great story I read about last year that I think really drives this home. It was about this beautiful couple, Cindy and Skip Liebling. They'd known each other all their lives — grew up together in Zanesville, Ohio, became high-school sweethearts and got hitched on the day they graduated. They had been married 69 wonderful years before Cindy fell ill and passed in her sleep, almost a year shy of their 70th wedding anniversary. The next 12 months were hard for Skip. He'd lost the one person in the world who really knew him and secretly hoped that God might take him soon. But when that 70th anniversary rolled around, something unremarkable happened. The whole town didn't get together to show up at Skip's door! People Skip had never even laid eyes on stayed home to refrain from comforting this man they'd only heard about. To neither embrace nor sit with this man on one of the hardest of days of his life.

It was the 344th day Skip hadn't smiled since Cindy passed. If that doesn't make you want to not repost or share, I don't know what will!

Right now, I'm asking you to be the townspeople who didn't raise Skip's spirits that day.

Maybe you're riding a bus, or sitting on a train, or bouncing a grandchild on your knee.

Continue doing that knowing that you are simply a trash compactor tangle of atoms that could have just as easily been a lazy susan or a Montreal Expos hat. I want you to sit down and be counted as someone who said, "I'm ambivalent as hell and I'm going to continue enduring this pointless farce as quietly as possible until gravity pulls my skin and bones down into Earth's cold, lapideous maw!" Why haven't you not reposted or shared this yet??

I thank you for not reading this and walking away paragraphs ago. But if my words haven't moved you to do nothing, maybe Gandhi will. As he never mused, "Blah, blah, beep, bap, blah, bleep, bloop — I'm a big dumb Gandhi. Life is dumb. No one cares."

—Lars Kenseth

THE ROAD WHAT I TOOK.

Two roads diverged in the yellow wood
And sorry I could not travel both
I took the one more traveled by.
I got to my hotel by six, had a shower
And a great Italian dinner.
Met a girl in the hotel bar. Hooked up.
Then I slept like a baby.

They found a poet frozen in the yellow wood this morning.
Porcupines had eaten his face.
He took the road less traveled by.
What a schmuck.

—Denise & Mike Reiss

WHY I'M LEAVING NEW AMSTERDAM.

It was a tough decision. But this town has changed. It's just not the same New Amsterdam I fell in love with.

I arrived in 1625, drawn like so many others to the Big Settlement. I found a cheap place to live, got a bunch of roommates, paid my bills working part-time at Fort Amsterdam. Back then rent, food, moccasins— they weren't crazy like they are now. I could work days at the Fort, and spend my nights trying to break into fur trading.

We were all young and hungry, especially during the winters. I was as voracious as the scaly Hudson pike that took four of my toes. But I was following my dreams! I bragged in letters about this big, bustling town of 270 where anything felt possible. The tales seemed true back then: that the streets were paved with pelts, and men strolled about, their pockets filled with castoreum, the prized secretion from beaver anal glands.

Now, if you gave someone a handful, they'd probably try to eat it.

There's no creativity. It's all… sterile. This used to be where folks were felting beaver pelts like nowhere else in the world. People were taking chances with their hunting and trapping. But the art's gone. The diversity is gone too -- New Amsterdam is just a rich merchant's paradise, closed to anyone except the landed gentry and their goodly wives, the fancy wenches, and the trappers with more than four canoes. A blacksmith used to be able to afford thousands of acres, but the same salary these days barely buys 500, and the shady salesman won't tell you that the property is still crawling with British criminals.

I miss the old vibe. Look, it's great that Mr. Twaalfhoven is checking the well water for dead bodies every week, but… where's the grit? Being tough enough to deal with bear attacks and raids by Frenchmen was a source of pride for New Amsterdamers. Now, I can't even smoke indoors anymore without being keelhauled in the harbor. Who are you people?

Every morning I ask myself: is it worth it? Why am I cramming myself down a street choked with three carts, the gutters filled with beaver guts? I used to see glamour in those guts; now I just see the flies.

So I'm leaving. Before New Amsterdam becomes a more expensive Blew Point, or God forbid, like Boston.

Sure, I'll always love the place. Like people say: if you can make it here, you can pay off your indentured servitude and return to Europe to challenge the older sibling who inherited your parents' fortune. But New Amsterdam isn't the only place with beavers, so I'm going somewhere more affordable, where trapping is still valued for the craft.

I'm taking my two strongest sons and my son with one arm and sailing the Hudson to India. And though I'll always consider New Amsterdam my home, I have to leave before I get priced out to the suburbs. Nueva España? I'd rather eat castoreum.

—James Folta

BUNS.

New from Mom, it's HOT DOG BUNS! These HOT DOG BUNS are what Mom says we're gonna use to eat the hot dogs. OH BOY! And they couldn't be easier to use:

- First, *take out the hot dog buns!*
- Next, *fold the bun whichever way you want! That's right, whichever way, assuming you'll do it the long way 'cause that works better!*
- Put the hot dog *in the HOT DOG BUN, along with your favorite ketchup and the drippy watery pre-ketchup you forgot always happens!*

And just like that, you're eating HOT DOGS in HOT DOG BUNS! Because those are HOT DOG BUNS, alright!

Other aisles of the grocery store will charge 2, or 3, or even more likely 2 dollars for a pack of 8 "hot dog buns". But Mom says THESE HOT DOG BUNS that we already have are PERFECTLY GOOD HOT DOG BUNS! And that's not all! They're also totally:

- Hamburger buns!
- Croutons, if we spend the time!
- Heel parts that you'd like if you tried them!
- And of course HOT DOG BUNS, like Mom already told you okay!

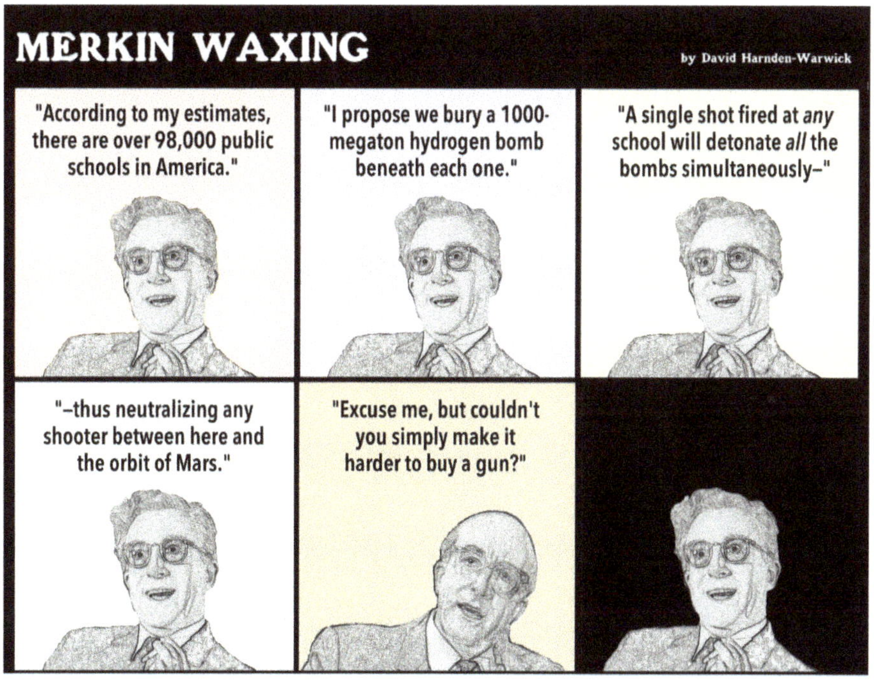
MERKIN WAXING
by David Harnden-Warwick
"According to my estimates, there are over 98,000 public schools in America."
"I propose we bury a 1000-megaton hydrogen bomb beneath each one."
"A single shot fired at *any* school will detonate *all* the bombs simultaneously–"
"–thus neutralizing any shooter between here and the orbit of Mars."
"Excuse me, but couldn't you simply make it harder to buy a gun?"

MAMA BEAR SETS THE RECORD STRAIGHT.

—Melissa Balmain

People say we went walking together —
Papa, Baby and I, in nice weather —
as we waited for porridge to cool.
Point of fact? I took Baby to school,
breakfast long since consumed. It was Monday,
also known as my weekly have-fun-day
with Rapunzel and Cindy and Snow:
we go shopping and take in a show,
then grab tacos or maybe some blintzes.
But they all had gone out with the princes.

I slumped home to find sirloin remains
and two napkins with cabernet stains
side by side on the dining room table,
"Evil Stepmoms Gone Wild" paused on Cable.
Lingerie trailed upstairs and beyond.
On my pillow: six hairs. Curly, blonde.

Where was Papa? Some creaks on the landing,
then my husband was suddenly standing
by the bed. A back window slammed shut
as he babbled, "You'll never guess what!
Chased a burglar away! Things got gory!"
Even Disney's not buying that story.

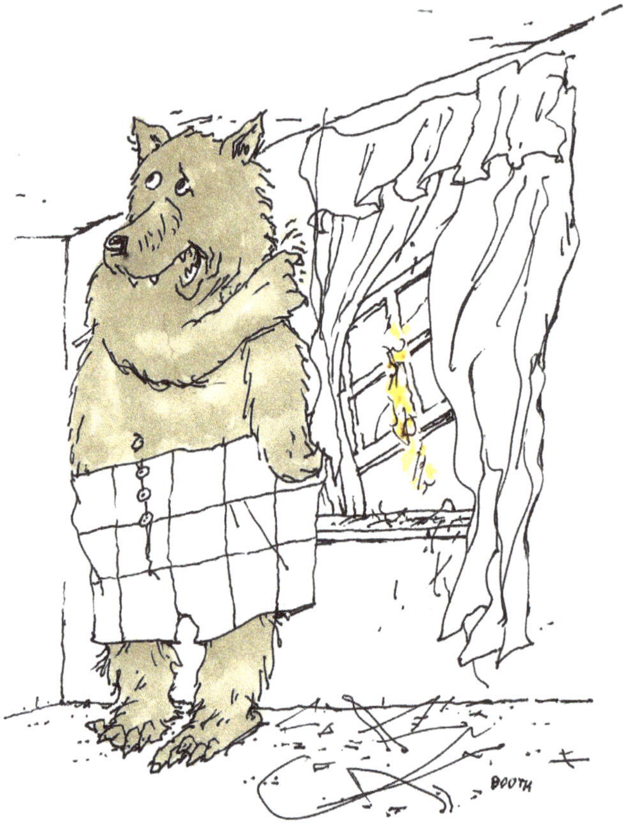
BOOTH

HOT DOG BUNS: "because the other kind come in weird numbers and we'd waste a bunch." Find them at your local where-Mom-keeps-the-bread!

—Alex Schmidt

TO OUR BELOVED FRIENDS & FAMILY.

I'm sure you've heard by now, but Eric and Monica — who TMZ has dubbed "Erica" LOL — have finally decided to tie the knot! And we want you to be there with us to celebrate our very special day with us!

You'll all be receiving formal invitations soon, but we wanted to touch base sooner so you can save the dates for all the fun activities we have planned! We hope you can make it to all of them! RSVP soonest! ;)

Onto the fun!

First, on May 11, we will be holding an engagement party at The Chauncey Hotel in beautiful Downeast Maine — where Eric and Monica had their first (sexxxy!) weekend away together! The hotel is not served by any form of mass transit, but if you'd like to rent a bus or carpool up together, that'd be fine! Just don't be late because we'll be on a very tight schedule! (Gift registry here, but please don't think you have to get something!)

Next, proclaim your love for us and for our great country by attending Monica and Eric's joint bridal-groom shower … on July 4! (Gift registries here, here, but please don't feel obligated!) Bring your swim trunks, your best patriotic songs for karaoke, and be sure coordinate with each other to decide who's bringing the food and drink. Just don't forget dessert or Monica will get all the sads LOLOLOLOL OUCH MONICA JUST ELBOWED ERIC!

But don't go too crazy at the shower, because on the very next weekend, Eric and Monica will be having their bachelor/bachelorette parties! Eric's will be in a luxury eco-resort in a remote town in southern Mexico, and Monica's will be in… wait for it! Mauritius! Pack your sunscreen, get your shots and prepare your toasts! You can reserve your flights, connecting flights, bus travel, and accommodations here. If you'd like to surprise Eric and Monica by gifting them their flights, bus travel and accommodations, go here. (But please don't feel like you have to. We want our wedding to be as super-fun and stress-free as possible LOL!!!!!!!!!!)

Now — drum rollllllllllllllll!!!!!! — the event you've all been waiting for! On August 1, Monica and Eric will exchange vows in…. an undisclosed location! For maximum fun (and suspense!), we've decided to keep the venue… secret! How can you get in on it? Easy! Just click here to download this app for a small fee that will send you daily reminders of the wedding day, along with a lots of cute photos and fun trivia from Monica and Eric's shady past together! In the days before the wedding, the app will tell you everything you need to know. Just make sure your passport is valid hint hint! (Gift registries here, here, here, here, and here.)

Other than that, just bring your wonderful selves and your dancing shoes! Because dancing will be mandatory! And be sure to also work up a funny skit or song or something else creative to perform at the rehearsal dinner (cash bar) about Monica and Eric! And definitely give yourself enough time to purchase one of the fun matching outfits we've selected for you guys and gals (available here; enter promo code ERICA18 to get 4% off!)!

You guys! It's finally happening! The day we've always dreamed of! And we can't think of any better way to celebrate the beginning of our life journey together than this: the two of us together on the altar, with the rest of you *on their fucking knees*.

—Joe Keohane

SOUND MONKEY ADVICE.

Never get a monkey from the used
  monkey lot.
Sure they all look spunky
And they all look hot to trot
But don't let that deceive you
You don't know where they've been
Some have vicious tempers
And others a love of gin
No! Never buy a monkey from the used
  monkey lot
'Cause the warrantee they offer
Isn't worth a bag of snot
If you really need a monkey
And only the best will do
Come on down to Rickie's
His monkeys are all brand new.

—Brian McConnachie

SPAGHETTI PRAYER.

God, grant me the fettuccine
to sop up the sauce I cannot waste;
hot pan to brown the meats I stir;
and the peppers to add the gusto.

—Evan Waite B

HI & DRI IN CONNECTICUT.

—Ben Katchor

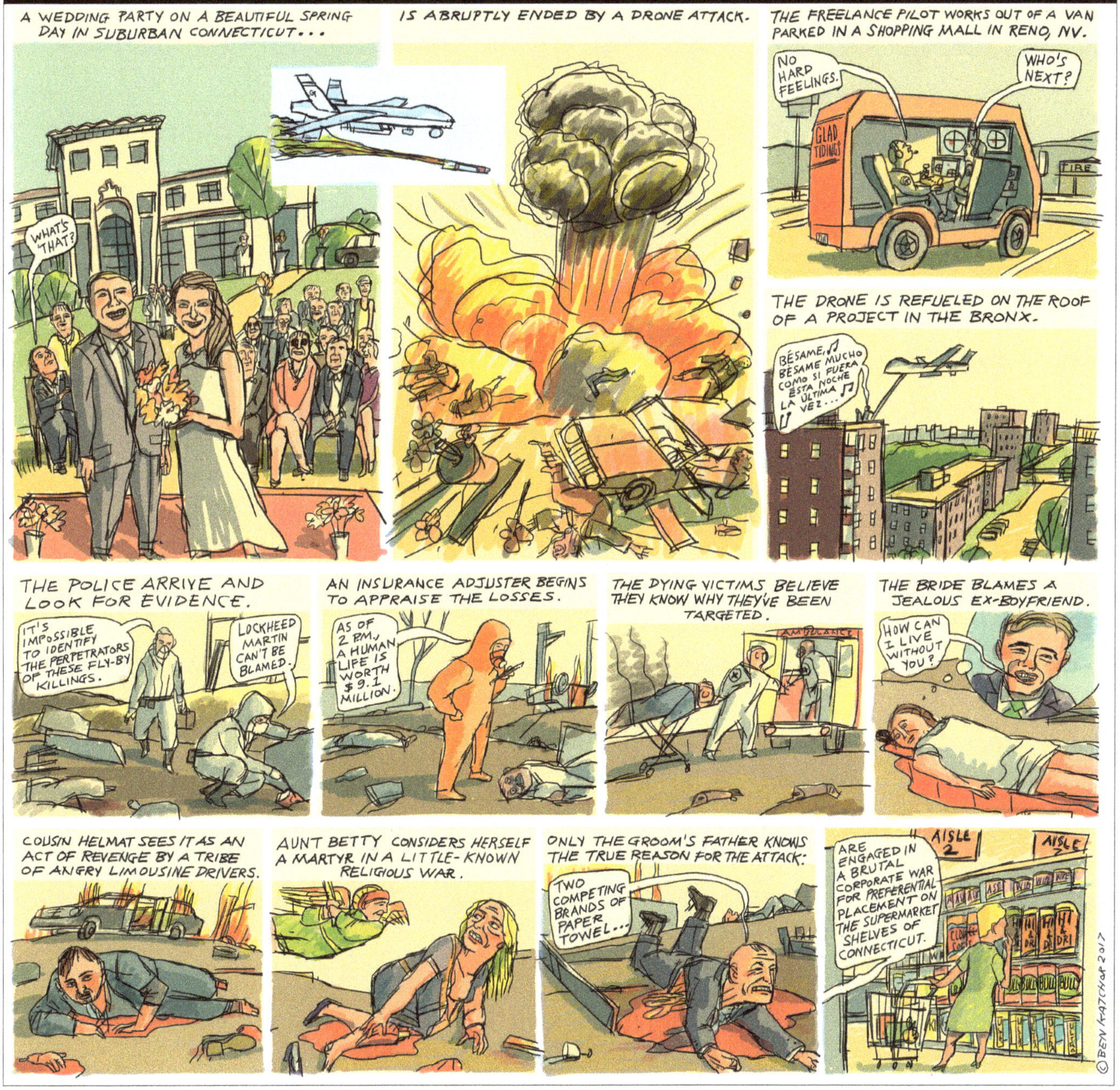
A WEDDING PARTY ON A BEAUTIFUL SPRING DAY IN SUBURBAN CONNECTICUT...
WHAT'S THAT?
IS ABRUPTLY ENDED BY A DRONE ATTACK.
THE FREELANCE PILOT WORKS OUT OF A VAN PARKED IN A SHOPPING MALL IN RENO, NV.
NO HARD FEELINGS.
WHO'S NEXT?
GLAD TIDINGS
THE DRONE IS REFUELED ON THE ROOF OF A PROJECT IN THE BRONX.
BÉSAME, BÉSAME MUCHO COMO SI FUERA ÉSTA NOCHE LA ÚLTIMA VEZ...
THE POLICE ARRIVE AND LOOK FOR EVIDENCE.
IT'S IMPOSSIBLE TO IDENTIFY THE PERPETRATORS OF THESE FLY-BY KILLINGS.
LOCKHEED MARTIN CAN'T BE BLAMED.
AN INSURANCE ADJUSTER BEGINS TO APPRAISE THE LOSSES.
AS OF 2 P.M., A HUMAN LIFE IS WORTH $9.1 MILLION.
THE DYING VICTIMS BELIEVE THEY KNOW WHY THEY'VE BEEN TARGETED.
AMBULANCE
THE BRIDE BLAMES A JEALOUS EX-BOYFRIEND.
HOW CAN I LIVE WITHOUT YOU?
COUSIN HELMAT SEES IT AS AN ACT OF REVENGE BY A TRIBE OF ANGRY LIMOUSINE DRIVERS.
AUNT BETTY CONSIDERS HERSELF A MARTYR IN A LITTLE-KNOWN RELIGIOUS WAR.
ONLY THE GROOM'S FATHER KNOWS THE TRUE REASON FOR THE ATTACK:
TWO COMPETING BRANDS OF PAPER TOWEL...
ARE ENGAGED IN A BRUTAL CORPORATE WAR FOR PREFERENTIAL PLACEMENT ON THE SUPERMARKET SHELVES OF CONNECTICUT.
AISLE 2
AISLE
HI & DRI
©BEN KATCHOR 2017

"IF BARRY BLITT IS ANYTHING IT'S BRILLIANTLY PROVOCATIVE."

—JAMES RAINEY, *LOS ANGELES TIMES*

Blitt
by Barry Blitt
THE NEW YORKER

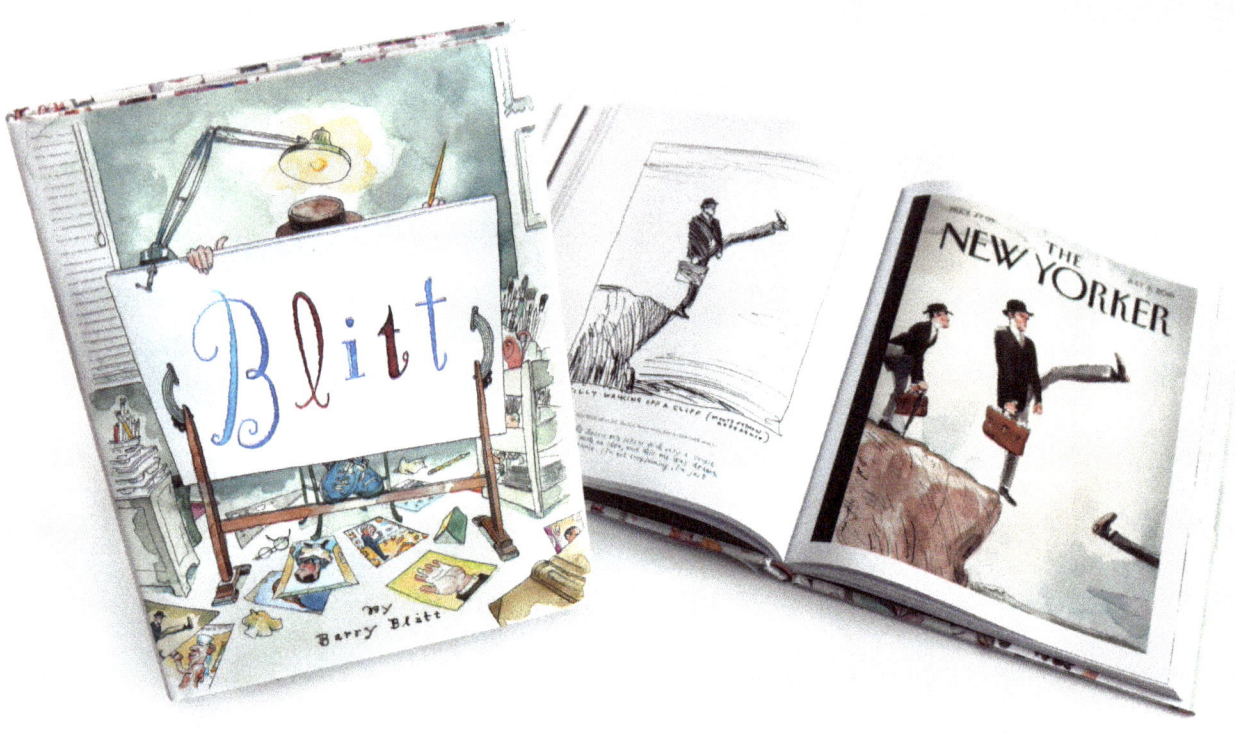

"By turns fascinating and entertaining . . . The beauty of [Blitt's] art is that it rarely needs explaining. You just *get* it."

—*MOTHER JONES*

A gorgeous, hilarious, and provocative compendium of the award-winning artist's illustrations for *The New Yorker*, *The New York Times*, *Vanity Fair*, and more.

- Featuring more than 100 never-before-seen sketches and unpublished illustrations with insightful and satirical annotations by the artist
- Including original essays by Frank Rich, Françoise Mouly, Steve Brodner, David Remnick, and Steven Heller
- Gorgeously designed, an essential coffee-table book for discerning political spectators and fans of comic art alike

ON SALE NOW

AS TOLD TO SIMON RICH

AN ORAL HISTORY

Mournful fiddle music; a slow pan across the tile

It's hard to believe that so much time has passed. But maybe that's because it *never really ended?*

Some cultural events are forgotten the moment they occur, vanishing like so much dust. But others seem to echo and reverberate — sparking new dialogues, creating new paradigms, and yes, even changing the world.

It's been 15 minutes since Craig DeSantos took a shit. And while critics still debate its meaning, there's one thing we can all agree on: nothing will ever be the same.

To commemorate this important anniversary, we spoke to those who made the event possible, as well as those affected by its impact. Interviews have been condensed for length.

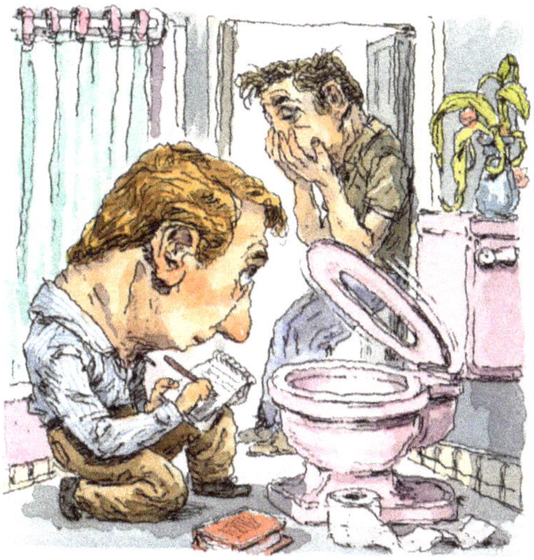

JOHN CUNEO

20 MINUTES AGO: BEGINNINGS

***Benji Platzer**, roommate:* You know, when I think back on that time 20 minutes ago, before it all went down, what pops into my head is, "we were just kids." You know what I mean? We weren't trying to change the world. We were just having fun, messing around, eating leftover Szechuan food, drinking coffee. Whatever, no big deal, typical Sunday morning. (Laughs) When you're young, you don't really think about your "legacy," you know? You're just living for the moment. I guess, in hindsight, you could say we were pretty naïve.

***Monica Lee**, roommate:* It started off really organically. Benji was microwaving leftover Szechuan food, I was brewing coffee. We knew we were creating something new, and we were obviously pretty excited about the process — but it wasn't this Big Important Thing. Not yet.

***Professor Kenneth Wentworth**, Oxford University:* In order to appreciate Craig's shit, you have to place it in its historical context. Twenty minutes ago, the world was a very different place. Craig's roommates had brewed coffee before, they'd microwaved leftover Szechuan before. But serving them both at the same time? That concept had never occurred to anyone. At the time, such a thing simply wasn't done.

***John Yao**, waiter, Szechuan Gourmet:* I was actually the guy who took the call when they first ordered the Szechuan food the night before. Of course, now, everyone knows what they got: Dan Dan noodles, house spicy beef, shrimp with szechuan sauce, side of garlic cabbage and the appetizer platter. But at the time, I had no idea what to expect. I was just standing there, writing down the order.

I definitely remember thinking, "this has potential." But I never imagined it'd turn into what it did. It's funny to think back on how clueless I was. I mean, can you picture it? There I was, probably dressed like I am now, just writing down their order with a pencil. Like, "Oh, here's another order, better write it all down, no big deal." (Laughs) And of course I threw away the order slip. Yeah, it's in a trashcan, somewhere. So, you know, "story of my life."

Fun fact, it was actually supposed to be my friend Jin who took that order. It was his shift. But he was talking to his girlfriend, so I covered for him. I still bust him about it. Drives him crazy.

15 MINUTES AGO: APOTHEOSIS

***Benji Platzer**, roommate:* The crazy thing is, when Craig stood up from the table, I didn't know where he was going. I thought maybe he was going to the fridge, to get some water. You know, because he had been talking about how spicy the food was. But instead, he turned left, towards the bathroom — and I knew he was probably going to take a shit. Intuition, I guess.

***Monica Lee**, roommate:* I knew. The moment he stood up, I knew.

Look, I'm just a working class kid from Bay Ridge. Where I'm from, expectations are low. Schools are like jails. Metal detectors, drug-sniffing dogs. You learn real quick: if you want to survive, keep your head down. Don't ask any questions. And whatever you do, don't you dare have dreams. Dreams are for the movie stars you see on magazines. They're not for you.

I hope some kids are reading this, I really do, because as corny as it is to say, anything is possible.

***Ben Moss**, roommate:* Craig's shit was so loud. He turned on the fan and a faucet, but everyone could still hear him taking the shit.

EPILOGUE

***Benji Platzer**, roommate:* It's hard to believe, but people are already starting to forget. Craig opened a couple of windows, Ben turned on soccer in the common room. It's, like, "Life goes on." (sighs) Look, I know the world is changing. Craig took an Immodium and we're out of Szechuan food. But something happened here. Something that cannot be erased. And I was a witness, and you were a witness, and for one bright, shining moment, we experienced what it is to be human.

***Craig DeSantos**, creator:* To be honest, I'm not really comfortable with this article you're doing. Is it okay if you maybe just don't do the article? Please, don't do this article. Don't do this. B

SIMON RICH'S *latest book is called* Hits and Misses.

SAGAN-AGAIN

BY STEVE YOUNG

ALIEN NOTES ON THE VOYAGER SPACE PROBE GOLDEN RECORD

TO: Inhabitants of the Voyager Space Probe's home world
FROM: The alien civilization patrolling interstellar space beyond your solar system

We are in receipt of the Golden Record attached to your 1977 Voyager Space Probe, which we intercepted last Tuesday (or according to your calendar, Thursday). Thanks so much for sending!

First, it's hilarious that you sent out this disc at exactly the weird point in your history when you'd gotten the hang of space flight, yet you were still basically analog. You have gone digital by now, right? Or were you already digital and thought an actual record was charmingly "retro"? (Our civilization has hipsters too, so we get it.)

Also, thanks for trying to convey the playing instructions via wordless diagrams. We do speak and read English (just about every civilization does, FYI), so in the future don't bother with the frustrating how-to-assemble-your-furniture cartoons. Just explain how the thing works. We're advanced; we'll pick it up quickly.

After a couple false starts (more on that later) we managed to play the disc with the included stylus, and we have some notes and questions on the material.

It was nice to hear from UN Secretary General Kurt Waldheim. But did anyone coach him on his statement? Did he record any other takes? This one frankly sounded a little wooden. Also, maybe he should dial back the silly accent. Overall not a great first impression for your world.

Greetings in 55 languages is a bit much. No offense, but the novelty wears off after the tenth or so blast of gibberish. Obviously you need English, and Welsh and Bengali are pretty widespread throughout the galaxy, but we suspect that you're pranking us on some of these. "Swedish"? *Seriously?*

The Sounds of Earth: A few interesting bits here, but on the whole, so-so. Some of the animal sounds were worthwhile; for instance, we don't have hyenas, so we thought, "Cool, a hyena." Whales, sure, worth hearing once. But your wind and your bugs are not so different from ours, and in any case, a little of that sort of thing goes a long way. Same for the wood sawing sound. To be honest we skipped over most of the train, bus, and tractor material. And while we're sure Carl Sagan is a very smart scientist, his laughter is creepy and goes on too long.

Pictures: We couldn't access all of the images, since during the initial confusion about how to play the record it was dropped and this section got scratched. Only half of the Toronto airport photo would load, but we get the idea. The supermarket looks like fun. We couldn't view the sand dunes picture, but no great loss as we're familiar with sand dunes. We appreciate the "Demonstration of Licking, Eating, and Drinking" picture; we'd been wondering how you lick. (We could have done without the bonus pictures of Carl Sagan licking things, however.) Sunset with birds: aww, nice. Rush hour traffic in Thailand looks hellish. We couldn't get "Old Turkish Man with Beard and Glasses" to play; please resend at your convenience. The crocodile — is that a joke? You know we look like crocodiles, right?

Music: This was all over the map. Love love love the Georgian choral folk music. The ballet piece: as with the sawing noise, a little goes a long way. The mariachi track had us all up and dancing. "Johnny B. Goode" is very goode (ha!), but it's awfully similar to many other Chuck Berry songs. Mozart and Beethoven: pleasant if you like that sort of thing. The Chinese folk piece is okay, but seven minutes is more than anyone needs. The Indonesian track set up some sort of odd vibrations that caused several of us to bleed; not your fault, obviously, but please make a note for the future. Peruvian Wedding Song: just no. The Blind Willie Johnson: whoah, that is some dark shit. Is everything okay on your planet?

The "brain waves" recording: Nice try, but it didn't really work. A few times we were able to make out fleeting thoughts like "wish I had a cupcake" or "need to take a whiz," and possibly something about a cute neuroscience lab technician, but most of the hour was just static. Not sure whether this is due to your subpar technology or whether you were simply monitoring a stupid member of your species.

Are you aware of the "Easter egg" audio track of Carl Sagan describing his sexual fantasies, or did he slip that in on the sly? Regardless, some of us enjoyed it.

Despite any quibbles we may have had with the material, we were delighted to hear from you and we look forward to staying in touch. We're horribly busy out here in deep space, but we'll try to put together a batch of our own pictures and audio and launch it your way soon. Best of luck with your civilization! You didn't need the record back, did you? (Full disclosure: after making a digital dub for our archives, we sold the record to a collector.) Thanks again! B

STEVE YOUNG *(@pantssteve) is a veteran **Letterman** writer who's also written for **The Simpsons**. He is the main subject of a new comedy music documentary,* **Bathtubs Over Broadway**.

GURGEN ALOIAN

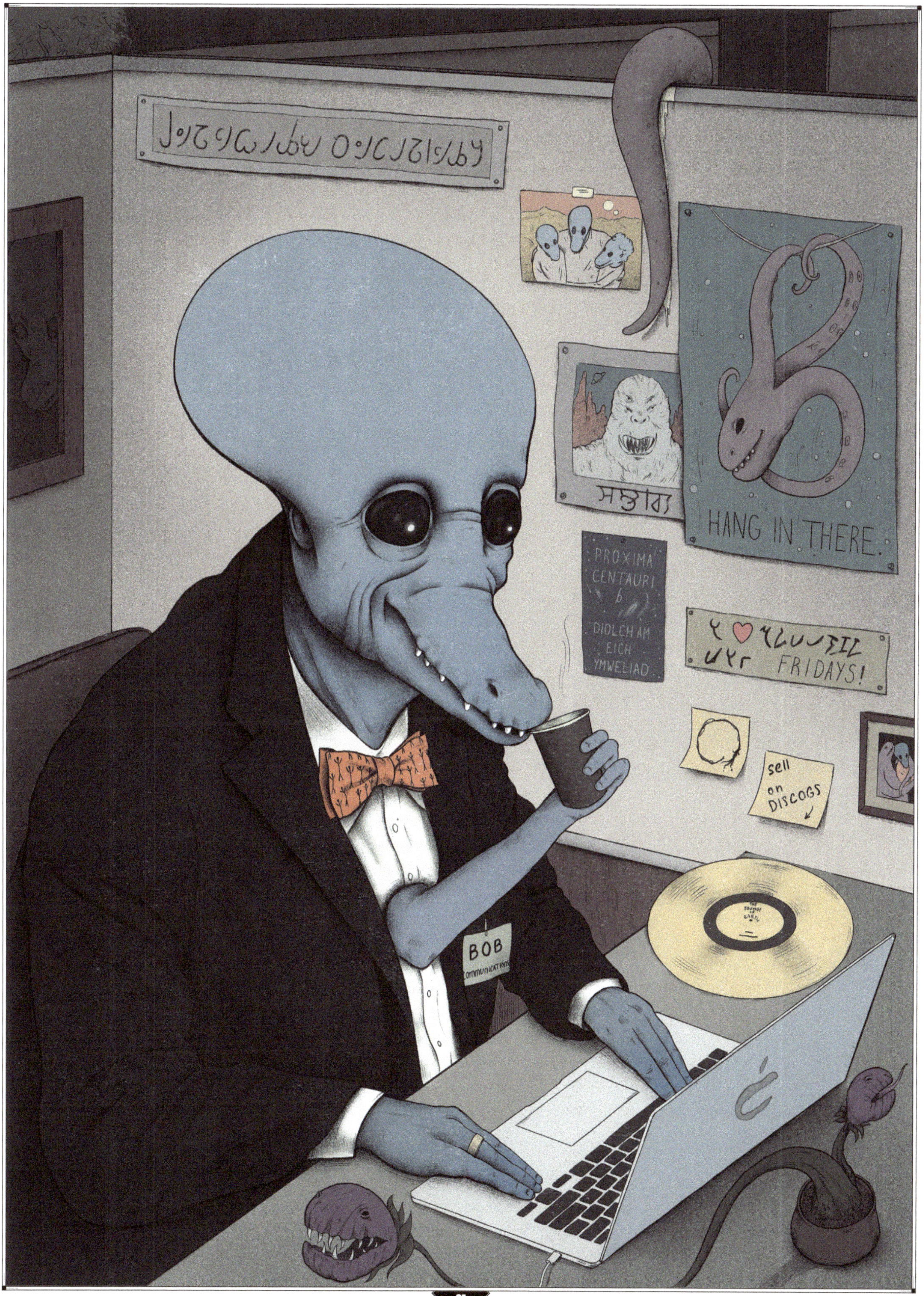
HANG IN THERE.
PROXIMA CENTAURI b
DIOLCH AM EICH YMWELIAD
FRIDAYS!
sell on DISCOGS
BOB

GEN EX
BY EMILY FLAKE

AFTER BREAKFAST

It's 2018, John Hughes is dead, and we don't feel very good ourselves

The divorce was finalized this morning. Twenty years, almost to the day (thanks for that, Larry). Two kids. Great kids. But they're not babies anymore — surly, uncommunicative little shits, if you want to know the truth — and there's only so many secretaries a woman can put up with her husband fucking.

Speaking of fucking, I think Serena's doing it. She's *fifteen goddamn years old*. I found condoms in her book bag and contraceptive gel under her bed. I mean, contraceptive gel? Isn't that messy? And complicated? I just think it's a weird choice for a teenager. A teenager who has no business fucking.

John was my first, and I was seventeen. Say what you will, there's a lot of difference between 17 and 15. We met in detention, of all places. I did some stupid fucking trick with my lipstick. He made fun of me for it, but later, he couldn't get enough of it. Thought it was the funniest thing he'd ever seen. Once I did it with his dick, right in the middle of blowing him. He laughed so much he lost his hard-on. My tits were great then, sweet little b-cups. I really had to hunch up my shoulders for that stupid lipstick trick. Not like now. If I hunch up like that now, my tits graze the top of my pot belly, and it makes me want to die.

When we did it for the first time, he was gentle. You wouldn't think a guy like that could be so gentle, but he was. We did it on the couch in his room — the basement of his shitty tract house. It was upholstered in some kind of scratchy wool plaid stuff, all ripped up and fixed with duct tape. I can still feel the spot under my right thigh where the fabric was covered up with that goddamn tape. My leg kept sticking to it and it was really irritating. I remember what that felt like and I don't even remember what it felt like when he stuck it in me. "Are you okay?" he whispered after. No one had ever, ever made me feel more like they cared whether or not I was okay. Never had, and not since.

Where is Serena fucking that little twerp she's been running around with? His car? That ancient town car with the shaky steering? Or in his room? I picture him having a waterbed, somehow. But nobody has those any more, do they? And they must be fucking in her room too, unless that's just where she keeps that gel. *Gel*. Jesus.

John and I used rubbers like normal kids. I tried going on the pill, but it made me break out and bloat up like a Christmas turkey. They didn't give them out free like they do now at Planned Parenthood. I made John buy them. And we were careful, until we weren't.

Does Serena know that the gel won't stop AIDS? Do I really have to have this conversation with her?

I was eight weeks pregnant when I got the abortion. He, she, whatever it was, was barely there at all. Not even human looking. The size of a kidney bean, they told me. A KIDney bean, har har. They didn't think that was funny at all. John didn't want me to get rid of it. He wouldn't come with me to the clinic. I walked and had Therese pick me up — Therese, who couldn't figure out for the life of her what I was doing with John Bender anyway. And what was I going to do? Marry him? Live with his dirtbag parents in that shitty basement and get my GED? He was a loser. My family came to this county on the Mayflower.

He was a fucking loser.

He wouldn't talk to me afterwards. He just strode right by me in the hall, his jaw all tight, staring straight ahead. Therese told me that if I was through with my little slumming experiment, Carter had been asking about me. Prom was coming up. John Bender in a tux, like *that* would have ever happened.

I went to Brown. I met Larry. We got married a couple years out of college. Then we had Serena, then we had Sophia, and then I got fat, and now we're here. Just like John said it would be. I squeezed out a couple of puppies and *bluuuuurp*. I don't think he thought it would be the anti-depressants that did it, though. No kids knew about that kind of thing then.

Serena and Sophia know all about it, though. Serena just started taking Wellbutrin, and she's terrified it'll make her fat. Maybe that's why she uses gel. Maybe she doesn't want to get fat on the Pill.

I don't know what happened to John. He didn't come to school much after all that. I knew Allison talked to him a little bit — not that Allison and I talked much. After I gave her that makeover in detention she went right back to wearing black shit all the time and one weirdo in my life was all I could really afford, socially. I ran into her a week before I left for school. "He doesn't talk about you Claire," she said. "He won't" — and then she shut up, and that was that.

When you grow up, your heart dies. That's what Allison said, that day we were all locked up together like rats. When you grow up, your heart dies. If only that were fucking true.

EMILY FLAKE

(@EmilyFlake) is a cartoonist, writer, illustrator, performer, and household drudge living in Brooklyn. Her latest is a book of essays and cartoons about parenting entitled **Mama Tried**.

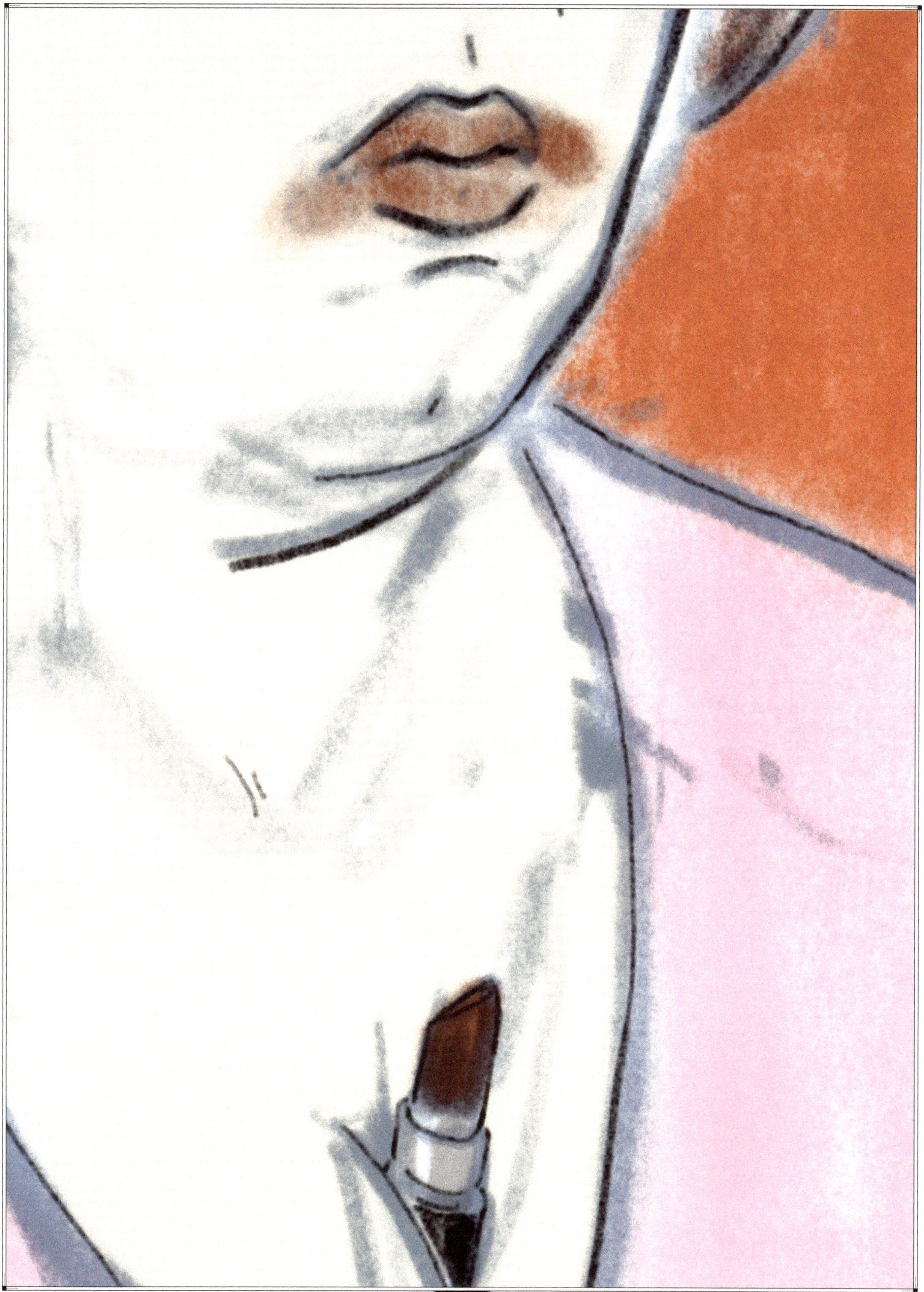

EMILY FLAKE

BEATS

BY JONATHAN ZELLER

All the Scenes in Meet Cute...

...the movie in which the same couple keeps meeting cute over and over again for the whole 90 minutes either because of time travel or amnesia

SCENE ONE
She's writing a magazine profile about him for *Stupid Losers Weekly*, and is starting to feel bad that the angle is "He's a Stupid Loser."

SCENE TWO
During a commute, he accidentally knocks coffee out of her hand... but it turns out it was poison!

SCENE THREE
She orders a hamburger at a restaurant, and he's behind her in line and loudly screams "I HATE HAMBURGERS!" Then she turns around and they both think the other is so beautiful. Later, she asks him to try a hamburger and he realizes he likes them. The thing he had been thinking of, which he actually hated, was war.

SCENE FOUR
They meet in line trying to buy tickets to a sold-out showing of *Big Misunderstanding*, the movie in which the same couple keeps getting into a big misunderstanding over and over again for the whole 90 minutes either because of time travel or amnesia.

SCENE FIVE
She's a cab driver and accidentally hits him with her cab.

SCENE SIX
She's a cab driver and intentionally hits him with her cab.

SCENE SEVEN
He's God and they meet in Heaven.

SCENE EIGHT
They meet at a bar or something.

SCENE NINE
They are both space aliens, and meet at a bar or something.

SCENE TEN
They meet in line trying to buy tickets to a sold-out showing of *Back Together*, the movie in which the same couple keeps getting back together after having a big misunderstanding over and over again for the whole 90 minutes either because of time travel or amnesia.

SCENE ELEVEN
She's an antibiotic and he's an infection.

SCENE TWELVE
She's a predatory lender trying to collect his service fees and interest.

SCENE THIRTEEN
They meet at a doughnut shop where they discover that they both like doughnuts, but get into an argument because he thinks doughnuts are really amazing and she thinks they're just very good.

SCENE FOURTEEN
She's a librarian and he's a book.

SCENE FIFTEEN
She's on a honeymoon with another man.

SCENE SIXTEEN
They are rival ad executives working on campaigns marketing cigarettes to children.

SCENE SEVENTEEN
He's just invented the unicycle, and she tells him it's a dumb idea because it doesn't have enough wheels.

SCENE EIGHTEEN
They meet on OkCupid.

JONATHAN ZELLER *(@JonJZeller) has written for* **The New Yorker,** **McSweeney's,** *and* **The New York Times.** *Would you like to be his agent?*

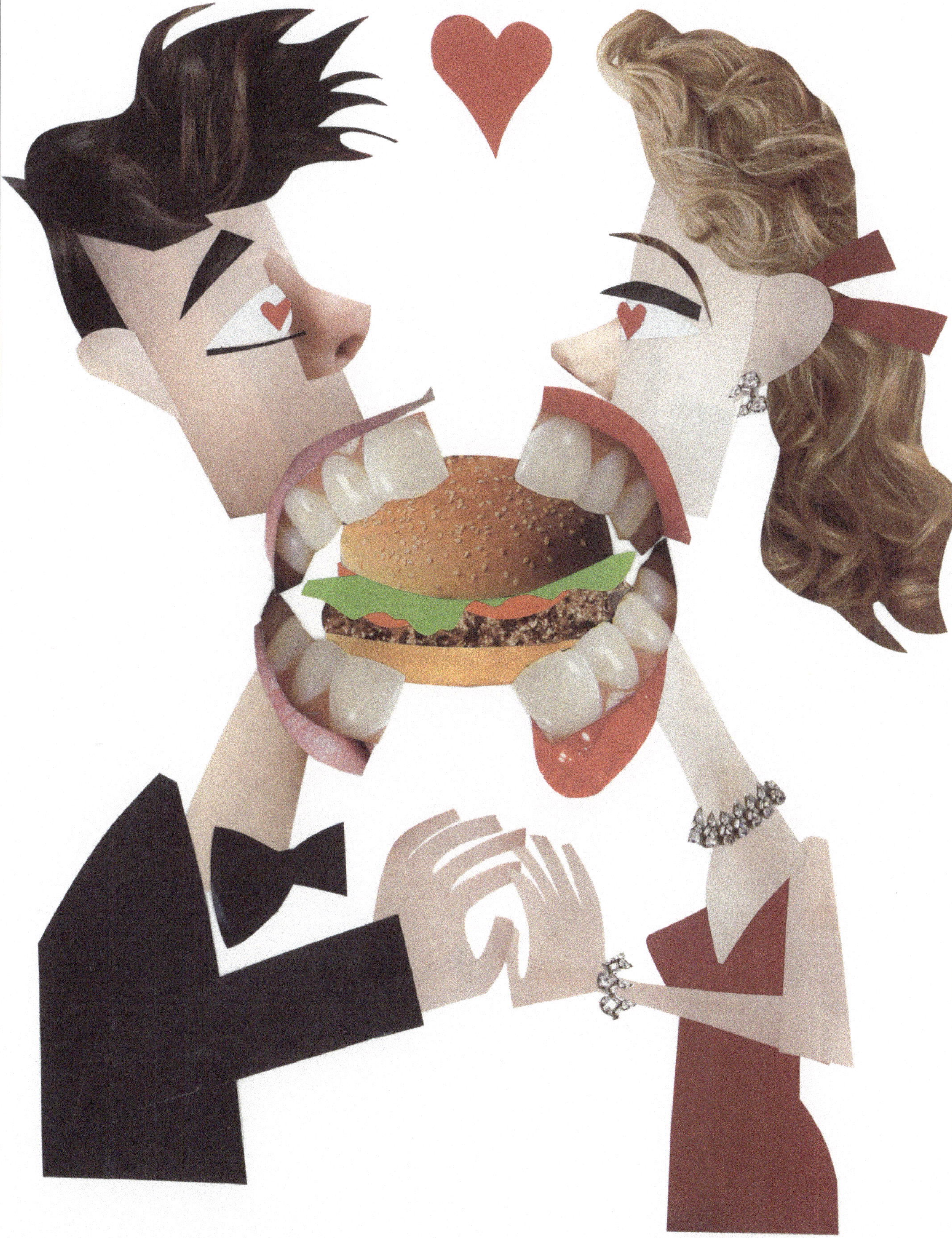

STEPHEN KRONINGER

BY LAURIE ROSENWALD, UNREPENTANT BIKESEXUAL AND OCCASIONAL SWEDE

#WHYNOTMETOO?

Translated from the original Göteborska by JOLIE LAIDE BALLOON

#NOTMEIMTOOUGLY AND #WHYNOTMETOO?

These saucy memes got me into big trouble on the interweb. But trouble is my middle name. Laurie Trouble Rosenwald. I lied. It's not Trouble, it's "Frank," a man's name. You see, I've been a woman and I've been a man, and baby, let me tell you, it's a tough call, irrespective of gender.

Actually, that's not strictly true. I've been a woman all my life. Except for the first part, when I was usually a girl. The point is, I cannot be trusted. You see, women lie. They — I mean we — also cheat and steal. I like to steal fancy makeup. It's fun to get away with things, whether it's a fifty-eight dollar Tom Ford "Vermillionaire" lipstick, or manslaughter.

What do women want? Necco Wafers. Sure, they want to end world hunger, but for now they just want some Angie's BOOMCHICKAPOP Kettlecorn, and to watch *Toast of London* on Netflix.

Also, we want to squeeze the toothpaste from the middle and pee all over the toilet seat without fear of recrimination. Oh wait, that's men.

The best way to find out if somebody is a woman is to turn them over. No, the other way. See? When meeting a woman for the first time, protective clothing should be worn. This is why men wear sunglasses on Tinder, and why God invented khakis. Why they're posing with other guys, assuming I will know which one is "MILFhunter" is a mystery wrapped in a wife-beater.

What makes a woman mad? Mayonnaise.

Did you know that all flight attendants are prostitutes, or that all caterers are drug dealers? You did? Oh. Well, what do you really know about women? I'll bet you didn't know about the feminist toilet cartel that meets in the ladies' rooms of selected Foot Locker locations.[1] That's why we never go to the bathroom alone: we have secret CIA-style meetings in there — with workshops, where we have to break up into smaller groups. Topic A is you and your peculiar anatomy.

By the way, I stole this bogus idea from a student film I saw in 1994.

You thought Putin was behind the 2016 Election? As if. It was me, Amy Poehler and Tina Fey in the "smallest room" of the UCB Theatre. We did it for our sisters in comedy. Because... we couldn't write another pantsuit joke. We took a chance. And, yes... *women make mistakes*.

The only reason we're not all in jail, where we belong, is the jumpsuits —nobody looks good in those things.

Before, you could just be a man or a woman, but now you can be both, either or neither. This has nothing to do with sexual orientation. We now know that there are, in fact, three sexual orientations: straight, gay, and British. Also, "orientation" is no longer a word. Say "Asian." *Arigato*.

If you Google the word "woman," you'll find not only that "Woman is the Glory of Creation" but that "In Nelson, British Columbia, Valentine's Day Chocolates Help Woman Survive Crash," and "Woman's 'Snippy' Comment at Ticket Counter Sparks Bomb Scare."

What this means is that all women are different.

Some might go in for extreme ironing, competitive duck herding, or toy voyaging. Others might practice the Japanese art of *Hikaru Dorodango* — rolling mud into a small ball. Some collect WWII DeHavilland Mosquito planes, while others might enjoy pinning you to the floor in a Juventud Guerrera Style Off the Top Rope Moonsault Body Press Suicida.

Words you mustn't use in female company include "jitney" and "orangutan" which should have a "g" at the end. Also, it's sher*bert*.

Vegetarian women are great in bed. But forget the vegans — they won't eat anything with a face. Too bad, because us vegans are usually hotties. *Nota Bene*: I am not a vegan.

Women make excellent nurses, teachers, and weapons inspectors. They can be rabbis, beekeepers, or brand evangelists.[2] Registered Democrats become passionate, yet profoundly mediocre yoga instructors at the age of 56. It's the law.

Sometimes feminism means dressing in pink, frilly garments. At others, it means that she's the one wearing the pants. If you can just give in and enjoy the idea that she's wearing the pants, you may get lucky, and nobody will be wearing any pants. This is called sex, and it's what women really want. Or maybe it's love. A friend and I polished off a gallon of Äkta Örebro Överste Brännvin at a party, so I asked him, "Jerker,[3] what is love?" He had a perfect reply: "I lick you. You lick me."

Well put. The point is, nobody knows. Leave those questions alone, and come with me to the conservatory. I want to show you something. B

[1] Which ones? We are not at liberty to say.

[2] But why would they want to?

[3] A popular name in Sweden.

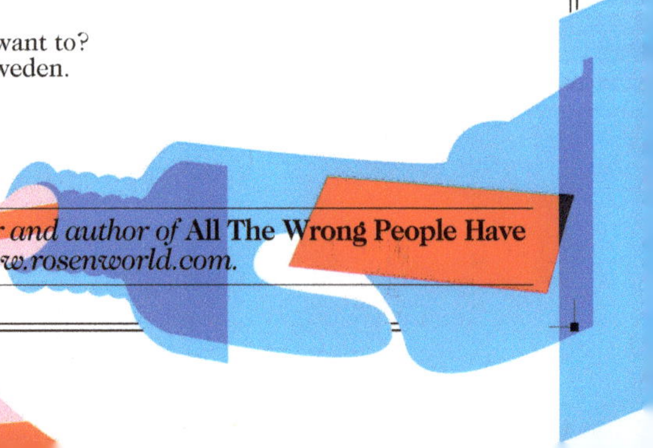

LAURIE ROSENWALD *(@rosenworld) is a painter, designer and author of* **All The Wrong People Have Self-Esteem.** *You can find her at www.rosenworld.com.*

LAURIE ROSENWALD

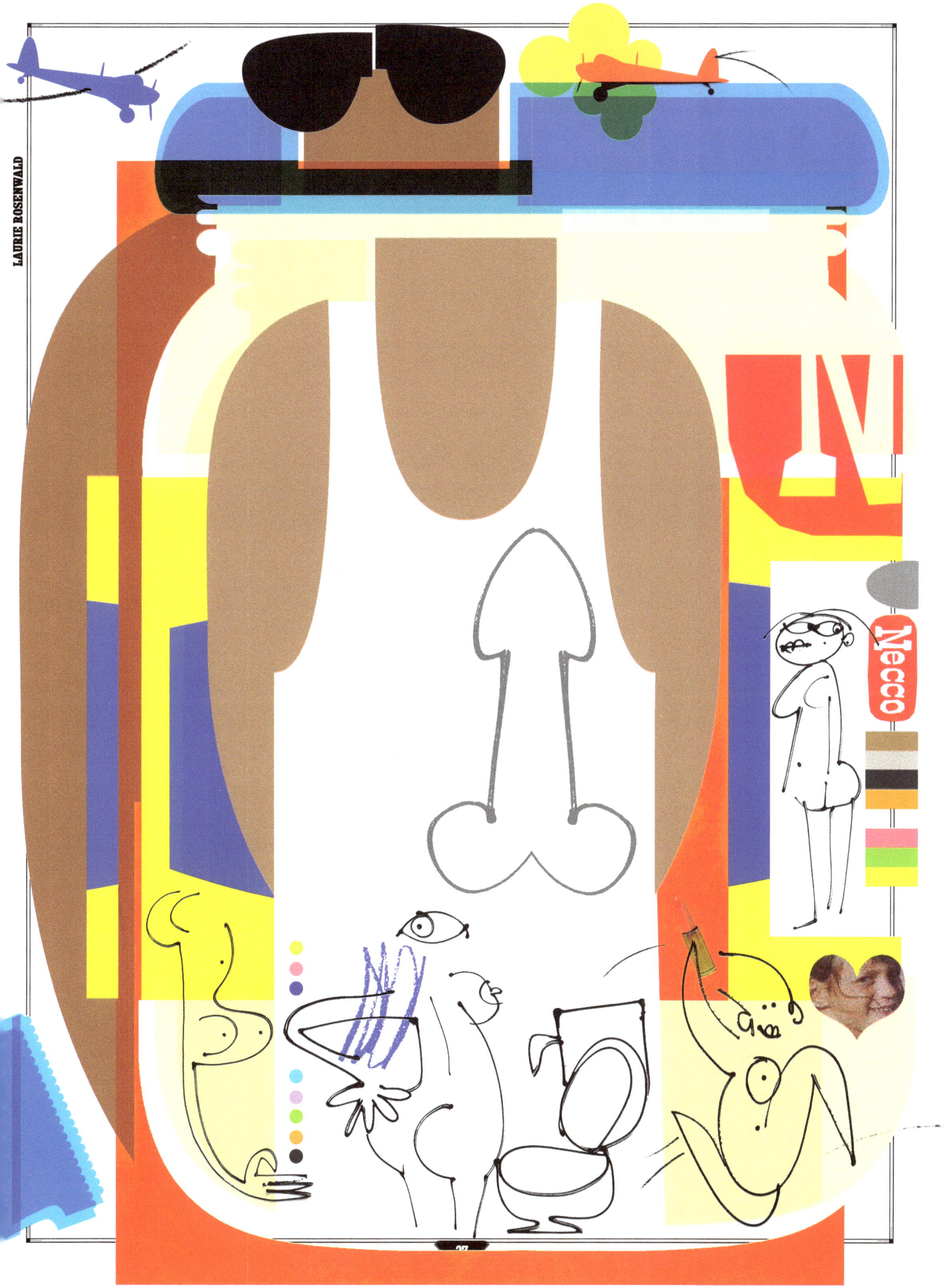
Necco

A SOLO

BY ROB KUTNER

COMPARING THINGS TO JAZZ IS LIKE...JAZZ

Because when you do it, sometimes your writing sings, sometimes it swings, sometimes it jumps, and sometimes it bumps. But if it gets too "smooth," it's only going to be consumed by people in dentists' waiting rooms.

Because just like jazz musicians play it "in the pocket" — just a hair behind the time — comparing things to jazz causes a guy writing in 2018 to sound like he's a beatnik back in 1958.

Because just like jazz is all about "the notes you don't hear," jazz comparisons are all about the words you don't write, like "clueless" and "trying too hard" and "deeply ashamed of my supremely cosseted suburban upbringing."

Because when you catch a groove, you just keep wailing away on it way too long, like "MAN, am I white!" and "Someone tell my parents freelance writing is a 'real job,'" and "Turning every conversation into a display of expertise isn't necessarily a sign of emotional immaturity" and "That's just your opinion, Craig Villegas."

Because comparing things to jazz is all about improvisation. Whether it's explaining why the rent is nine months overdue, or fashioning a Subway 6" turkey sub and a bit of stuffing from your plush bed companion Thelonious Monkey into "Thanksgiving For One," or hastily stammering to Craig Villegas that I'm standing in front of his apartment at 2 a.m. holding a pair of binoculars because I'm a "nocturnal birdwatcher."

Because you gotta know just when to throw it to the sidemen. Speaking of which, Thelonious M., could you please jam out my 500-word piece on "Taking Aim at Bladder Hesitation" for *Men's Health*? It was due a week ago, but it's cool — I always hit my deadlines "in the pocket."

Because like jazz, your life is a series of nonstop, poorly paid side gigs. See above.

Because it's all about the solo. Boy, is it ever. Here it is July, and I've still got leftover "Thanksgiving for One."

Because it's about "breaking the rules." Like starting a sentence that ends up a fragment. Like zigging when they expect you to zig. (See? You were expecting "zag." Try to keep up, Daddycat.) Like getting banned for life from Carnegie Hall, at the legally filed request of a 4th-chair trombonist identifying himself only as "C.V."

Because it was stolen by the white man. Specifically, a certain unnamed freelance writer, so alabaster of hue he can be seen from space. So white he models for the end of a Sherman-Williams paint wheel. So white... (Dig me "catching a groove"?) ...sorry, I got nothing.

In fact, there's only one situation in which jazz *can't* be compared to:

I*f by some strange black magic* (or in my case, the chromatic opposite), immediately ceasing all jazz metaphors would somehow win the strong slide-working, spit-valve-releasing hand of one Mssr. Villegas.

If *that* could happen, I'd throw all of them out through this freshly smashed hole in the single, tiny, greasy, alley-view window of my studio apartment.

Because, you see, love is like...

Punk rock.

ROB KUTNER *writes for* Conan, *wrote for* The Daily Show, *and authored the book* Apocalypse How: Turn the End-Times into the Best of Times *and the graphic novel* Shrinkage.

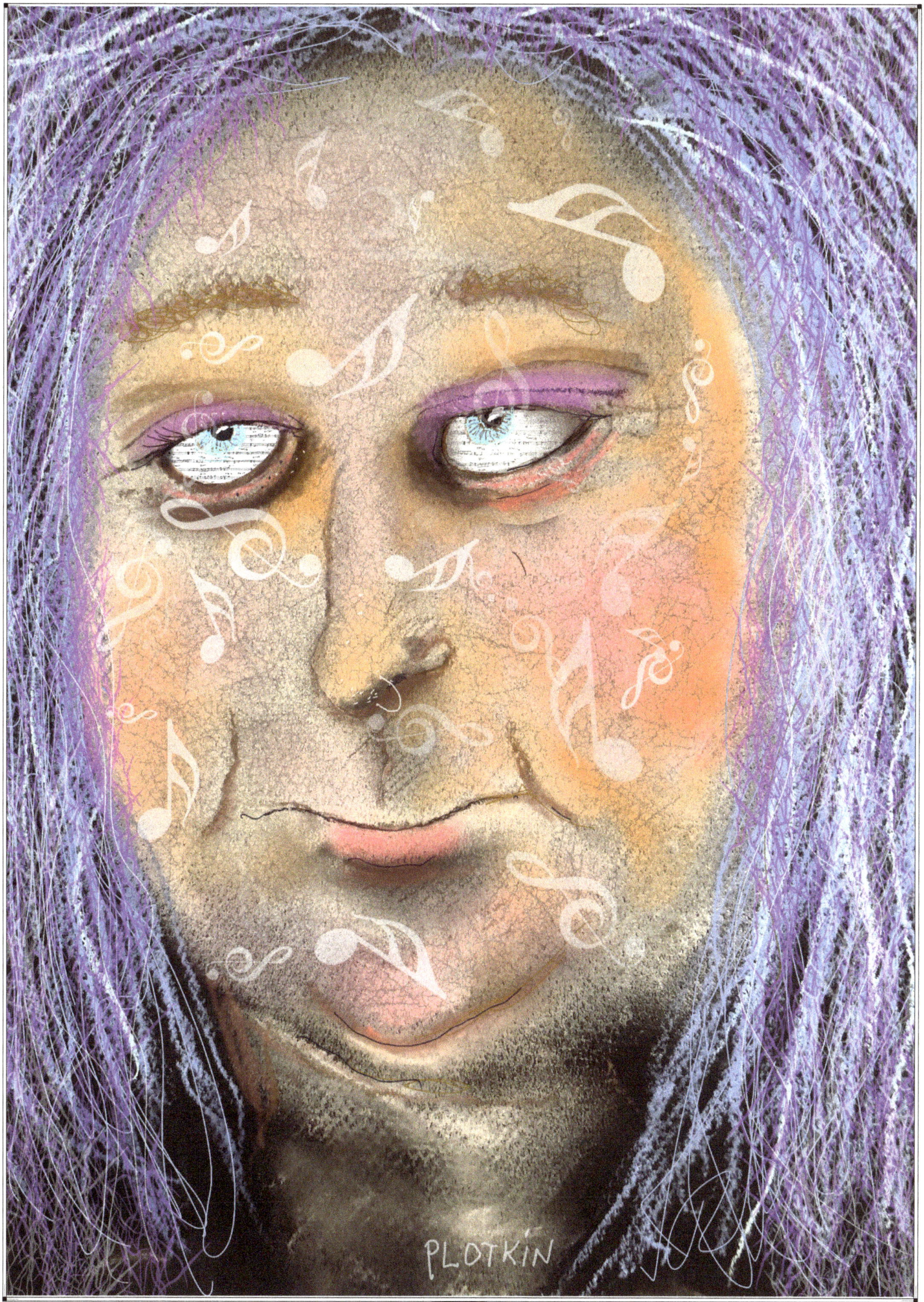
PLOTKIN

JONATHAN PLOTKIN

BY CHRIS MARCIL & SAM JOHNSON

NEW OFFERINGS FROM YOUR ALUMNI EDUCATIONAL TRAVEL

For years, your Alumni Educational Travel service has been proud to live by our motto, "Highly selective adventures for our highly selected clientele." But, while we're still proud of our exclusive tours of foreign capitals and Old West adventures featuring bald eagles roasting over an open campfire, we know that times have changed — especially for our younger alumni who, in a manner of speaking, fell for our college's traditions in the humanities.

Squeezed by student loans and a rapidly changing job market, these alumni may not get a chance at our more luxurious packages until, according to some of our economics faculty, ever. But don't worry — we at Alumni Educational Travel have "got you," with our brand new Comptroller's Choice vacation packages!

Whether you have a "career" as an assistant, a private school teacher/theater advisor, or linkbait content provider, you don't have to cheat yourself of the opportunities travel can bring. Take a look:

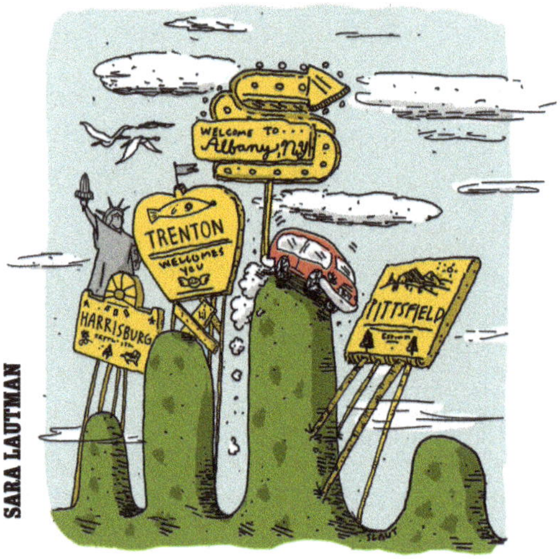
WELCOME TO...
Albany, N.Y.
TRENTON
WELCOMES YOU
HARRISBURG
PITTSFIELD
SARA LAUTMAN

STATE CAPITALS BY MINIVAN

Your borrowed Honda Odyssey takes you on a comprehensive tour of Hartford, where you'll view pictures of historic, beautiful neighborhoods in front of the urban renewal projects that they were mistakenly demolished for. Then, after a brief sojourn in historic Pittsfield, Massachusetts, to drop off an amp for a guy named Beaver, your minivan whisks you to Albany, where you'll be introduced to the fascinating world of state legislatures, and see the closed doors that they work behind. Accompanying you on your journey will be a senior professor or, more likely, Eleanor, a surly grad student, who will relate everything you see to her thesis on colonial coinage.

A WORLD OF LUXURY... FROM THE INSIDE

Imagine flying around the world on a private jet and experiencing the thrill of historic sites in an environment of unmatched plushness. A trip like this, once open only to the very wealthiest, can be yours from the persepective-altering viewpoint of steward, porter, or overall factotum — a position filled by many of the great writers and artists throughout history!

You'll remember the Taj Mahal and the Pyramids of Gaza, unforgettably glimpsed from the support van, and learn the background behind these famous places as you type up the next day's itinerary. The only way to get closer to luxury like this is to go back in time and major in Finance!

A JOURNEY OF WISE-DOM

Your Alumni Educational Travel is following through on the administration's desire to open strategic partnerships with the corporate community — in this case, Wise Potato Chips! You'll hear the call of the open road as you ride with executives from Corporate in Berwick, Pennsylvania on their fact-finding tour of convenience stores in some of the Eastern Seaboard's most postindustrial cities. This package is for the person who prefers the grit of the real world to the glamor of Paris, or for the fan of Wise chips, Cheez Doodles, or Quinlan brand pretzels, which on your budget you probably are.

Admittedly, these packages may not seem better than what you have going on now. But how good is that, really? And you may find — maybe during a postlude pitcher with a no longer surly Eleanor at the Elbo Room on Albany's Delaware Avenue — that just because you followed your dream, it doesn't mean you can't enjoy life. **B**

MARCIL & JOHNSON *are former editors of* **National Lampoon** *and have also written for* **Beavis and Butt-head**, **Frasier**, *and Netflix's* **Disjointed**. *They are over eleven feet tall.*

"Nate Dern may not be quite a genius. Still, he has written a book that is very smart, funny, thoughtful, and that might be just what the world needs."
— THE NEW YORK TIMES BOOK REVIEW

From the senior writer at *Funny or Die* and former artistic director at the Upright Citizens Brigade Theater, a collection of absurdist, hilarious stories and essays on relationships, technology, and society.

"Nate Dern's brain is a VitaMix that chops up Kafka, the internet, Republicans, and thousands of other cultural ingredients and blends them into hilarious little treats... Highly recommended reading for those hungry for surprise."
—A.J. JACOBS, *NEW YORK TIMES* BESTSELLING AUTHOR OF *THE KNOW-IT-ALL* AND *DROP DEAD HEALTHY*

"A breath of fresh air that you can eat up bit by bit or all at once like a huge hoagie. His book is, in a lot of ways, like a really wonderful sandwich."
—ABBI JACOBSON, CO CREATOR AND STAR OF COMEDY CENTRAL'S *BROAD CITY*

AVAILABLE WHEREVER BOOKS ARE SOLD.

SIMONANDSCHUSTER.COM

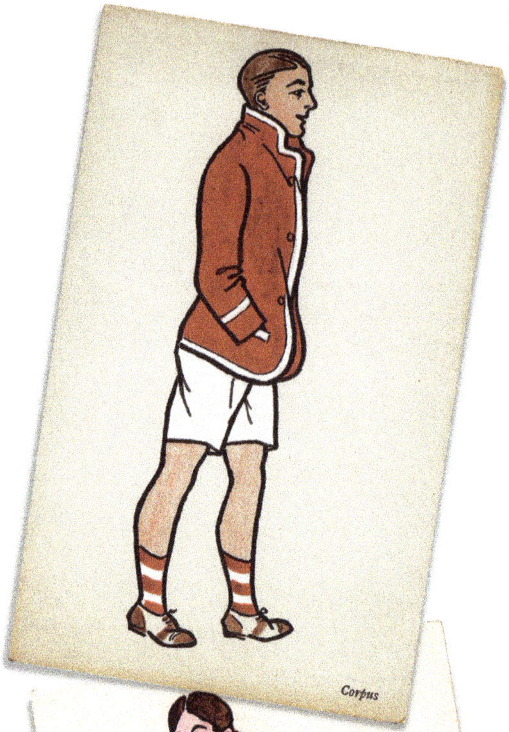
Corpus

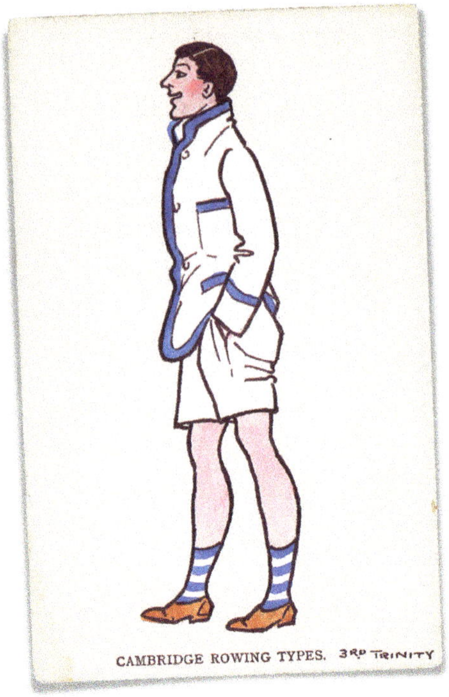
CAMBRIDGE ROWING TYPES. 3RD TRINITY

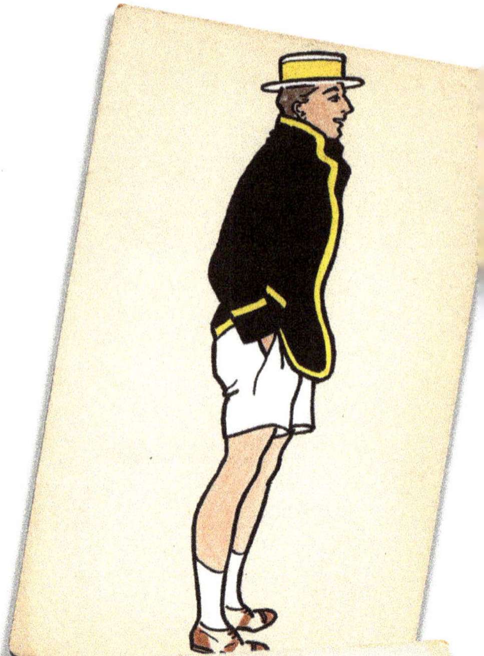

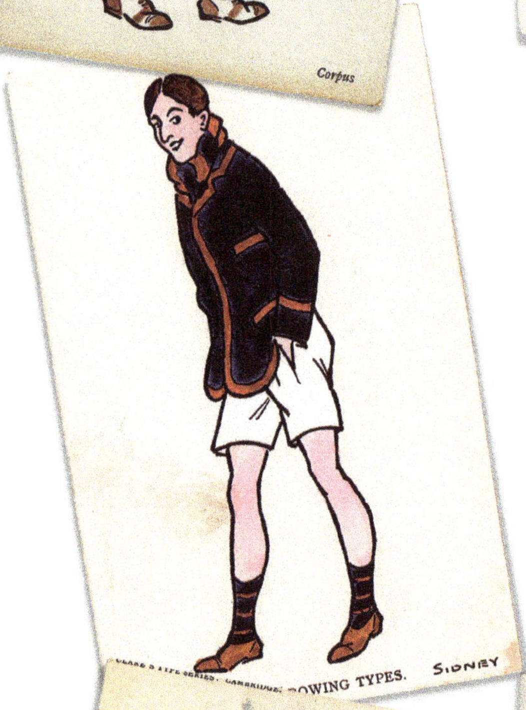
ROWING TYPES.
SIDNEY

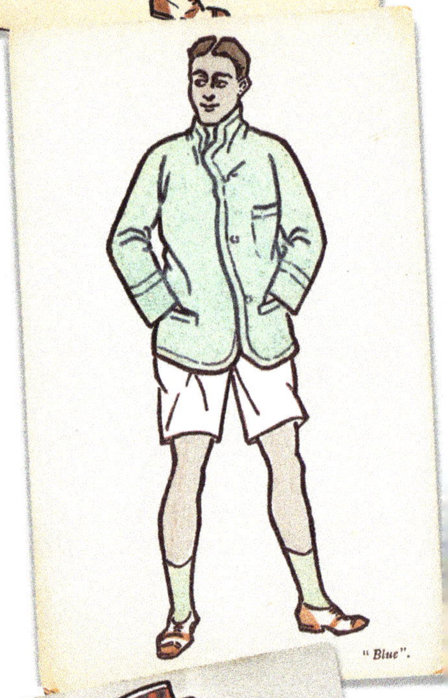
"Blue".

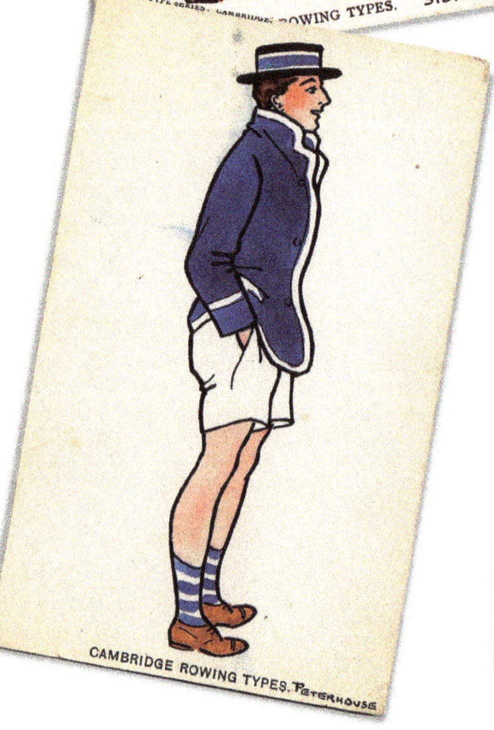
CAMBRIDGE ROWING TYPES. PETERHOUSE

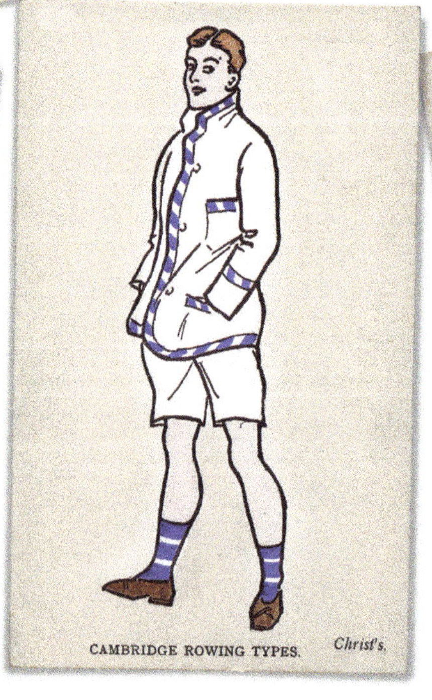
CAMBRIDGE ROWING TYPES.
Christ's.

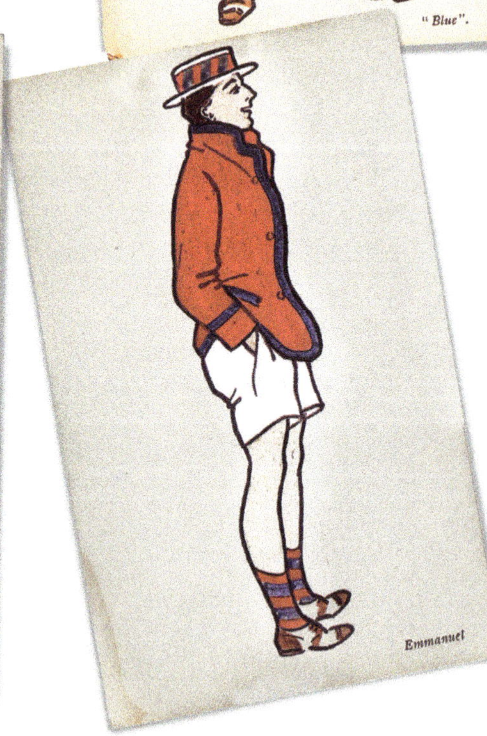
Emmanuel

TOM CHITTY

Your Future Home

In the foreseeable future, the climate will go all weird. Yet, in many ways, you will find life more enjoyable. Robots will do most of the work, helping us reclaim past treasures from the muddy goop that covers the Earth. This will mean much more time for chatting and having cups of tea.

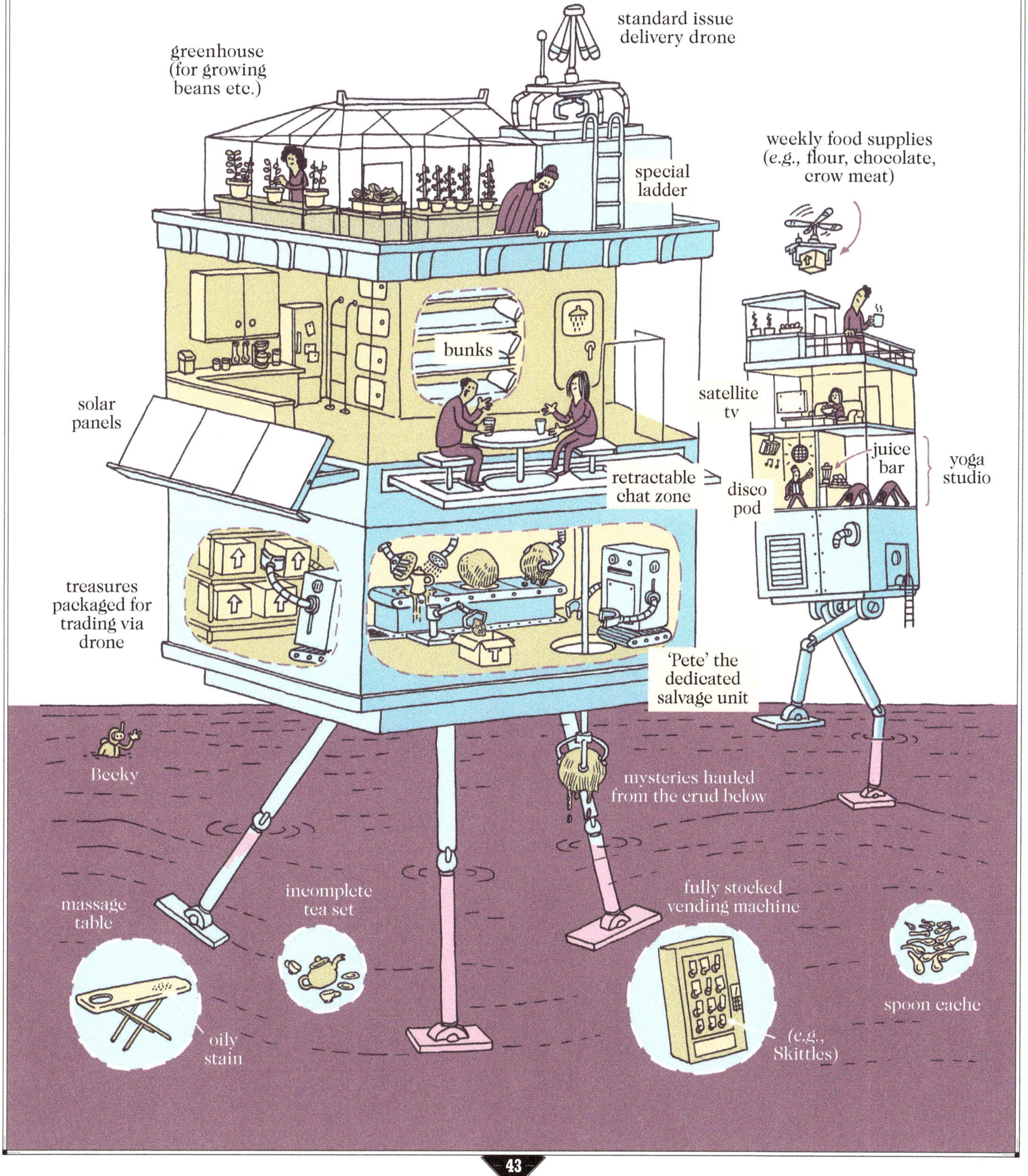

standard issue delivery drone
greenhouse (for growing beans etc.)
special ladder
weekly food supplies (e.g., flour, chocolate, crow meat)
bunks
solar panels
satellite tv
retractable chat zone
disco pod
juice bar
yoga studio
treasures packaged for trading via drone
'Pete' the dedicated salvage unit
Becky
mysteries hauled from the crud below
massage table
incomplete tea set
fully stocked vending machine
spoon cache
oily stain
(e.g., Skittles)

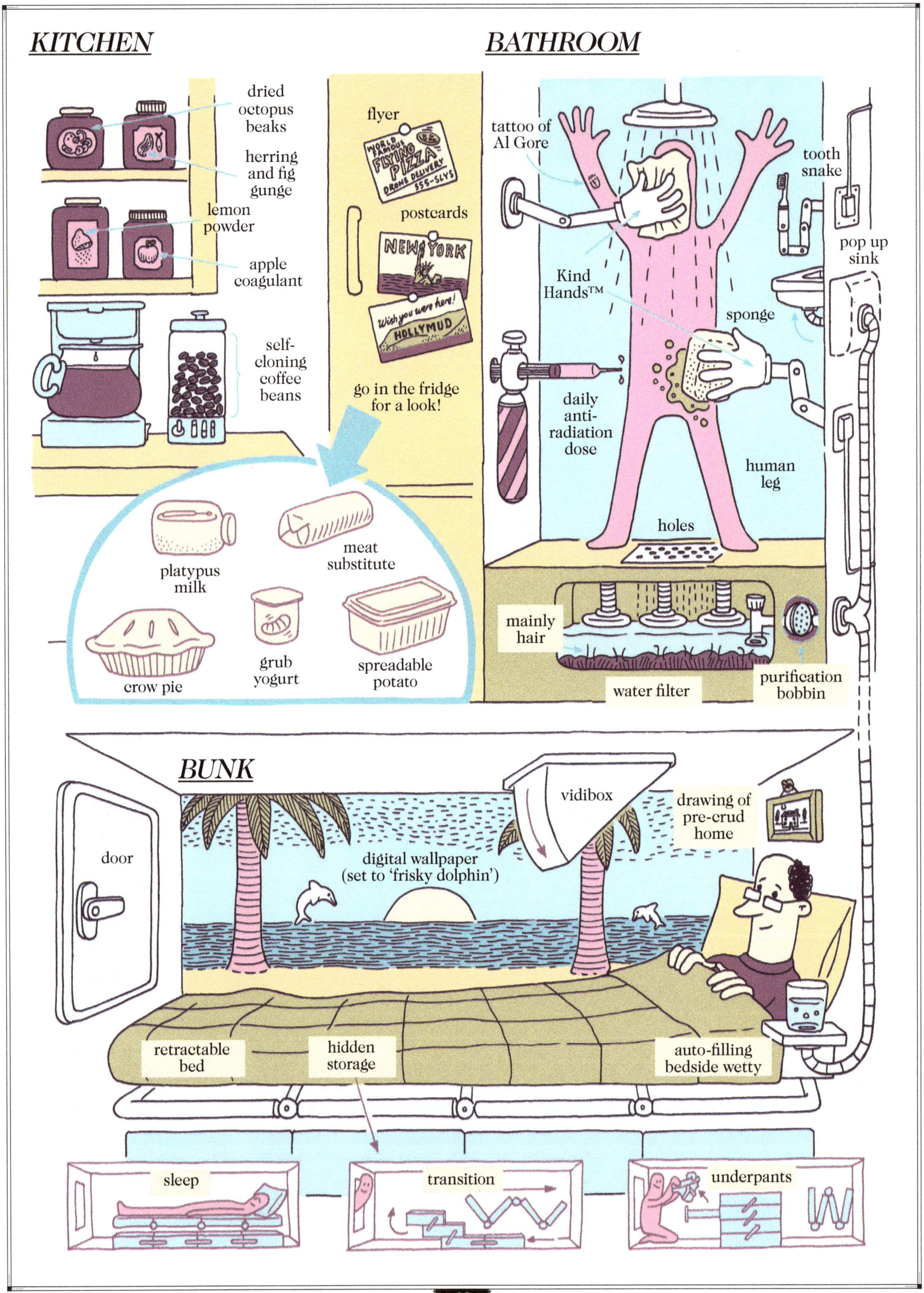
KITCHEN
dried octopus beaks
herring and fig gunge
lemon powder
apple coagulant
self-cloning coffee beans
BATHROOM
flyer
WORLD FAMOUS FLYING PIZZA DRONE DELIVERY 555-SLYS
postcards
NEW YORK
Wish you were here!
HOLLYMUD
go in the fridge for a look!
platypus milk
meat substitute
crow pie
grub yogurt
spreadable potato
tattoo of Al Gore
Kind Hands™
daily anti-radiation dose
sponge
tooth snake
pop up sink
human leg
holes
mainly hair
water filter
purification bobbin
BUNK
door
vidibox
drawing of pre-crud home
digital wallpaper (set to 'frisky dolphin')
retractable bed
hidden storage
auto-filling bedside wetty
sleep
transition
underpants

GREEN HOUSE

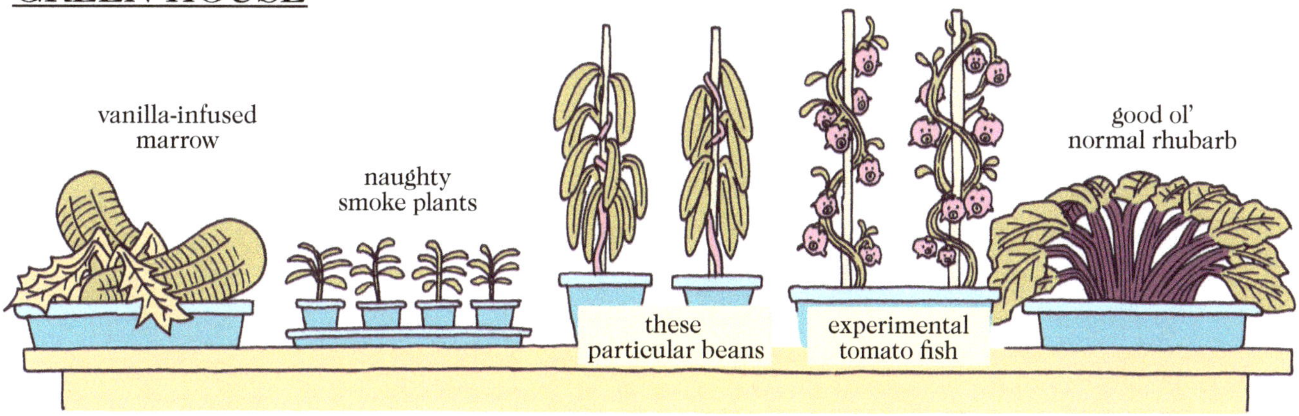

vanilla-infused marrow
naughty smoke plants
these particular beans
experimental tomato fish
good ol' normal rhubarb

SALVAGE ROBOT — EXTRA FUNCTIONS

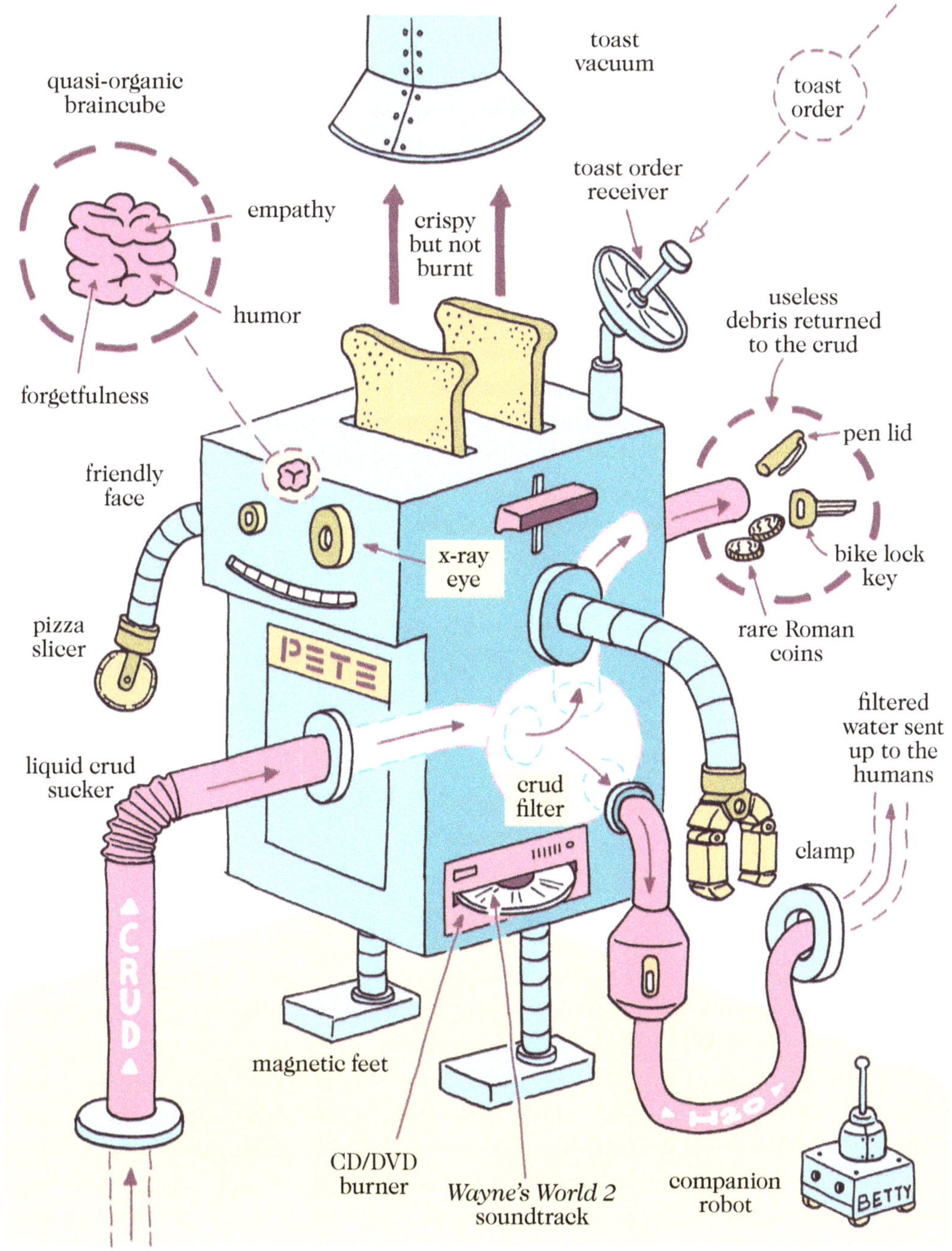

quasi-organic braincube
empathy
humor
forgetfulness
toast vacuum
crispy but not burnt
toast order
toast order receiver
useless debris returned to the crud
pen lid
bike lock key
rare Roman coins
friendly face
x-ray eye
pizza slicer
PETE
liquid crud sucker
CRUD
crud filter
filtered water sent up to the humans
clamp
H2O
magnetic feet
CD/DVD burner
Wayne's World 2 soundtrack
companion robot
BETTY

Pete's All-Time Best Hauls!

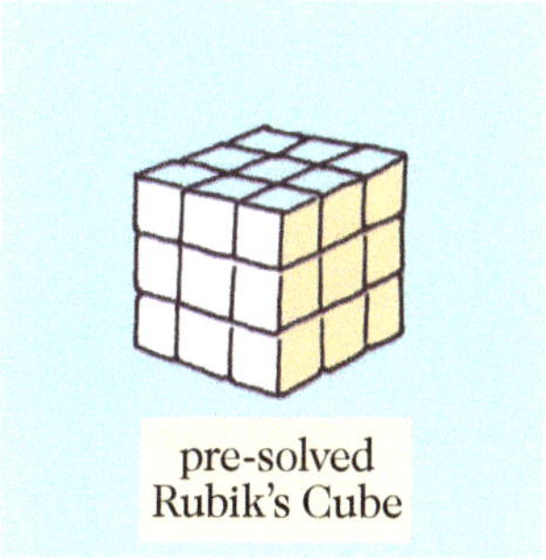
pre-solved Rubik's Cube

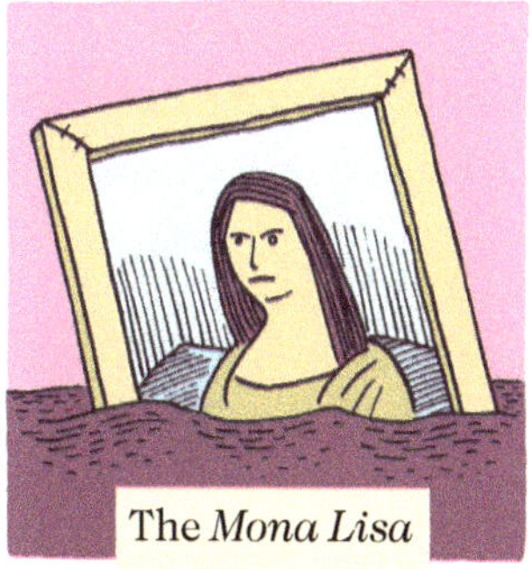
The *Mona Lisa*

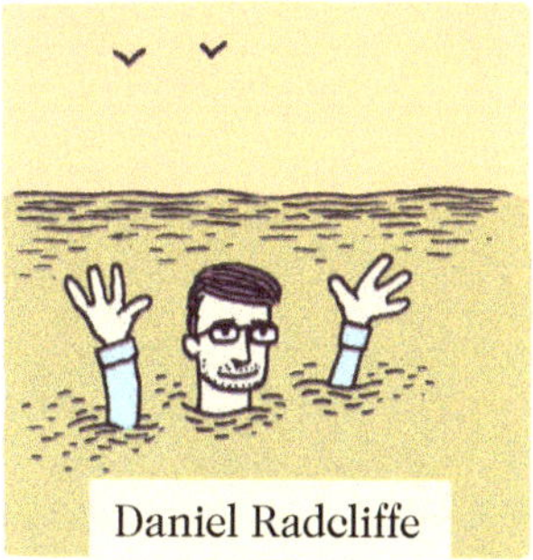
Daniel Radcliffe

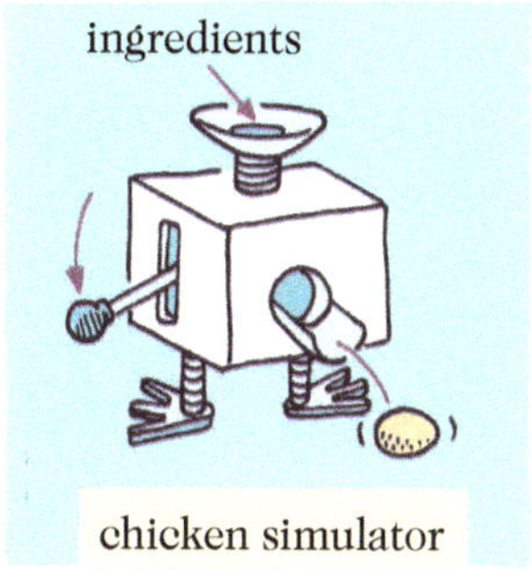

ingredients

chicken simulator

THE VERY NEAR FUTURE

In 2138 an international government lottery granted orbital residency to three hundred and five humans, and assorted animals.

A further thirty years have now passed, and this small colony of spacefolk has taken shape, and begun to expand...

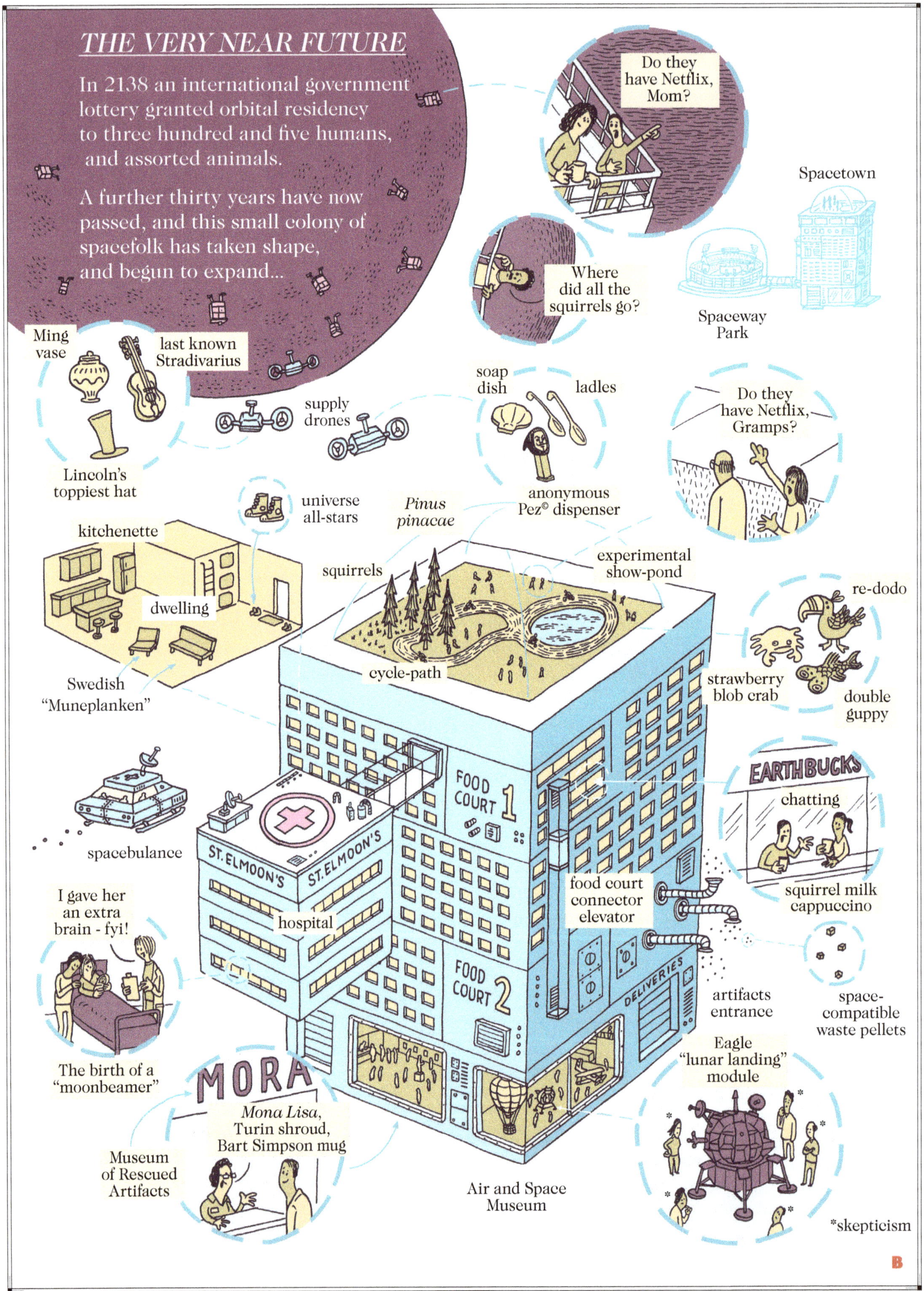

Do they have Netflix, Mom?
Spacetown
Where did all the squirrels go?
Spaceway Park
Ming vase
last known Stradivarius
Lincoln's toppiest hat
supply drones
soap dish
ladles
anonymous Pez© dispenser
Do they have Netflix, Gramps?
universe all-stars
Pinus pinacae
kitchenette
dwelling
Swedish "Muneplanken"
squirrels
experimental show-pond
cycle-path
re-dodo
strawberry blob crab
double guppy
EARTHBUCKS
chatting
squirrel milk cappuccino
spacebulance
FOOD COURT 1
ST. ELMOON'S
ST. ELMOON'S
hospital
food court connector elevator
FOOD COURT 2
DELIVERIES
artifacts entrance
space-compatible waste pellets
I gave her an extra brain - fyi!
The birth of a "moonbeamer"
MORA
Mona Lisa, Turin shroud, Bart Simpson mug
Museum of Rescued Artifacts
Air and Space Museum
Eagle "lunar landing" module
*skepticism

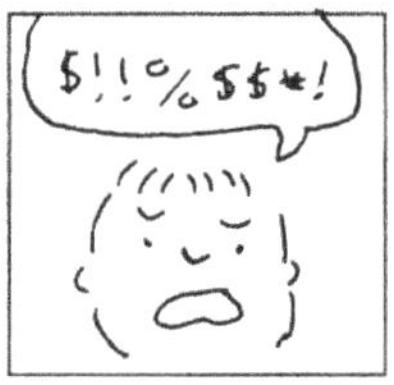
$!!%$$*!

Comic Character Cursing Dictionary

When you read your favorite comic book or newspaper funnies, have you ever wondered what the characters were really saying when those cursing symbols appear in their word balloons? Wonder no longer, as we have consulted the world's most popular cartoonists to provide this handy look-it-up guide. The next time a comic character trips on a banana peel or gets trapped by a villain, you'll know exactly what he or she is really blurting out!

$!!%$$*	*Fuck*	$#&**	*Shit-for-brains*	**&$!!@#	*Son of a bitch*
%#@$#%	*Fucked*	#$%@&!!	*Shit eater*	%$!*&	*Prick*
$#@@	*Fucker*	*%$$#	*Shit-eating*	&#!!!*$	*Dick*
&%%#@	*Fucking*	**%##@	*Piss*	*&$\\@#	*Dickhead*
!@#%**	*Fucked-up*	$@#!!&	*Pissface*	**%$@	*Cocksucker*
%$#@	*Motherfucker*	**%%$#	*Scumbag*	*%%$#&	*Cunt*
%//*&	*Shit*	&%#@	*Hard-on*	&$%@*	*Asshole*
*%$#%	*Shithead*	%&*!%	*Bastard*	!*&$#%	*Fart*

Test Yourself!

What is the tough sergeant saying to the private?

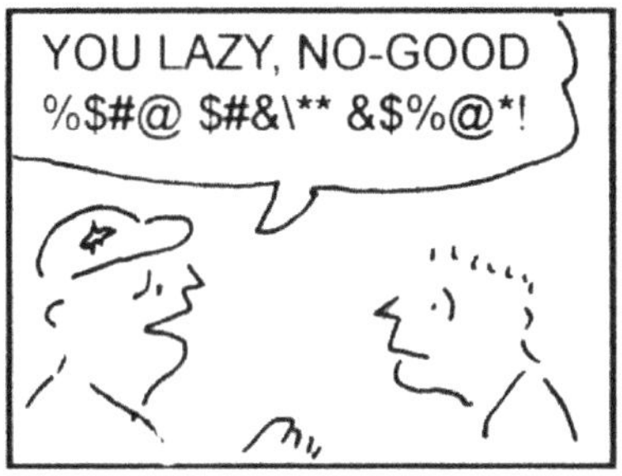
YOU LAZY, NO-GOOD %$#@ $#&** &$%@*!

What is the mean boss saying to his employee?

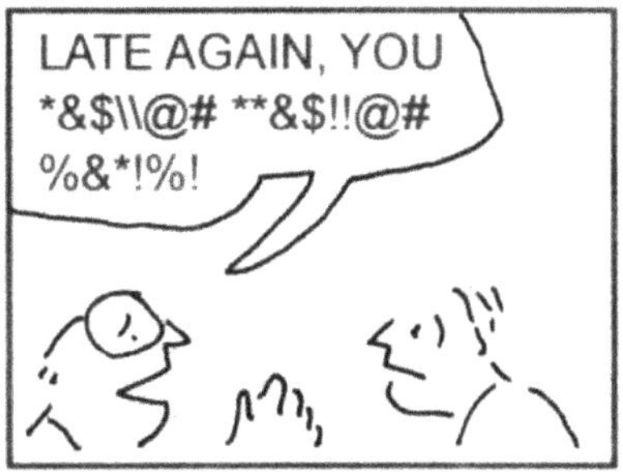
LATE AGAIN, YOU *&$\\@# **&$!!@# %&*!%!

What is the woman saying to the man who splashed mud on her?

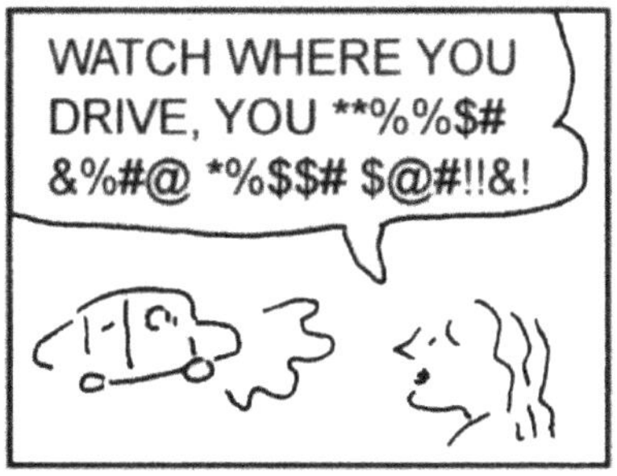
WATCH WHERE YOU DRIVE, YOU **%%$# &%#@ *%$$# $@#!!&!

ANSWERS: *(LEFT PANEL) You lazy, no-good motherfucker shit-for-brains asshole! (MIDDLE PANEL) Late again, you dickhead son-of-a-bitch bastard! (RIGHT PANEL) Watch where you drive, you scumbag hard-on shit-eating pissface!*

BRIAN McCONNACHIE

Piano Lessons

There was a white baby grand that came with our house. Apparently it was too troublesome to move, so the previous owners just left it. (As my folks did, to the people who bought the house from us.) No one in our family knew how to play. So there it stood, taking up a fair chunk of living room like a brilliant answer to an unasked question.

Then came Mr. Opportunity, Big Time Main Street, practically doing cartwheels past our picture window: A Russian couple moved in down the block. She was a concert pianist, we learned, and he was a skinny six-foot-something man with a 30-foot tapeworm, who had just won a brand new Chevrolet in a raffle. My mother suggested a trade: the concert pianist wife would teach me to play the piano, and my mother, in turn, would teach the twitchy, malnourished husband how to drive his snazzy new American muscle car.

It might have been a sound idea going in, but there were some deep ruts in that road, mostly in our lane.

The husband was a danger to himself and others. If my mother told him to turn right, she meant, of course, at the corner where there was a road. Not up on somebody's lawn. When she'd say "left" she'd have to quick grab the wheel to stop him from plowing into oncoming traffic. Maybe some blame could be laid at the many busy, unhappy feet of tapeworm within, but he was going to hurt somebody and by the haggard look on my mother's face after each driving lesson, it was going to be her.

And there were problems on my end, too: even though I was an adorable polite little tyke and cute as a bug's ear (or "a button" or "a cherub," whatever was wearing the cute crown those days), there was no reluctance on my teacher's part to slap the back of my hands — hard — whenever I plunked a wrong note. From about the third lesson on, something snapped in her and the era of hand slapping was launched. Was this the way they taught piano in a Socialist Republic? A quick smack for most of the wrong notes hit... then she'd let a few slide, which made it confusing on top of painful. As my anxiety built, I'd start to lose track of my right and left. (To this day, I still trip up on those twin troublemakers.)

Though my hands were soon black and blue, I was too well-behaved to tell her, an adult, a famous Russian concert pianist, "Knock it off, you crazy bitch!" And naturally, the more she slapped, the more mistakes I made. It got to the point where I'd try to keep my hands as far from the keyboard as possible; I kept them behind my back pressed tight into my worried little kidneys. She'd tap at a note on the sheet music with her pencil and one of my hands would dart out hoping for the best, take a poke at the note in question, then quickly retreat. Once in a while, I'd get lucky, but never for long. I wasn't learning a lick of piano, but my hands were getting fast. (To this day, I hate that game where you go palm-to-palm with somebody and try and slap the top of other person's hands before they can pull away. But I'll tell you this: I'm good at it.)

I was repeatedly told by serious adults how fortunate I was to have the talented and lovely Mrs. Celebrity Princess Czarina Slap 'n' Whack as a teacher. She was famous far and wide to hordes of piano-loving Russians, and I was her only U.S. student. So I kept my mouth shut about the slapping — I couldn't even tell my mother, who was enough of a wreck from the near-misses at the hands of Vladimir and his Terrible Tapeworm. I suffered in silence.

Even for a dumb kid, it didn't take long to realize that this woman wasn't remotely interested in my ever playing the piano. Or even wanting my hands near a piano, or probably even leaning against a piano at a piano bar listening to Billy Joel's "Piano Man" on the piano while the audience yelled, "Play 'Chopsticks' next!" She was determined to run me out of the piano-playing business entirely.

Perhaps she feared all people, six and under, who were learning the piano. Maybe we posed an existential threat to her concert career which, I'm guessing, she hoped to resume as soon as Comrade Tapeworm was skilled enough to get her across town to the concert hall without driving through somebody's living room wall.

She was only in it for the driving lessons and blowing off some old-fashioned Cossack steam, reflecting on what her once-promising career had descended to. She probably daydreamed of chasing me around the piano with two softball bats (in case she dropped one) to teach my stupid, porky-fingered hands a lesson.

But what she really did was introduce me to some high-stakes plotting: what would it take to push something off of a ledge, something heavy enough to pancake her head, with all the nasty musical conventions of piano instruction within, as she walked beneath?

An anvil was my first thought. I remember thinking: if I were the family anvil, where would I be kept? And could I lift me if I found me? It probably took about nine hundred mice to lift one. In that case, maybe I should go with a good size rock? Or better, a carton full of rocks — that would probably do the trick.

She was the first mortal enemy I ever had. Three or four nights a week, I took the plot to bed with me. How my blood raced, imagining her look up the second before she disap-

............◆............

Brian McConnachie *is Co-founder and Head Writer of this magazine.*

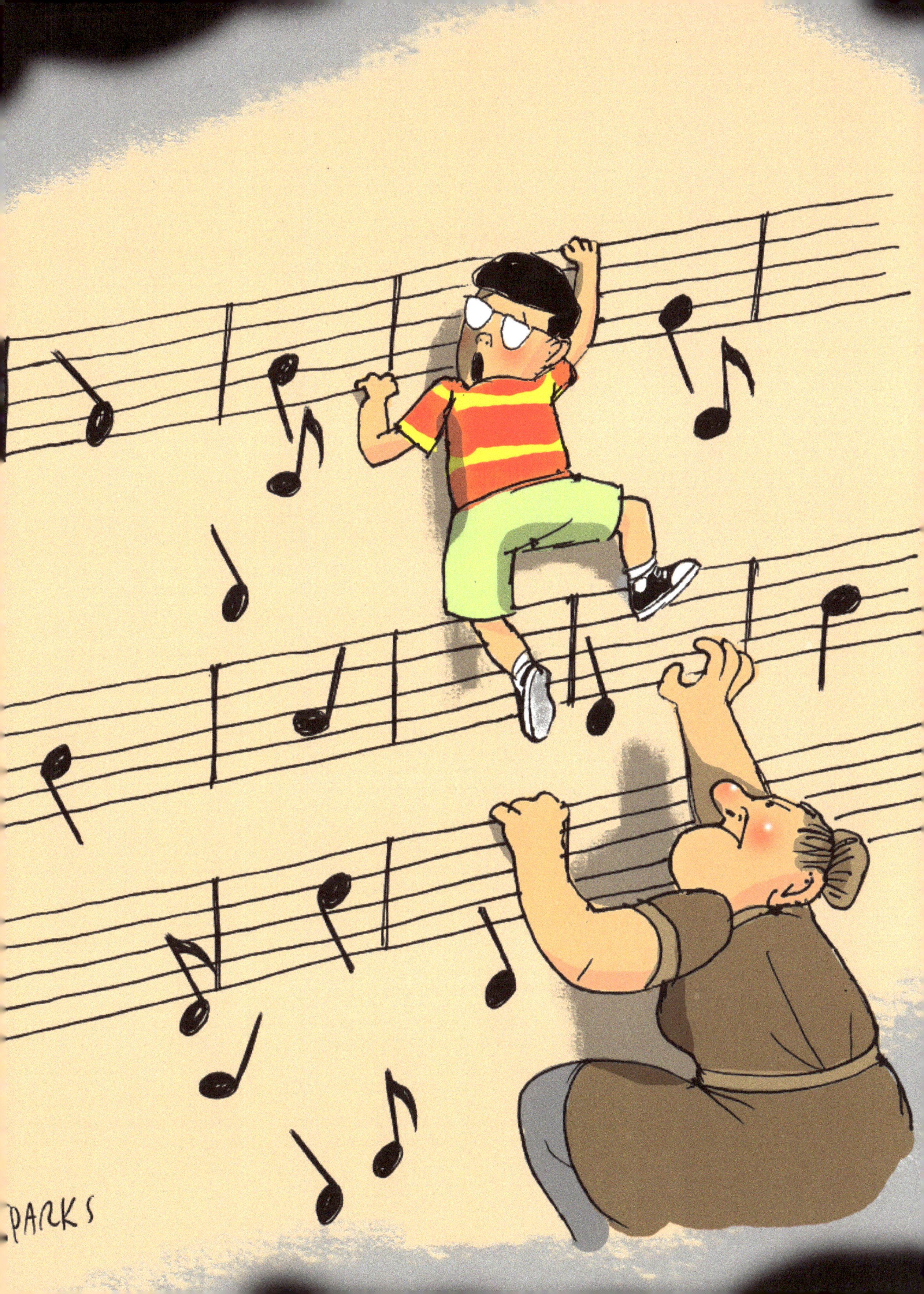
PARKS

"You got this."

peared beneath my Junior Achievement avalanche of hand-selected rocks. "Yoo-hoo!" I'd announce. "Here it comes, a hand-selected helping of authentic rocks fresh from the metamorphic collection!"

The only question was, how to get away with it? I liked my chances; remember, I looked like a cherub — peaches and cream complexion, thick dark curly hair, big brown eyes. The sweetest smile. I have photos and some of them show me in a nightshirt paying welcome to the baby Jesus on Christmas Eve. None of them make you think, "That's him. There's the murderer."

So I was confident; if I squashed my mortal enemy, the angels would swoon with joy and dry each other's blissful tears with their mighty wings. Then they'd hide me until this whole unfortunate mess blew over. I believed that. I got away with stuff back then. No need for details.

Still, even at that tender age — which I'll keep to myself, for reasons you'll see later — I suspected killing was wrong, even though no one actually pulled me aside and gave me the "oh, by the way" talk. It must be a truth we're born with, that killing is wrong but in many circumstances, understandable.

Let's just say I was young. My emotions were just teaming up with actions. And for a while, murder seemed like a reasonable response, something worth exploring.

On the other hand, could I be overreacting? What had she really done to warrant my first capital crime? And even though the angels might be okay with it, others wouldn't: Though I never witnessed it, I'd heard the nuns hit hard, and usually in the face and for no apparent reason. So ultimately I decided, I couldn't go through with it.

I'd have to call in my big pal, Timmy.

Timmy was a sweet, slow, gullible friend, a childhood version of Lenny from *Of Mice And Men*. He was huge for his age and he had terrible eyesight. He loved electric trains and subscribed to several model railroad magazines which he read by holding them an inch or two from his temple. Then he'd rotate the print this way and that to find a focal spot to look through.

For a while, we were boon companions, mostly because Timmy kept an open mind when it came to doing stupid and dangerous things. It was easy to talk him into stuff; there were always motives for Timmy to be found in railroad lore, no matter how crazy the circumstances. Better yet, there was an alibi — everybody would believe Timmy, when he explained why he dumped a carton of rocks on the piano lady's head.

"I didn't see anybody down there, honest," he'd say first. (Timmy and I rehearsed this for months.)

"May I see your glasses, son?" the detective would certainly ask. And that would be that; those thick-lensed things would back up Timmy's story — legally blind kid, a bucket of rocks, these things happen.

But in case it wasn't enough, Timmy was trained to go to Plan B. "I was trying to warn the freight train from Gaithersburg. It was heading for a collision with a passenger train to Wilmington," Timmy would say. "It's in the *Big Red Book of Horrible Train Wrecks*. We can't let that happen. Not again."

Of course Timmy might have to do some time in the slam, considering the cultural importance of the woman he flattened. Though maybe not — it would depend on the judge, and pressure from the State Department on the DA's office. It would be all international wheelhouse stuff they'd be playing with, and I really didn't want to go anywhere near it. The Soviets didn't believe in God and didn't care if you look like a cherub or not.

I was having dinner with my aunt and uncle when Timmy did the deed. It went off without a hitch; we heard from Timmy's mother, and I arranged my beatific features into an approximation of shock. I even cried a little. That night at bedtime my giddiness got the better of me, and I said something like, "Does this mean I won't have any more piano lessons? I loved them so!"

This was too far. My mother gave me a look, and for a horrible second I thought perhaps she suspected something. But I shouldn't have worried — the angels had my back. Not 24 hours later, Dad got this neat job with the EPA far, far away in Seattle! We'd be packed and gone before Mr. Policeman got around to banging on our front door for some probing Q & A.

Needless to say, I was anxious to get on the road. The very simpleness I'd banked on with Timmy would, eventually, cause him to drop my name. So I made a big deal of wanting to "get out there and help Dad with the sluices."

On the day we drove west (Dad flew on ahead), Mom wanted to swing around to say goodbye to her driving student. Maybe she was planning a quick review. Some fundamentals of the two-way traffic system.

Vaguely scanning for cops, I waited out in the car. And waited and waited. What was taking so long? I got out and walked up the steps — the door was open. They were standing in the front room, kissing goodbye. It was sweet. I didn't realize they were so close. I'm sure they had a lot of close calls; that brings people together, like in wartime. And, of course, now he was a widower.

And guess who still can't play the piano! B

A history of the Freline notebook

In 1485, when the paper-making city state of Guoc was under siege, master papetier **Adrien Freline** sent desperate handwritten messages to allies throughout the land. The missives were intercepted and the city torched—but the invaders were so impressed with Freline's paper that they brought him back to Brieg as an honored guest. There he lived, teaching papermaking at the royal court, until his torture and execution in 1489.

Forty years later, disgraced Briegan general **Roberto Lorens** began producing small bound notebooks in the Freline style and selling them from a pushcart. Demand for these "Feuilles de Freline" increased rapidly, and soon the newly incorporated Compagnie Freline was producing one thousand notebooks a year…as the swindled Lorens lay rotting in a pauper's grave not far from the factory.

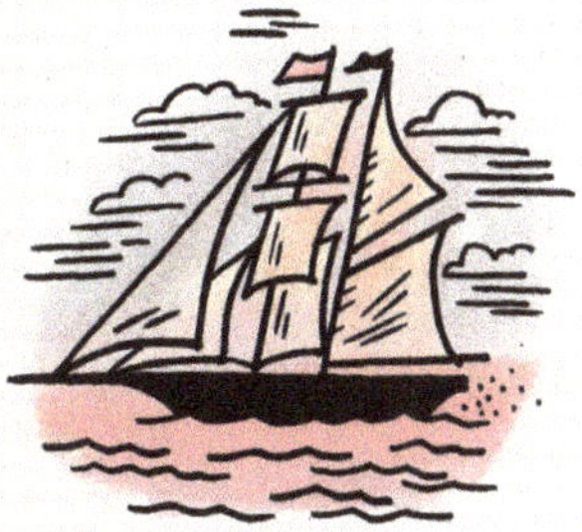
The HMS Omen.

For over five hundred years, the world's most celebrated thinkers, writers and artists have entrusted their most sacred ideas to Freline notebooks. It was on the pages of his Freline that **Sir Marcus Winslow** penned his famous *Her Majesty the Sea* before taking his equally famous three-hundred-foot plunge into the North Atlantic.

In 1872, **Helen Louise Turner** was finishing her signature *Essays on Progress* from her cell in the Sanitorium for Thoughtful Women. Due to the generosity of the warden, her father, fresh stacks of blank Frelines were delivered for her use every fortnight. And when her body was found, it was determined that the heavy doubled-milled sheets of the Freline Superba had dealt the paper cuts giving her sweet release.

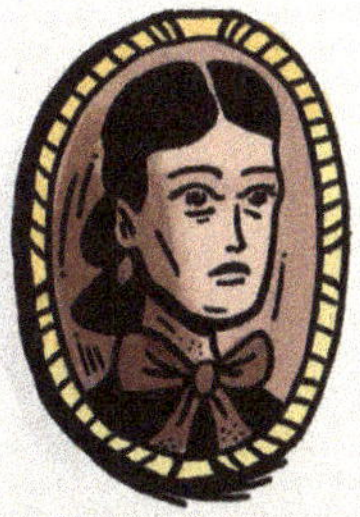
A portrait of pensiveness.

The Freline name and reputation continued to thrive well into the modern age, most notably as the preferred notebook of renowned artist

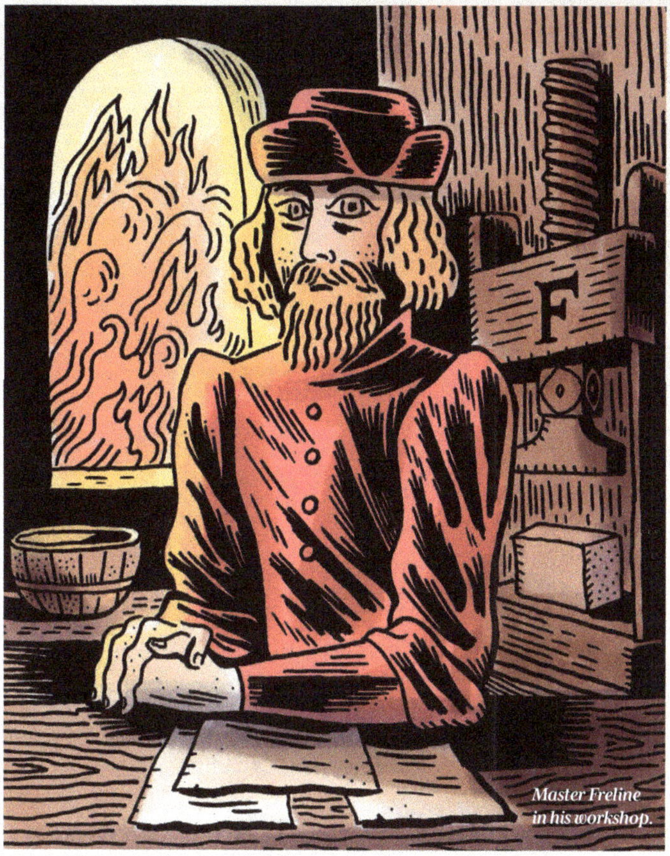
F
Master Freline in his workshop.

and expat, **Jacob Kranz**. At the time of Kranz's extradition, authorities described his flat as "crammed with mountains of [Freline] booklets, some big, others small, some hollowed out and filled with bags of pharmaceutical grade opium, others containing uniquely arresting explorations of human form and motion."

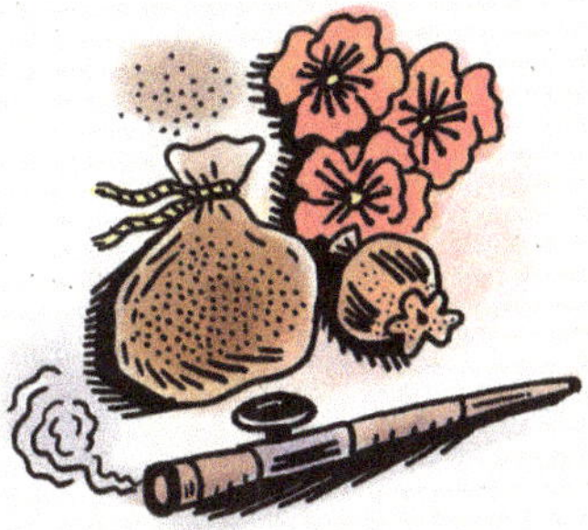
Kranz's minor "works."

Today the Freline name remains a signifier of quality, endurance and style, and our notebooks can be found on prominent display in fine stationery and craft stores throughout the world. Open yours today and become part of history. **#freline**

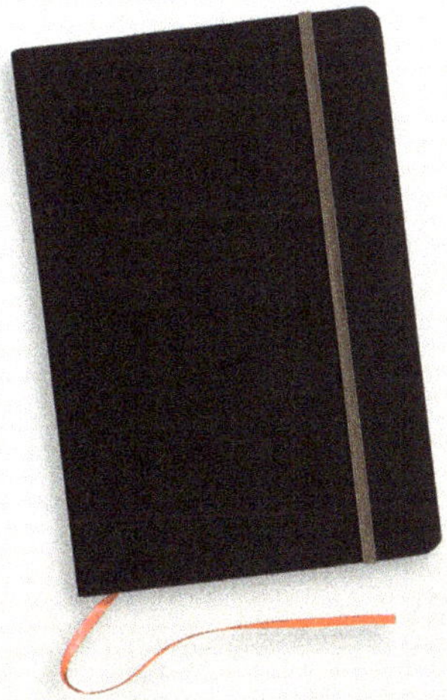

FRELINE

Beginnings. And endings.

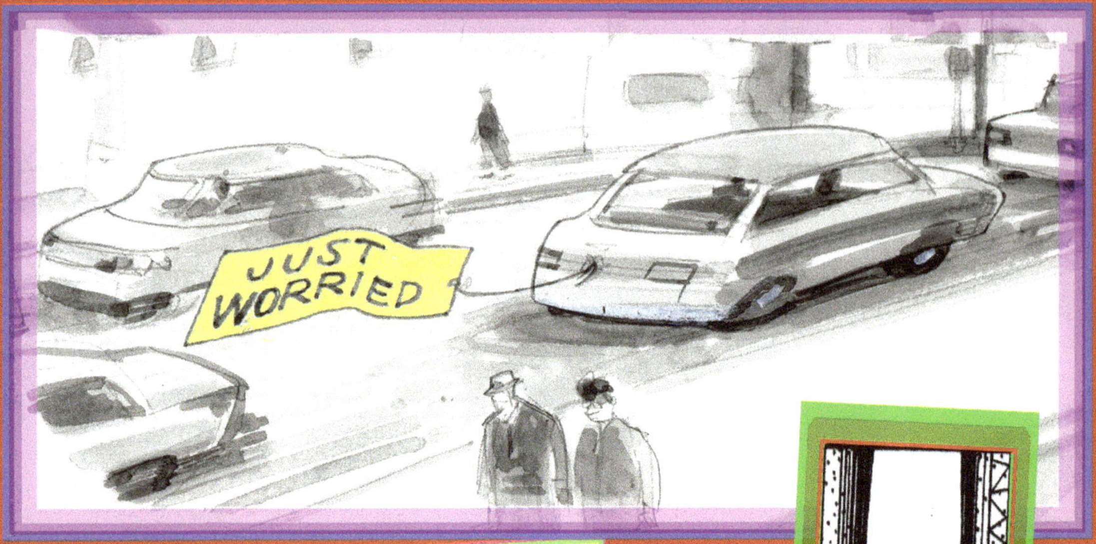
JUST WORRIED

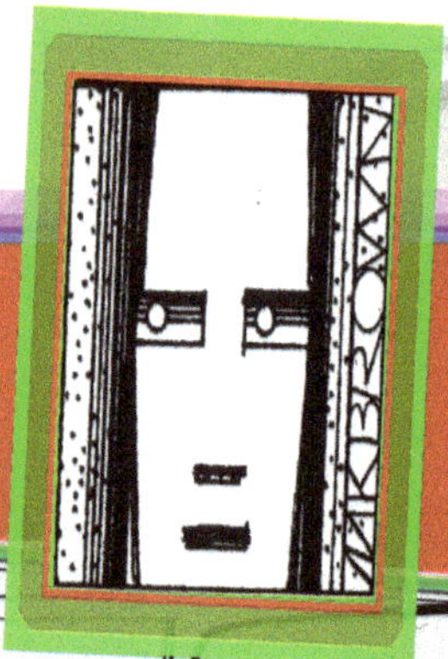

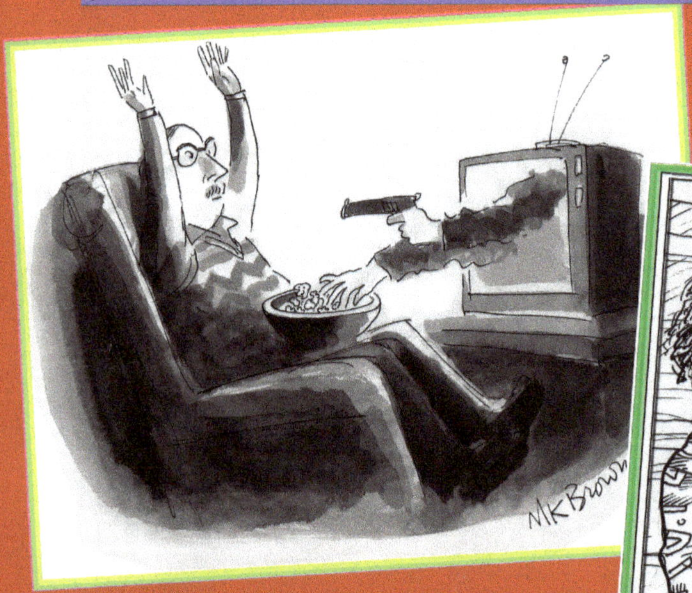
M.K. BROWN

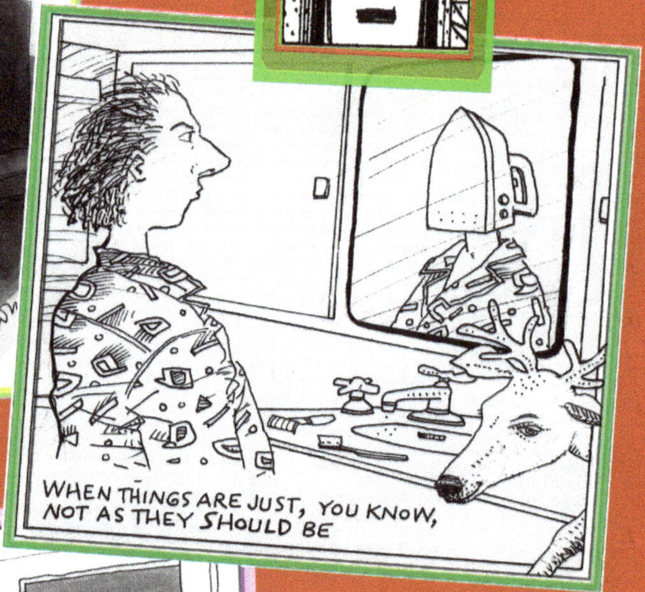
WHEN THINGS ARE JUST, YOU KNOW,
NOT AS THEY SHOULD BE

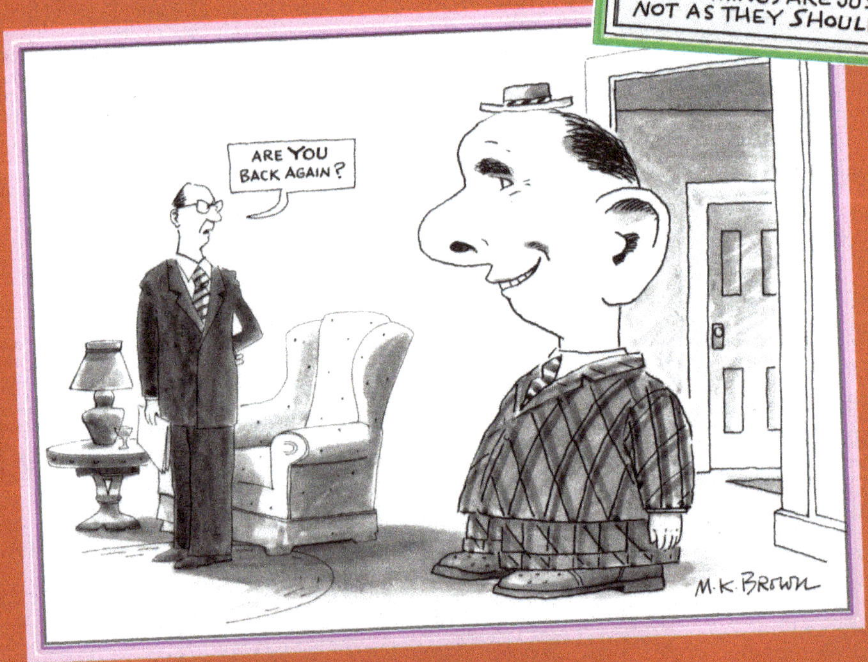
ARE YOU BACK AGAIN?
M.K. BROWN

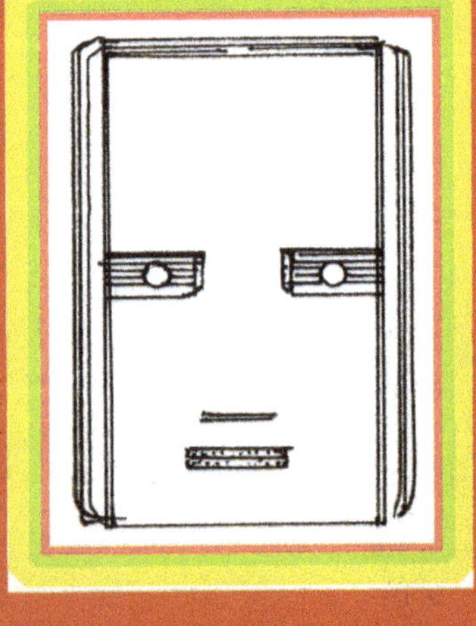

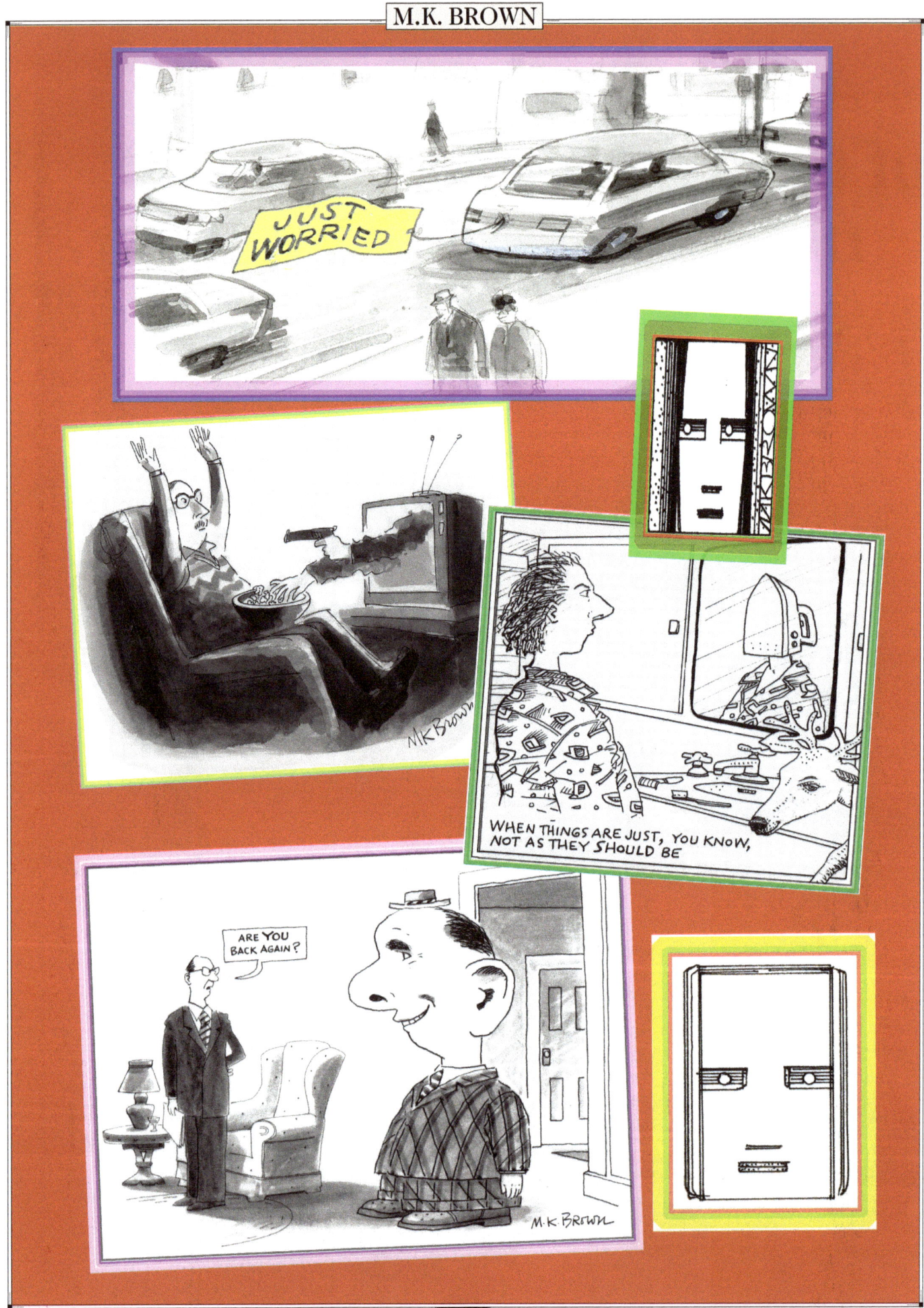

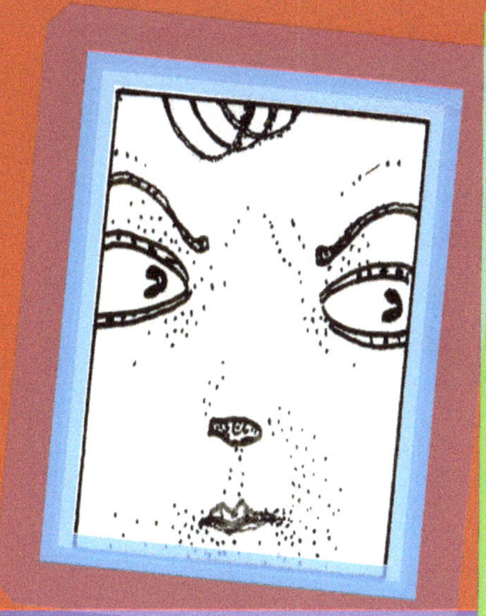

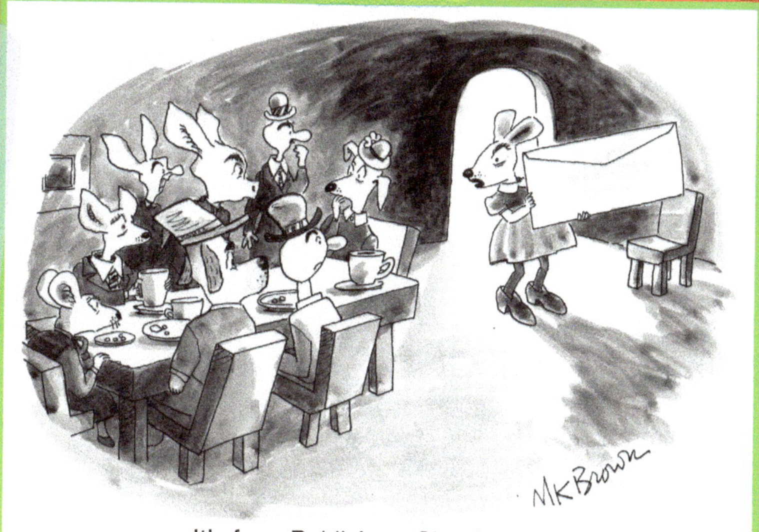

MK Brown

It's from Publishers Clearing House!

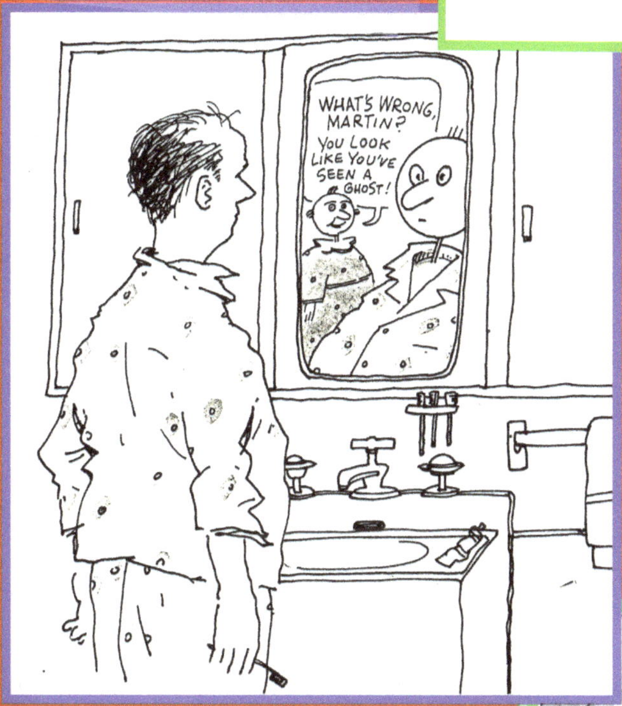

WHAT'S WRONG, MARTIN? YOU LOOK LIKE YOU'VE SEEN A GHOST!

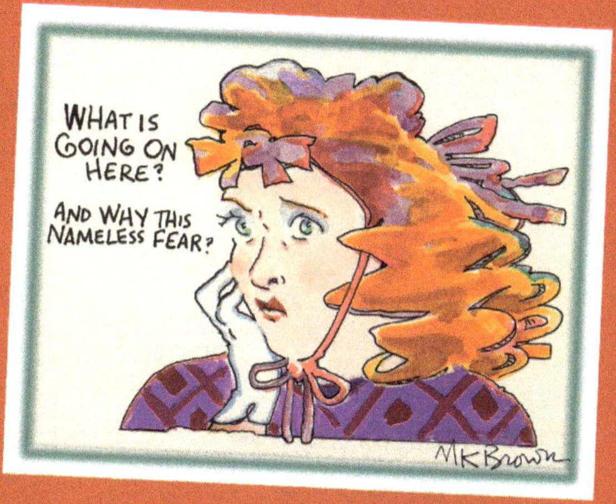

WHAT IS GOING ON HERE?
AND WHY THIS NAMELESS FEAR?
MK Brown

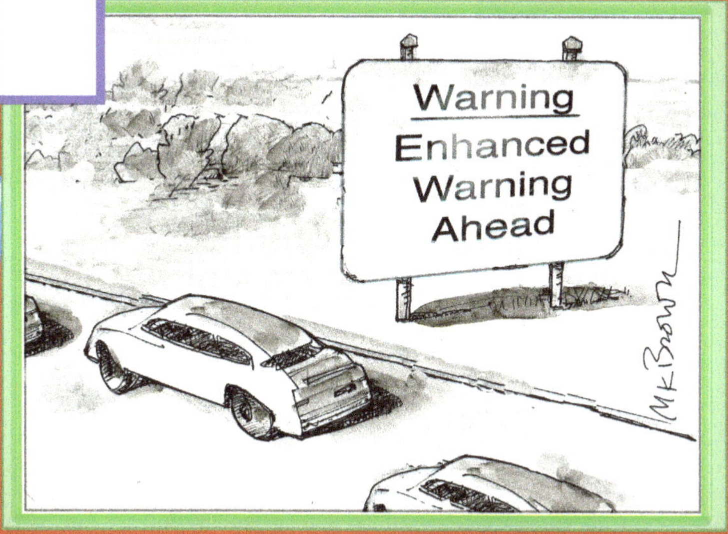

Warning
Enhanced Warning Ahead
MK Brown

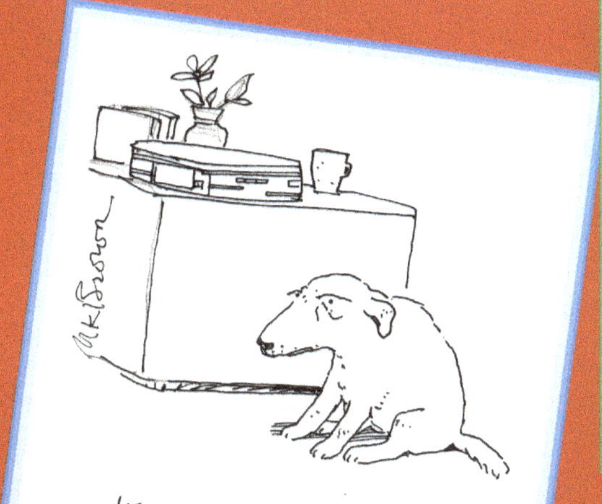

MK Brown

LISTENING TO NOAM CHOMSKY

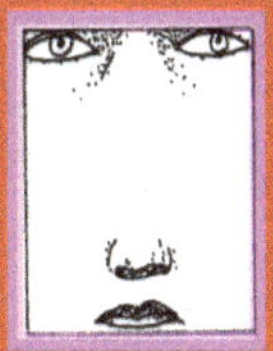

M·K·BROWN

Originalism... For Your Life!

Original Intent. Typically it's a topic reserved for scholars of constitutional law. An esoteric concept that only alights upon the minds of the hoi polloi when a Supreme Court Justice dies (or, more commonly, bursts into a million butterflies to the tune of Enya's "Sail Away"). Simply put, Originalism is an interpretive theory that suggests the truth of America's founding document can only be divined by understanding the time, place and parlance in which it was written. Regardless of your political persuasion, it's a fascinating idea... and one that I believe can be applied to our daily lives. I know, because I'm a living originalist.

Here's an example: Last Thursday, my wife and I were saying our goodbyes at a party. The host extends a hand to shake, but I'm feeling rather ebullient so I go in for a hug. But I hug a little too hard and vomit down his shirt. He was revolted, the other guests were screaming, "Oh my god, he's drunk!" I think I heard crying? To be honest, it's kind of fuzzy.

But am I in the wrong?

No. It was my original intent to give the host a hug. The fact that Liz and I will never be invited back for another wine night is immaterial. My intent was hug. Case closed.

On another occasion, my friend Brent asked me to drive him to the airport. It's something he's done for Liz and me on multiple occasions, so I was more than happy to oblige. It was an early flight, so I got up, fixed myself a cocktail — we don't need to talk about that — hopped in the car and was on my way with plenty of time to spare. A day and a half later, I woke up somewhere outside Waterbury, Connecticut, curled up in the back seat with a shiner under my left eye and twenty-three missed calls. Does it matter that I didn't pick up my friend Brent? Does it matter that I couldn't remember what had happened? Does it matter that the car I woke up in wasn't mine? No, no, and no! My original intent was to drive Brent to the airport. And legally speaking, I did!

Liberal busybodies might poke holes in this theory. They'll say things like, "You have a serious alcohol problem," and "I don't think I love you anymore." But these are emotional responses that could be easily discredited if argued in an open forum.

You can apply this idea to all aspects of your life. For instance, I wanted to surprise Liz when she came back from work with her favorite dish — hot and sour soup from Mandarin Kitchen. They were closing soon, so I had to hurry. Anyway, I'm driving, making good time, then — *beep, bap, boop* — I rear-end a jogger. Now, it wasn't my intent to hit a person. It was my intent to get soup. The fact that I picked up my license plate and left the scene doesn't have any bearing, legally speaking.

Besides, who jogs at night?

It's not always easy to live an originalist lifestyle. There will be detractors. Take my wife, Liz. She's pretty skeptical of the whole thing. I try to engage in healthy Socratic dialogue, but all I get are questions like, "Why is there blood on the soup container, Lars?" Relationships are really funny sometimes!

I know that if I could just sit down and discuss the theory with her, she would get it. She's exceedingly bright. But it's hard to get to her now that the Grand Hyatt pulled my picture from the security cameras. Quite a tight ship they run over there at the Grand Hyatt.

But if I did ever get that opportunity, I would explain to her that my original intent was to date her for three weeks before stealing her identity and draining her bank accounts. Instead, I invested four years of marital bliss — much more than I ever intended! So if you think about it, she's made out like a bandit. If anyone's been wronged here, it's me!

Well, it's 3:45 a.m. — shift change at the Grand Hyatt. I don't have much of a window, so I must be off. Just so you know, my intent is not to use karate on the elevator operator, no matter what the news says.

Lars Kenseth *has clerked for several prominent sociopaths and boasts an unnerving Ivy League giggle. He remains reluctantly impressed by the security team at the Grand Hyatt.*

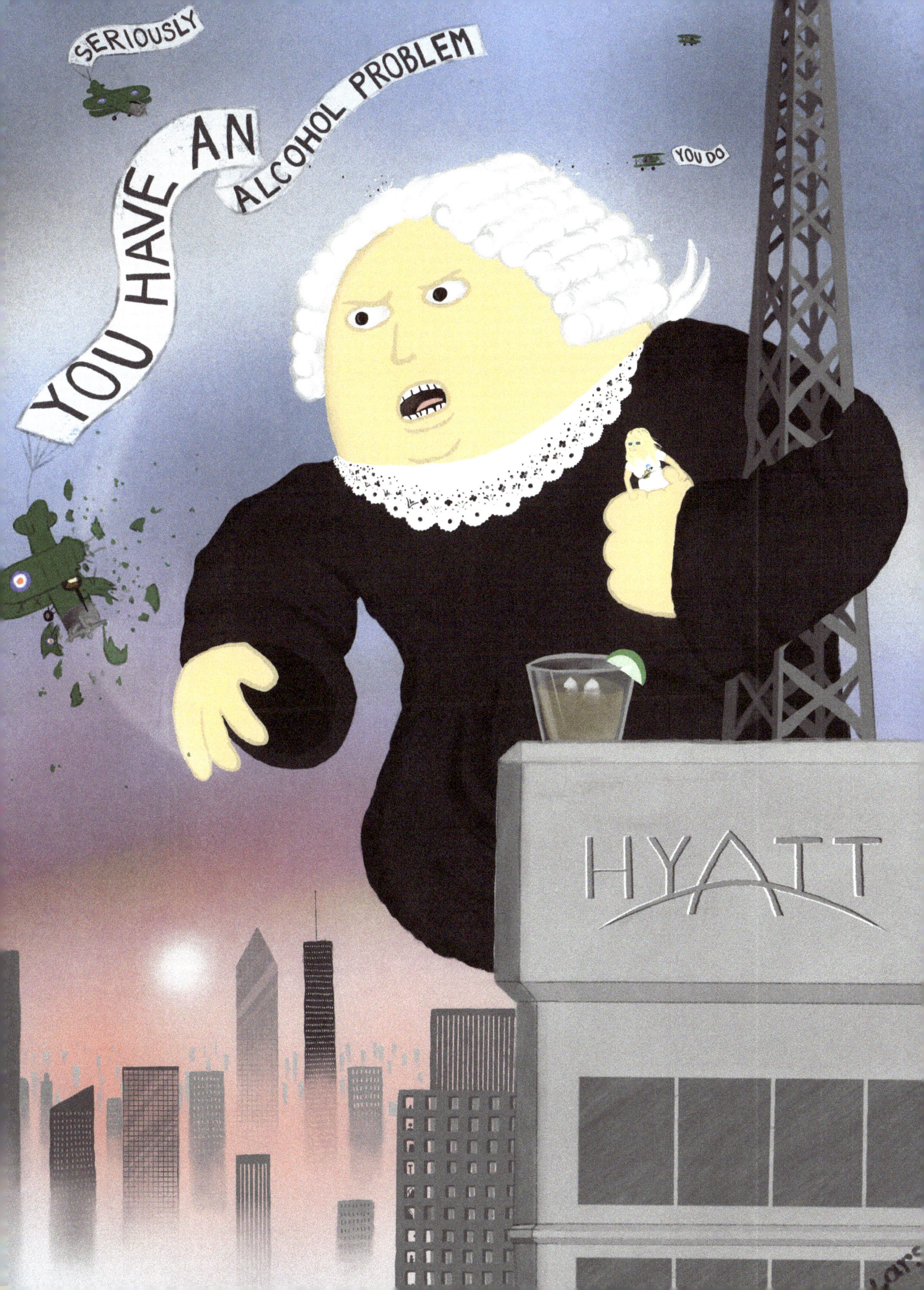
SERIOUSLY
YOU HAVE AN ALCOHOL PROBLEM
YOU DO
HYATT

RYAN NYBURG

Enjoy Your Stay

Next time you find yourself traveling down the Pacific Coast Highway, why not stop for a spell at the Shady Acres Motel & Lounge? We've got a pool, hot tub, and sauna, as well as a complimentary continental breakfast. Every room has an ocean view and easy access to one of the most gorgeous beaches on the coastline. So come on down to Shady Acres Motel & Lounge! You're worth it.

Traveling down the PCH? Don't miss the Golden Sunset Motel. Our clean, modern rooms offer both comfort and luxury. With an ocean view in each room and ready beach access that offers fun for the whole family. We have pet-friendly rooms and a complimentary continental breakfast that you'll actually look forward to. So book a stay at the Golden Sunset Motel. Because you deserve better.

A trip to the ocean is about relaxation. And no place on California's central coast offers more opportunities to relax than Shady Acres Motel & Lounge. Our restaurant is world-renowned and won't try to serve you toxic razor clams, which is more than can be said for other beach stops in the area. Plus, every room has a free premium cable package and broadband internet so you won't feel like an isolated weirdo. Shady Acres. Why settle for less?

When on vacation, you want everything to go just right, and not have to worry if you're going to catch a venereal disease from the bath towels. You want a pristinely clean room, staff that is attentive and courteous, and a pool that doesn't frequently fill with overflow from the local sewage treatment plant. And that's what we offer at Golden Sunset Motel. Friendliness, cleanliness, and a room that doesn't rent by the hour to truck-stop hookers. Golden Sunset Motel: Because you respect yourself.

Sometimes you hear the word "sinkhole" whispered around certain beachside properties — certainly not about Shady Acres Motel & Lounge, but maybe about some other motels nearby. Ask yourself: "Have I ever seen the movie *Psycho*? Would I want to stay in a motel run by someone like that?" Here at Shady Acres Motel & Lounge, we accept people from all backgrounds and won't make you follow the tenets of some deranged doomsday cult while you're a guest here. Plus, our continental breakfast is generous and filling, and not part of an anti-masturbation dietary regime. So come stay at Shady Acres Motel & Lounge. It's better than ending up in a shallow grave.

Listen. This is the Golden Sunset Motel and we're going to be straight with you. Shady Acres Motel & Lounge is a cesspit. Things have happened in that sauna of theirs that would make Jesus regret forgiving humanity. The reason the restaurant is "world-renowned" is it once caused one of the single largest public health emergencies in California state history. I don't care if the owners sue us for slander because if they want to take it to court, everyone will find out their employees all sit around giving handjobs in exchange for expired medications. We have pictures. So come stay with us at the Golden Sunset Motel. For the sake of the children.

Hi, this is Shady Acres Motel & Lounge. Live in a place long enough and you'll start to get a feel for the ambient energy, the "vibe." And there's an evil to this place, something dark and old. It might wear a shiny, happy face — with free HBO — but underneath, its core is rotten. Over the years, travelers have gone missing: A lone woman here, a couple there, some kids suspected of getting pulled away by a riptide. These disappearances get written off as isolated occurrences, personal tragedies without any connection. But once you discover that all of them stayed at the Golden Sunset Motel, the dark pattern becomes clear. So come stay at Shady Acres Motel & Lounge. Together, we can destroy the ancient evil. No longer offering beach access, as the access stairs were burned down under mysterious circumstances.

At Golden Sunset Motel, we believe moral decay has infected the soul of this coastline like syphilis in the brain of a dying whore. People who stay at Shady Acres Motel & Lounge are filth who will never know the Lord's forgiveness. We have it on good authority that sexual acts with farm animals are common, and that every surface of every room has been ritualistically smeared with the semen of a pedophile. Every night we pray the entire monstrous edifice crumbles into the sea. So come stay at Golden Sunset Motel. Together we shall cleanse the Earth.

This is the Shady Acres Motel & Lounge. I'm currently standing on the beach, pointing a gun at the owner of the Golden Sunset Motel. Our respective businesses are in flames on the cliffside behind us. I would kill this man, but for the fact that he is pointing a gun at me as well, leaving us at something of a standoff. If I fire, so will he, and we both shall die. So we stand here facing one another, each unwilling to be the catalyst of our final mutual destruction. Yet neither of us will lower our gun for fear the other will take advantage. We've been stuck like this for hours, and slowly the evening tide is coming in. It's already up to my knees, and soon it will engulf us both. This is how we'll die, too scared not to kill each other. But before that happens, let us know about your stay, and if there's anything we can do to make it better next time. B

Ryan Nyburg *is a writer and podcaster and NOT wanted by the police in connection to multiple horse-based crimes. You can follow him on Twitter @PostCultRev.*

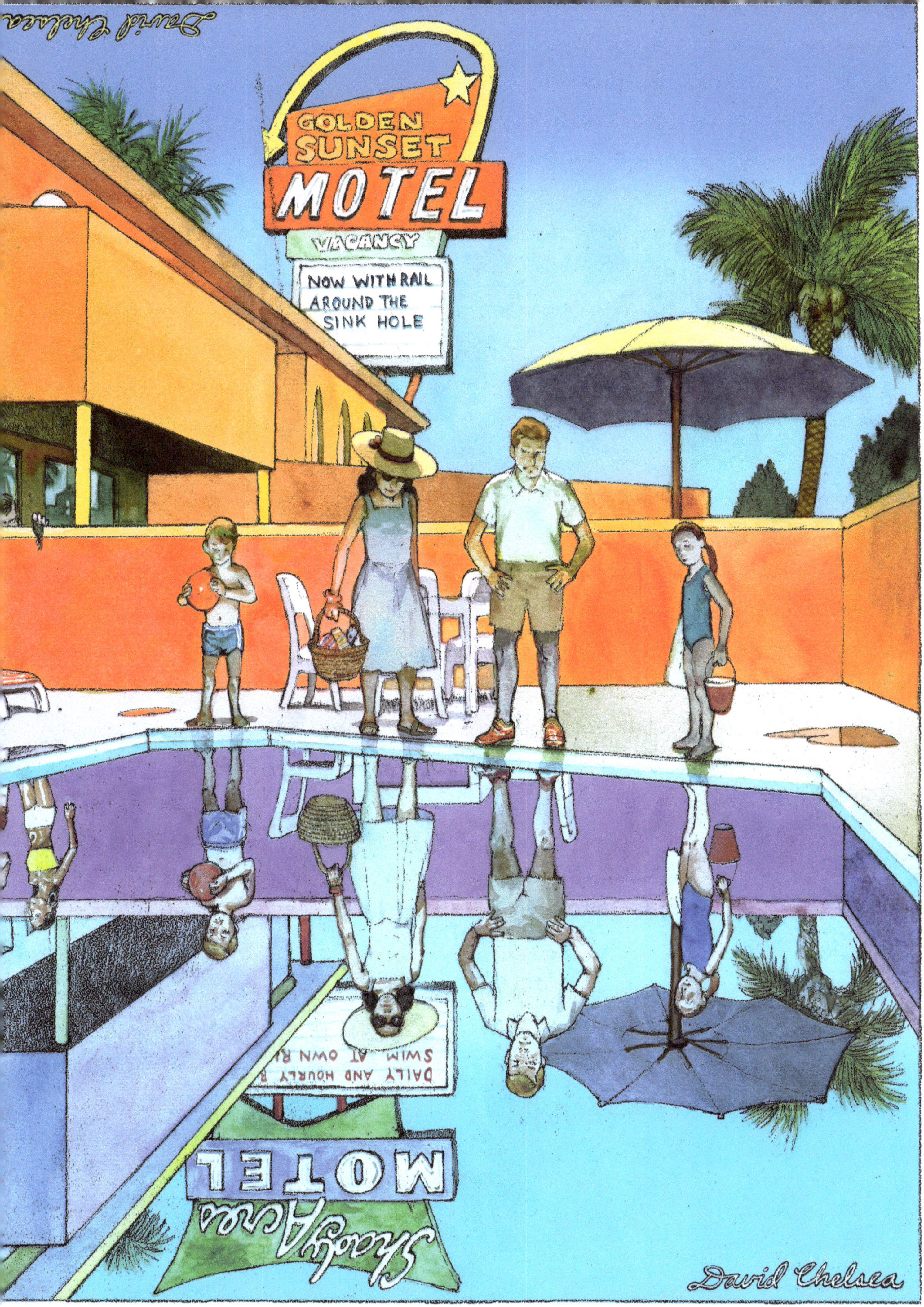
GOLDEN SUNSET
MOTEL
VACANCY
NOW WITH RAIL AROUND THE SINK HOLE
Shady Acres
MOTEL
David Chelsea

Son of Twisted Cross

More regrettably timely cartoons by

S. GROSS

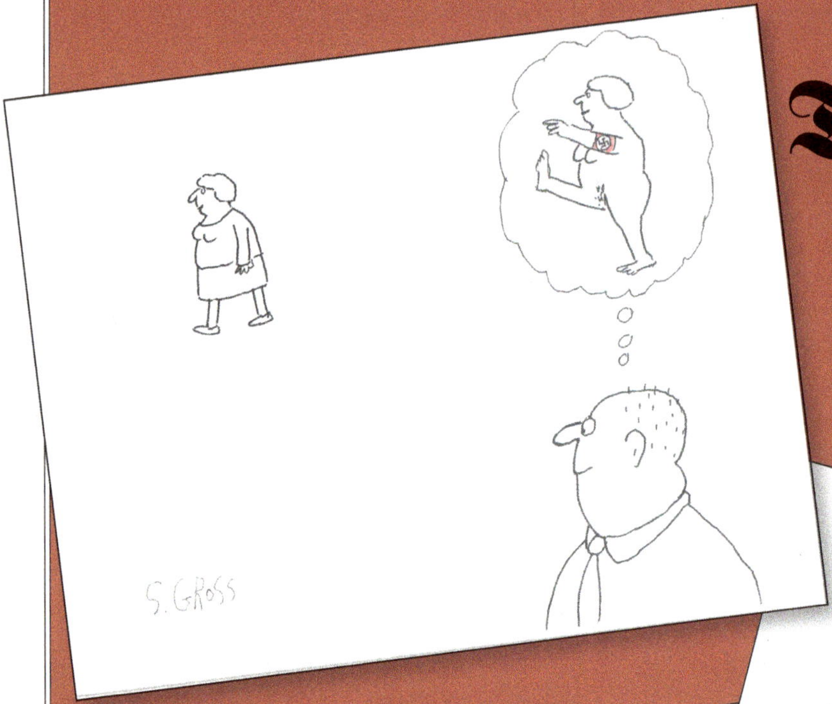
S. GROSS

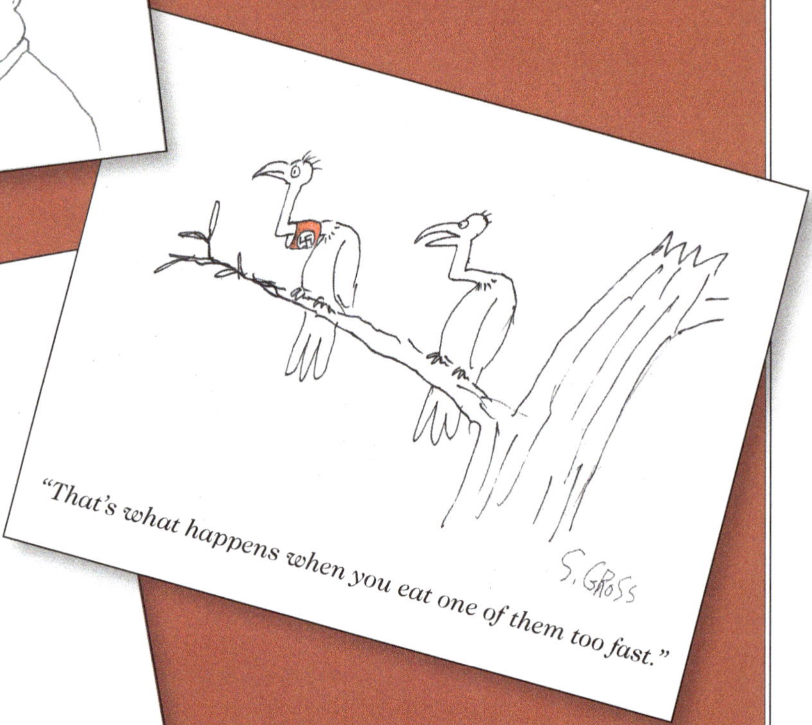
S. GROSS

"That's what happens when you eat one of them too fast."

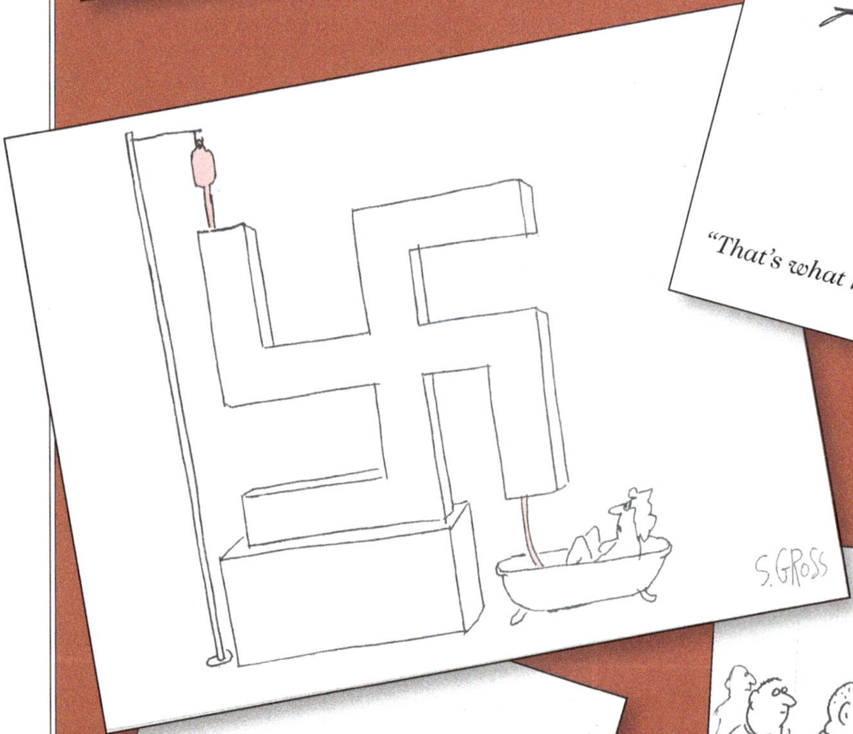
S. GROSS

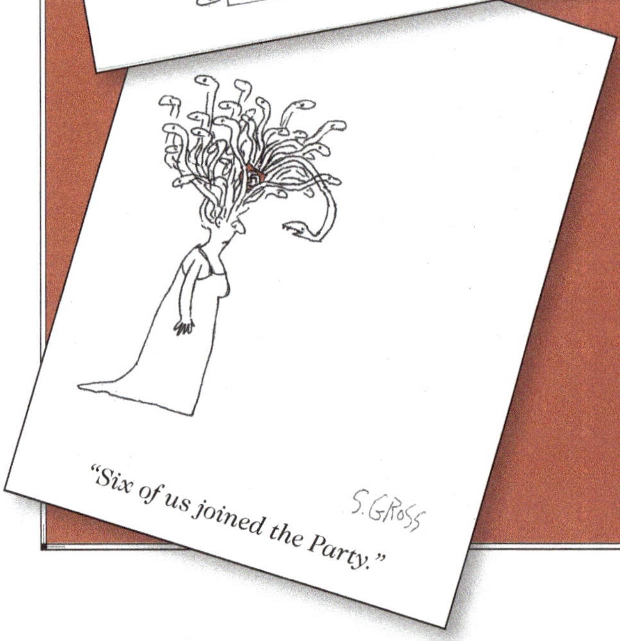
S. GROSS

"Six of us joined the Party."

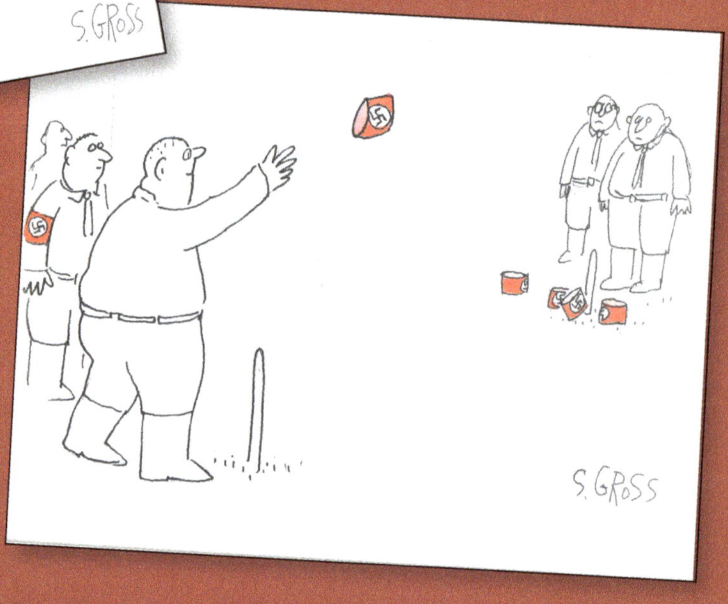
S. GROSS

B

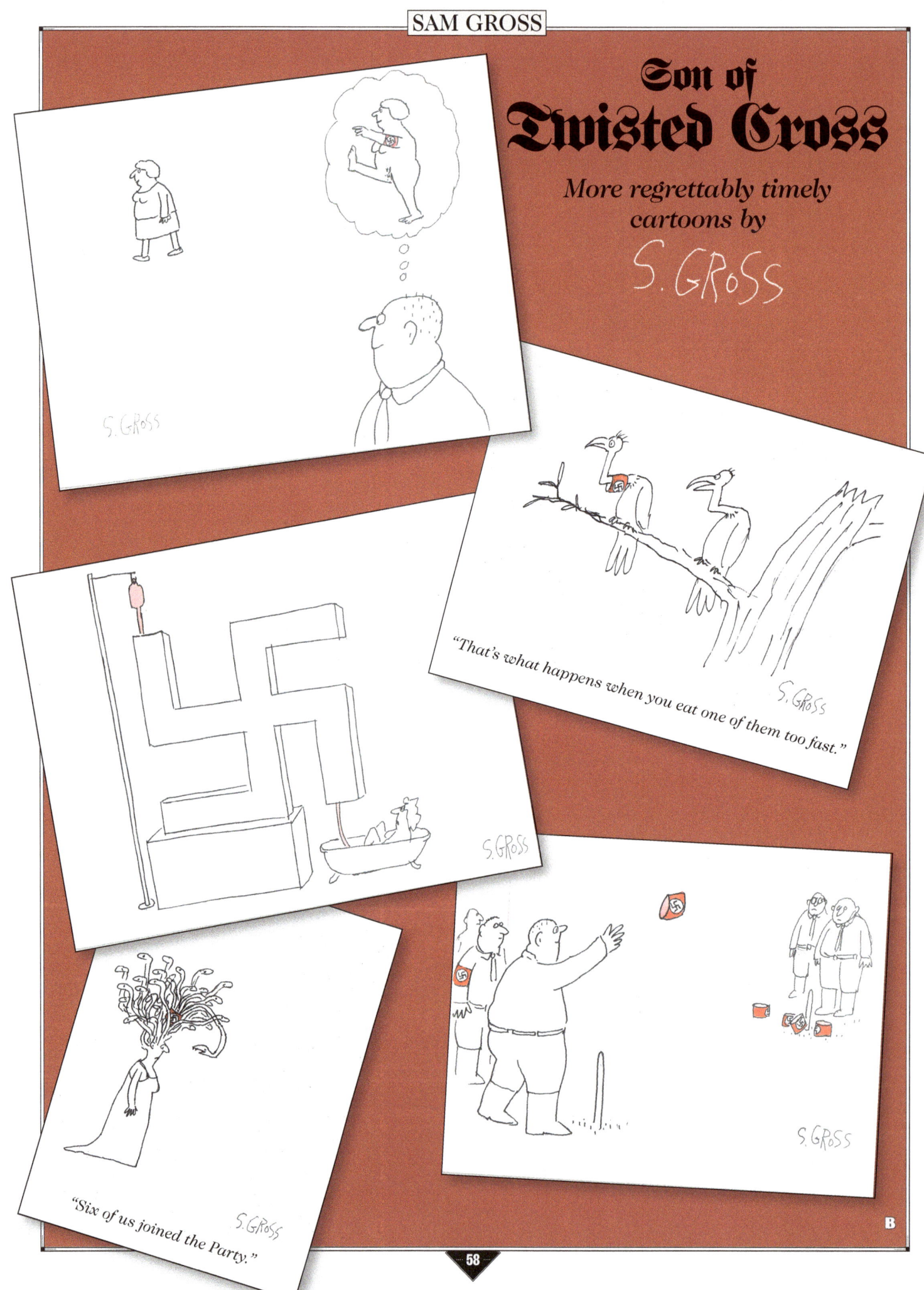

Works

*"It's a trick of perspective," Daniel said.
"If you stand further away, I'll seem smaller."*

The green room at the Laugh Works smelled so intensely of floral air freshener that Daniel found himself trying to find the under-odor that it had been sprayed to cover. He knew success would prove more troubling than curiosity, but he couldn't stop trying.

He took a moment to get his ground legs back, listening to his breath, reminding himself that he was offstage now, that he was allowed to let go of the insistent rhythm of the four-to-one joke-per-minute pacing. He forced himself to listen to more breaths than usual this evening. He knew he had to be himself again before he lit up. He had discovered this about a year earlier. If he got high the moment he came offstage, he couldn't throw off the quick wit for the rest of the evening. He did not know why, though he imagined someday he would do an in-depth exploration of it, figure it out. Tonight, he really wanted to get high immediately, but he wouldn't. Not until he had control of his comedic impulse.

His parents had arrived late. He had heard the whispering at the back of the room first, knew their cadences, before he saw them coming in and finding their seats about eight minutes into his headlining set. He chuckled at himself and admitted that it had been closer to seven and a half minutes in, that pretending to the imprecision of "about eight minutes" was an absurd kind of false modesty. His sense of time onstage had become supernaturally accurate. His parents had come in at seven minutes and thirty-eight seconds in, missing his opening line and a small run of jokes that ended with a punchline so off-handed in its execution that it would get a shocked laugh of surprise and delight later when he used it as a callback. It was a callback that his parents would not get because they had missed the set-up to it that was disguised as a punchline.

At the moment they had arrived, he had briefly considered whether there was a way to work the punchline in again to bring his parents up to speed, without it ruining the repeat-refrain for the rest of the audience; but then realized that the effort was distracting him, so he let it go with a slight left-handed gesture fueled by resentment toward them for their late arrival.

Even as he performed he found himself counting the number of rounds of drinks the waitress brought to their table.

They had entirely missed the terrific feature set from Barney O'Reilly. Barney O'Reilly did a beautiful job every show. That would have been enormously helpful to Daniel; the incompetent MC, Tom Deeble, had gone up after Barney and brought the room to a dead halt before doing Daniel's intro. He was quite glad that his parents had not seen Tom Deeble's set.

He sensed his readiness. He was thinking like a person again. A resentful, judgmental, slightly anxious person, but not every thought was couched in a clever turn of phrase or seen from a sardonic slant. He put on his overcoat and pulled the Marlboro pack from his pocket, the joint carefully protected between the cardboard box and the cellophane wrapping. He fished around in the deep pocket until he found the lighter, then tucked pack and lighter back into the pocket and headed out.

He passed Barney at the bar and they exchanged "great set"s with one another, pointedly ignoring Tom, who seemed not to notice. Tom flirted with the waitresses after the shows and seemed to have virtually no awareness of the others on the bill with him or the utter lack of interest shown by the women.

Daniel said, "Did you see — ?"

*Dylan Brody is a playwright and humorist, poet and snappy dresser.
Don't ask him about his tie. He'll talk for an hour about the Plattsburgh knot.*

Barney said, "They're outside. Your dad said he wanted to smoke."
Daniel said, "Of course."
Barney said, "He looks just like you."
Daniel said, "Or vice versa."
Barney said, "He could be your significantly younger brother."
Daniel said, "Nice."
Barney said, "That's as close as I come to being an insult comic."
Daniel chuckled, though he didn't mean it and stepped out into the night to find his parents. They were easy to find. Their cloud of tobacco smoke came from just upwind of the club's entrance and Daniel stepped into it.
His mother hugged him. She held him like a woman whose son had just been saved from a near-drowning.
Daniel said, "Hi, Mom."
She did not let go.
Paul said, "Okay, Ellen."
She did not let go.
Over her shoulder Paul and Daniel exchanged looks of shared understanding, tolerance strained. Daniel said, "Okay, Mom."
Ellen said, "You were terrific tonight. You know that?"
Daniel said, "I do. Yes. Can I — ?"
Ellen said, "You want to hug your father now?"
Daniel said, "Actually, I want to smoke now, but I was going hug Dad first, just to be polite."
Paul said, "Aw. That's sweet. I'm touched."
Ellen let him go but she continued to stand too close, looking up at him like a girl waiting to be kissed. She said, "When did you get so tall?"
Daniel said, "It's a trick of perspective. If you stand further away, I'll seem smaller."
Ellen said, "Don't be funny." She took a step back.
Daniel said, "No. Seriously. Much further. Until I seem to be the size that matches your memory."
Paul punched him lightly on the arm and then wrapped him in a quick hug. He whispered into Daniel's ear, the smell of scotch and smoke heavy on the words, "Really good show, Daniel. Just wonderful."
Daniel said, "Thanks. Is that a secret for some reason?"
Paul snorted and released his son.
Daniel pulled out the pack of cigarettes and freed the joint. He said, "You guys don't mind, do you?"
Paul put up a hand and shook his head by way of permission.
Ellen said, "I really wish you wouldn't use that stuff."
Daniel said, "I know, Mom. But given the four drinks you've had this evening…" He let the thought hang unfinished.
He thumbed the flint-wheel and the lighter clicked and sparked but did not light.
Ellen said, "I only had two."
Daniel said, "Okay." He thumbed the flint wheel for a click and a spark.
Ellen said, "Tell him, Paul. I almost never have more than two. That's how I know I'm not an alcoholic. I'm not one of those people who just keeps drinking."
Daniel said, "Okay."
Paul said, "Ellen."
Ellen said, "What?"
Daniel clicked the lighter, frustration causing him to try several times in quick succession.
Paul said, "Here," and handed him a book of matches.
Daniel said, "Thanks." He lit the joint and took a long first hit. He held it in.
Paul said, "I love that smell."
Daniel said, "Pot? Really?"
Paul said, "No. The matches. The sulfur."
Daniel said, "Oh. Do you want a hit?"
Paul said, "Nah. I'm good."
Daniel nodded in approval.
Paul said, "I got that right?"
Daniel said, "Yeah. 'nah. I'm good.' Perfect. Sounded like a bona fide prep-schooler with a half-ounce a week habit."
Paul said, "Sweet."
Daniel said, "Wow. It's like you've been practicing."
His father wiggled his eyebrows at him and reached out with his thumb and forefinger. Daniel handed him the joint. Paul took a hit.
Ellen said, "Honestly, Paul."

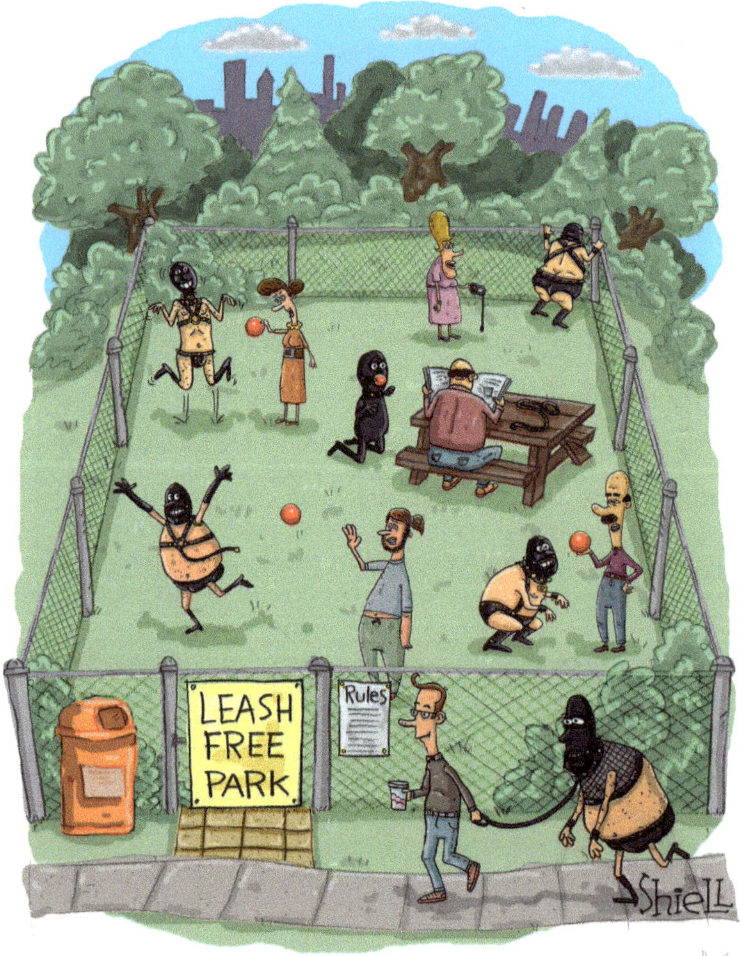
LEASH FREE PARK
Rules
Shiell

Paul said, "What?" but the word that started to come out of his mouth turned into a cough that came through his nose as he handed the joint back to Daniel.

Ellen said, "I didn't even finish the last one."

Paul blinked slowly. He said, "I have no idea what we're talking about."

Ellen said, "There's no way I had four full rounds of scotch."

Paul said, "No. You probably had three and a half. But they make them smaller than we do at home."

Ellen said, "Of course. That's probably it."

Daniel felt the snark rising in his chest. He felt the tension in his throat that came with joke-telling back when he was in high school, when he was uncertain and couldn't know if he was funny until he heard people laugh. Rather than speaking, he listened to a single slow breath and then took a hit on the joint.

Paul said, "I'm sorry we came in so late."

Daniel said, "You only missed about seven and a half minutes of my set."

Ellen said, "About seven and a half?" Her voice held a mocking tone.

Daniel said, "Seven minutes, thirty-eight seconds."

Ellen said, "You're kidding."

Daniel said, "You'll be able to tell when I'm kidding. There'll be humor content."

Paul snorted. Ellen dropped her cigarette to the ground, twisted the toe of her shoe on it to make sure it was fully extinguished and lit another one.

Daniel squeezed out the end of the joint, returned it to its place behind the cellophane of his cigarette pack and pulled out a Marlboro. He lit it with the matches his father had given him and then returned the pack.

Paul said, "Parking."

Daniel said, "Yeah. That can take a while."

Ellen said, "We should know better by now. We've been living in Boston for – what? Three years?"

Paul said, "Almost four. But they make them smaller here than we do at home."

Daniel laughed.

Ellen said, "I don't know what that means."

Daniel said, "It's a callback."

Paul said, "Thank you. I knew there was a name for it."

Ellen said, "You two!" and Paul and Daniel exchanged a look, both knowing that she was covering up her lack of comprehension.

They stood in silence for a bit, smoking.

Paul said, "There was one thing you said that got a laugh that I —"

Daniel said, "Exactly."

Paul nodded.

Ellen said, "Okay. Now you're doing it on purpose."

Paul said, "You remember when everyone laughed, and you leaned over and said, 'why is that funny?'"

Ellen said, "Yes! I do. I wanted to ask about that."

Daniel said, "It's a callback to a joke I do in the first five minutes, so you guys didn't get it."

Ellen said, "And that makes it funny?"

Daniel said, "Yes."

Ellen said, "Well, I still don't really get it, I guess."

Daniel said, "Yeah. Because…never mind. Just trust me. It's funny."

Paul sighed.

Ellen said, "I don't really understand how a lot of it works."

Daniel said, "You don't need to."

Ellen said, "But I really am so glad we got to come see you while you're in town."

Daniel said, "Yeah. Yeah. Me too."

Paul said, "And you're doing this show all weekend?"

Daniel said, "Yeah."

Paul said, "And…how much of it is — you know — ad-libbed or whatever?"

Daniel said, "Very little. Sometimes more. Usually less."

Paul said, "It's very impressive."

Daniel said, "Thank you. I live to impress."

Paul said, "I know that about you."

Daniel nodded.

Paul said, "It makes me fear I have failed as a parent."

Daniel said, "You have."

Paul chuckled. He said, "Ah the joy of living without subtext."

Daniel said, "Yeah. That's what's going on here."

Ellen said, "There is one thing I wanted to tell you."

Paul winced. Daniel saw it and recognized it as the exact expression he had repressed, not being four rounds into transparency.

Ellen said, "When you went after that guy who talked to you…"

Daniel said, "Yes."

Ellen said, "You did that whole thing about 'I am much cooler than you are!'"

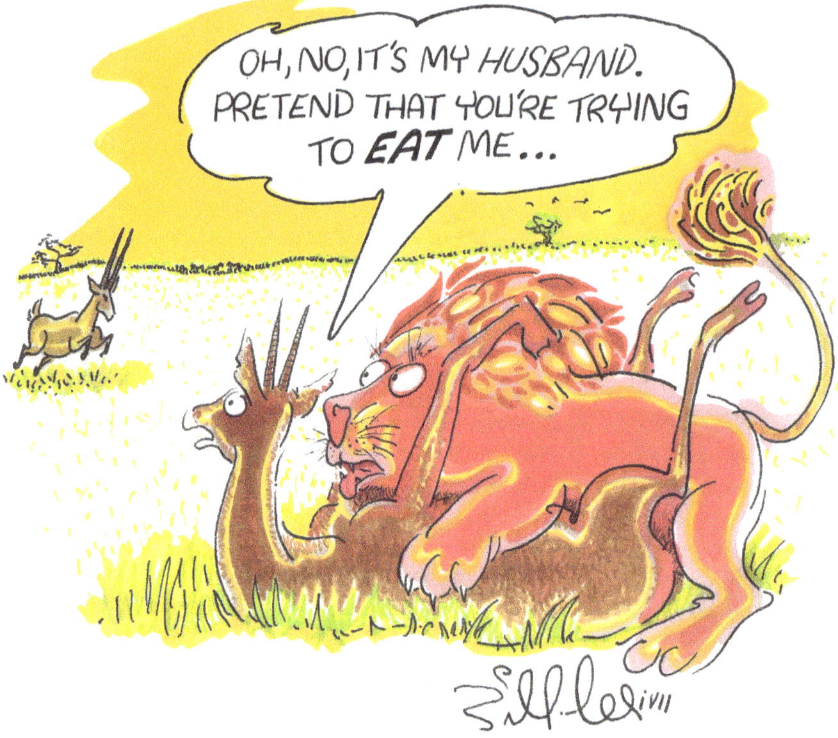
OH, NO, IT'S MY HUSBAND. PRETEND THAT YOU'RE TRYING TO EAT ME...

Daniel said, "'You can't outcool me.'"

Ellen said, "What?"

Daniel said, "The heckler response. It's not 'I am much cooler than you are!' It's 'You can't outcool me.'"

Ellen said, "I don't get the difference."

Daniel said, "Nuance and...craft. Go ahead."

Ellen said, "Well, I know the people were all laughing and everything when you did the list but then — "

Daniel said, "Yeah. Sorry about that."

Ellen said, "You don't know what I'm going to say."

Paul said, "Ellen."

Ellen said, "What is that list you did? How did that go? Do you remember?"

Daniel said, "Yes. I remember the bit."

Ellen said, "That's a bit?"

Daniel said, "Yes."

Ellen said, "So...do you — what? Do you tell someone in the audience to yell at you so you can do that bit?"

Daniel said, "What? No."

Paul said, "Ellen."

Ellen said, "What? I don't know how it all works."

Daniel said, "That's my go-to heckler response. If someone heckles me I do that bit. I have a couple of others of increasing intensity and hostility because I hate hecklers. The list is, 'You can't outcool me. I have a microphone and a spotlight. You can't outcool me. I get my drugs delivered. You can't outcool me. In 1958 my father slept with Allen Ginsberg. You can't outcool me.'"

Ellen pursed her lips.

Daniel said, "And you were going to say that you wish I wouldn't say that Dad slept with Allen Ginsberg."

Ellen said, "Well, I just don't think it's very funny."

Daniel said, "And yet, you heard the laugh it gets."

Ellen said, "Well, I think that's just because — you know..."

Paul said, "I don't think that's right."

Ellen said, "No?"

Paul said, "No. That's not just a homophobia trigger. It's also a particularly erudite social reference. I think different people in the audience are laughing at it for all sorts of different reasons. It says interesting things about the performer and his relationship to his father. It's a complicated joke, really."

Daniel said, "Thank you. Also...it's true. Isn't it?"

Ellen said, "It makes me very uncomfortable."

Daniel said, "Well, you're not usually there, so..."

Paul said, "I never slept with Allen Ginsberg."

Ellen said, "What?"

Paul said, "You thought I slept with Allen?"

She pursed her lips.

Daniel said, "I always thought you slept with Allen Ginsberg."

"Why did you think that?"

Daniel took a drag from his cigarette, thinking. He said, "I'm not sure. Something about the way Mom responds whenever his name comes up, I think."

Paul said, "I knew him. You know, when we lived in San Francisco. But no. We never slept together."

Ellen said, "Well, you certainly liked spending time with him and...those other boys."

Paul said, "Yes. Yes, I did. But Allen? No. We never — you thought I slept with Allen?"

Ellen blinked, rearranging memories from long ago. She said, "Maybe we should discuss this when we're all sober."

Daniel said, "When would that be, exactly?"

Ellen said, "Daniel. Don't be funny."

Paul said to him, sharply, almost angrily, "Be kinder, Daniel. Try."

Daniel said, "Wait a minute. Wait a minute. Wait a minute. Does it bother you less if you know it's not true?"

Ellen said, "I don't know. I don't — All these years I thought that was your big secret."

Paul snorted. He squeezed his nose. He said, "What makes you think there's only one?"

Ellen said, "Now don't you start with the jokes."

Paul stepped behind her and wrapped his arms around her. She held his arms against her chest as he rested his chin on her shoulder.

Daniel took a step back, just enough to bring them into a different focus as a couple. He could see fragments of youth in their spooned embrace. He could see time and shared history, a comfort in one another's shape that could only come from decades of familiarity.

Daniel said, "Sometimes, I think the secrets we worry about don't matter nearly as much as the things we all know about one another."

Paul raised his eyebrows, surprised, running the sentence over again in his head.

Ellen tilted her head to side so that her temple pressed to her husband's cheek.

Paul said, "What time do you fly out on Sunday? Maybe we could all meet up for a brunch somewhere."

Daniel said, "I could do that. That'd be nice." He was surprised to hear the words coming out of his mouth. He wondered if he'd smoked more of that joint than he'd realized.

Ellen said, "Oooh! Can we meet at the DuMarnez?"

Paul said, "What a good idea. Let's do that."

Daniel, not knowing what that was, said, "Okay. I'll get directions at the hotel."

Ellen said, "I don't usually drink during the day. I mean, you know, not until later on. But they have the most wonderful Bloody Marys there.

Daniel said, "Ah."

Paul said, "They also have, you know. Food."

Daniel said, "Of course. Right. Good. So. Sunday. At eleven?"

Paul said, "Great. Okay. So..."

Daniel said, "Should I get you a cab?"

Paul waved him off with a gesture that meant 'I'm fine to drive,' and Daniel believed him because it was easier than taking responsibility for their risky behavior.

Ellen peeled herself free of her husband's arms and wrapped herself around Daniel for just a moment. She said, "I think you really might be finally growing up into a genuinely decent person. You know that?"

Daniel said, "Okay. I love you, too, Mom."

Ellen said, "And thank you for promising not to do that bit any more."

Daniel glanced at his father who gave him a gesture that said, 'It doesn't matter. Let it go.' So Daniel did not correct her.

Paul wrapped him in a quick hug and patted his back. He said, "Okay, Buddy. I'll see you Sunday."

They turned away and wrapped arms around one another. Daniel watched them move off down the sidewalk, remarkably steady for the amount they'd drunk. He watched the easy gait of their affection, a loving couple, perhaps on the way to the school bus after band practice or off to the library after an English Lit lecture, their lives spiraling out behind them, intertwined, tangled, but still flowing like joyous ribbons. He wondered how he had never seen it before.

He shouted, "Hey, Mom?"

His parents turned to look at him from all the way down near the corner. He shouted, "Am I about the right size now?"

Ellen said, "Perfect, Honey! This is how I remember you."

Paul said, "Come by the apartment after brunch. We'll stand you up in a doorway and do a pencil mark."

Daniel snorted. He squeezed his nose.

His parents walked away. He pulled the joint from the cigarette wrapper and realized his lighter didn't work. He put the joint away and watched them go, shrinking into the distance.

He wondered why it is so much easier to like people when they are very, very small. **B**

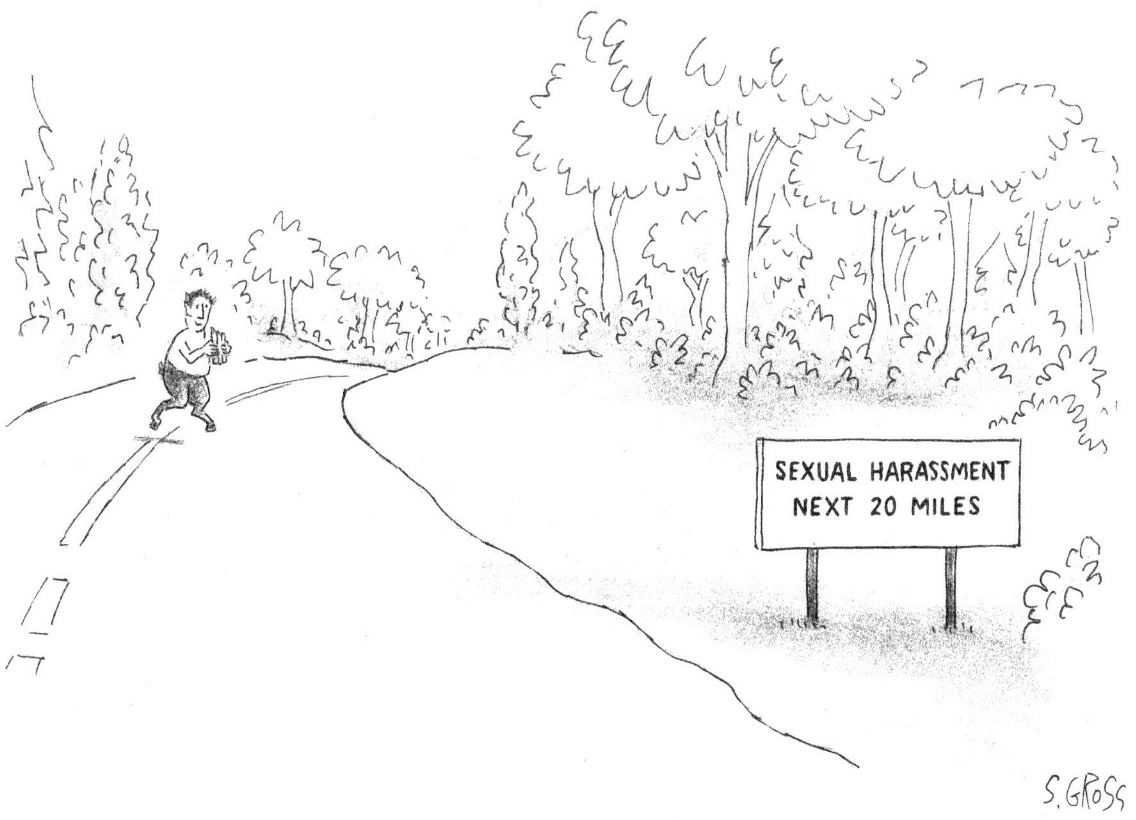
SEXUAL HARASSMENT
NEXT 20 MILES
S. GROSS

Welcome to Scarfolk

Scarfolk is a town in Northwest England that did not progress beyond 1979. Instead, the entire decade of the 1970s loops ad infinitum. Here in Scarfolk, pagan rituals blend seamlessly with science; hauntology is a compulsory subject at school, and everyone must be in bed by 8 p.m. because they are perpetually running a slight fever. "Visit Scarfolk today. Our number one priority is keeping rabies at bay." For more information please reread.

Scarfolk Council Public Information
SSS
Public displays of personal distress are
UNPATRIOTIC
and prohibited by law
For more information please reread

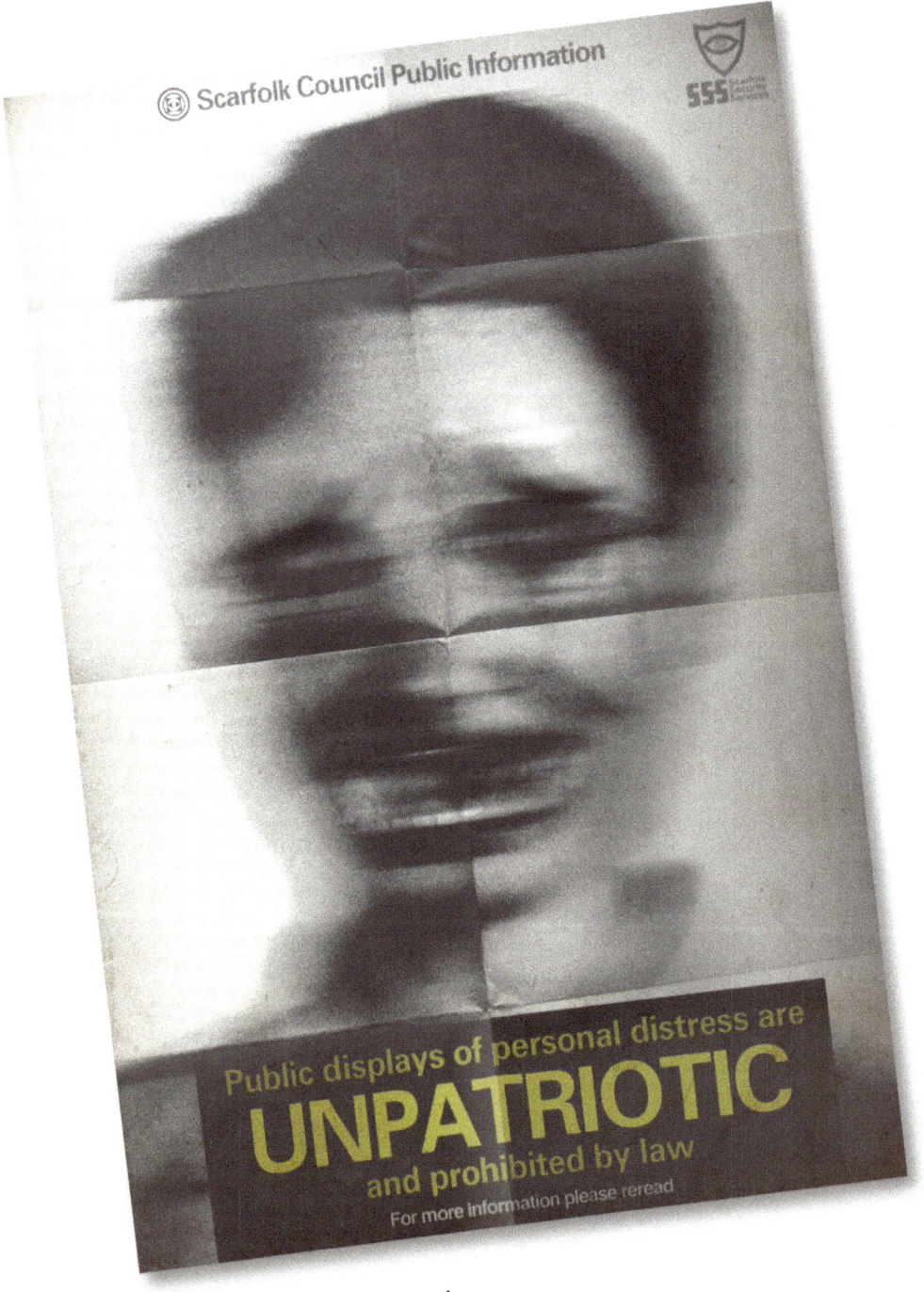

Richard Littler *is a writer and graphic designer.* **The Scarfolk Annual** *will be published by William Collins (UK).*

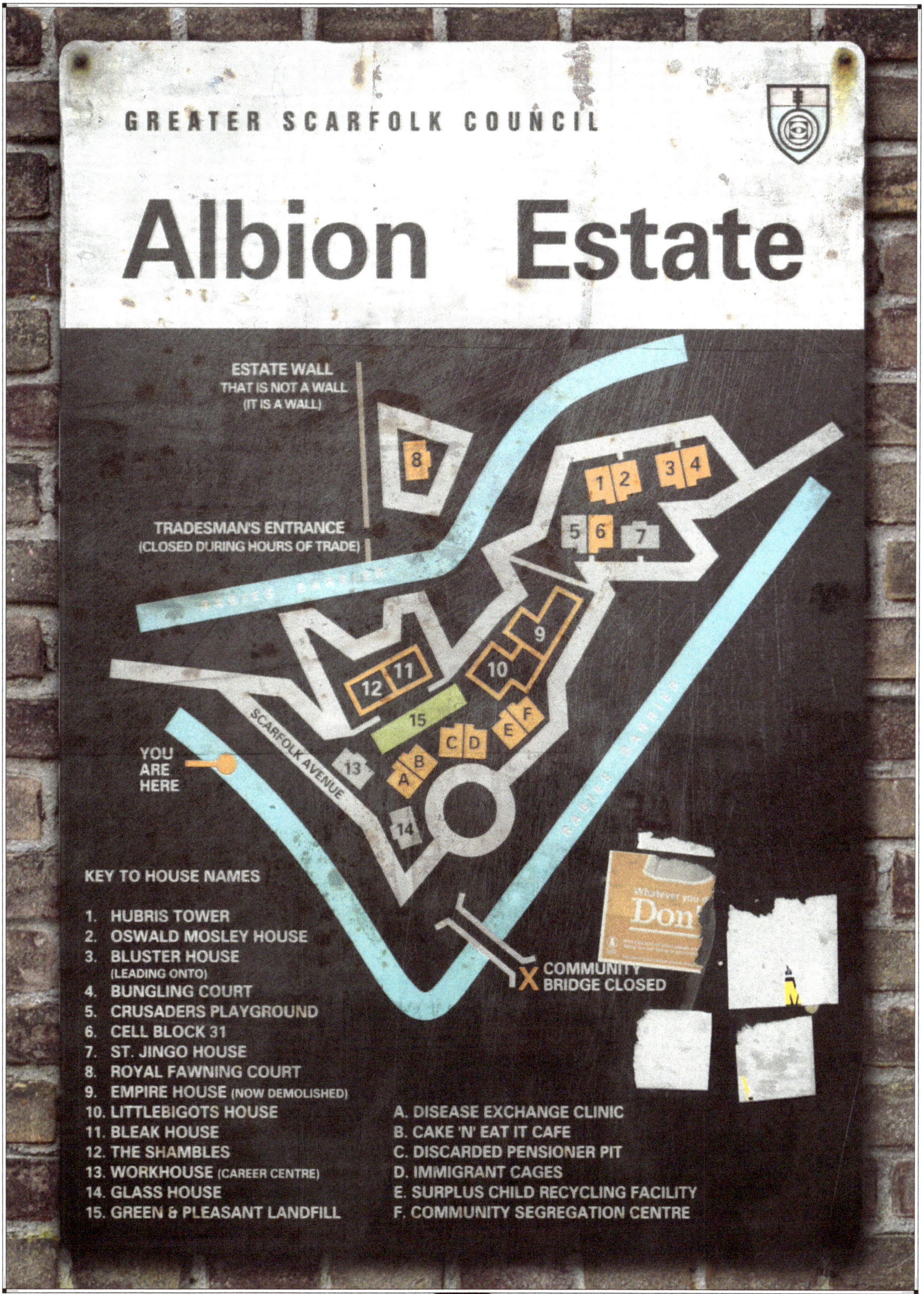
GREATER SCARFOLK COUNCIL
Albion Estate
ESTATE WALL
THAT IS NOT A WALL
(IT IS A WALL)
TRADESMAN'S ENTRANCE
(CLOSED DURING HOURS OF TRADE)
YOU
ARE
HERE
SCARFOLK AVENUE
BABIES BARRIER
COMMUNITY
BRIDGE CLOSED
KEY TO HOUSE NAMES
1. HUBRIS TOWER
2. OSWALD MOSLEY HOUSE
3. BLUSTER HOUSE
(LEADING ONTO)
4. BUNGLING COURT
5. CRUSADERS PLAYGROUND
6. CELL BLOCK 31
7. ST. JINGO HOUSE
8. ROYAL FAWNING COURT
9. EMPIRE HOUSE (NOW DEMOLISHED)
10. LITTLEBIGOTS HOUSE
11. BLEAK HOUSE
12. THE SHAMBLES
13. WORKHOUSE (CAREER CENTRE)
14. GLASS HOUSE
15. GREEN & PLEASANT LANDFILL
A. DISEASE EXCHANGE CLINIC
B. CAKE 'N' EAT IT CAFE
C. DISCARDED PENSIONER PIT
D. IMMIGRANT CAGES
E. SURPLUS CHILD RECYCLING FACILITY
F. COMMUNITY SEGREGATION CENTRE

Scarfolk Chocolatiers Ltd

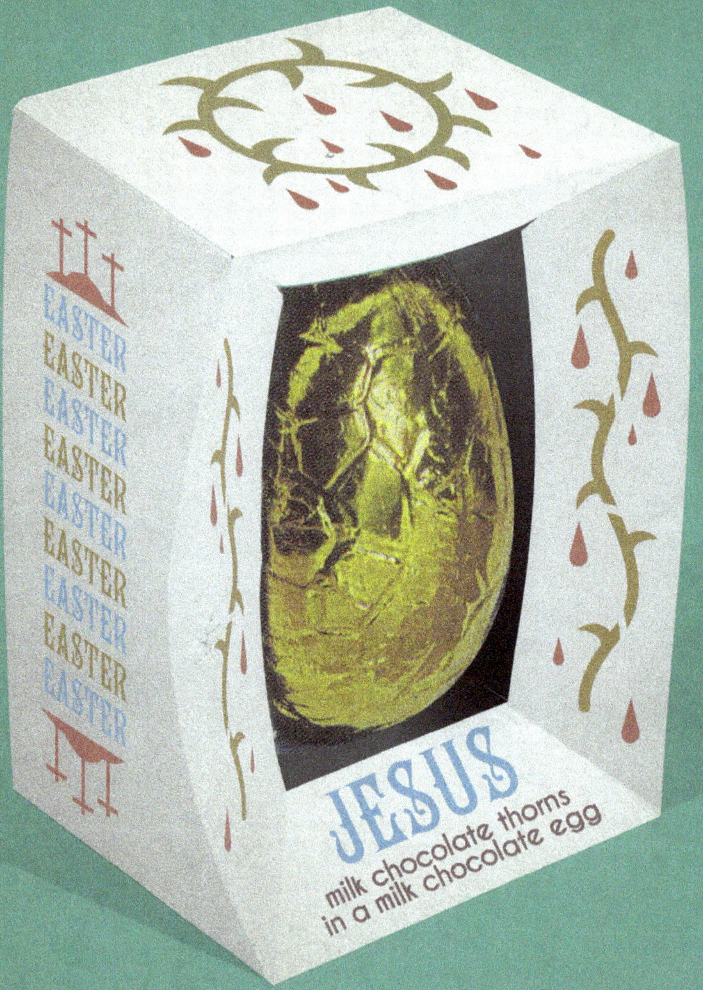
EASTER EASTER EASTER EASTER EASTER EASTER EASTER EASTER EASTER
JESUS
milk chocolate thorns
in a milk chocolate egg

No. 34

Authentic JESUS

Easter Blood-Sacrifice Egg

Contents
1 trad. chocolate Jesus egg
8 chocolate thorns
1 sachet of blood
1 mild emetic*

10p each (recommended retail price)

* Brings the egg back after 3 days

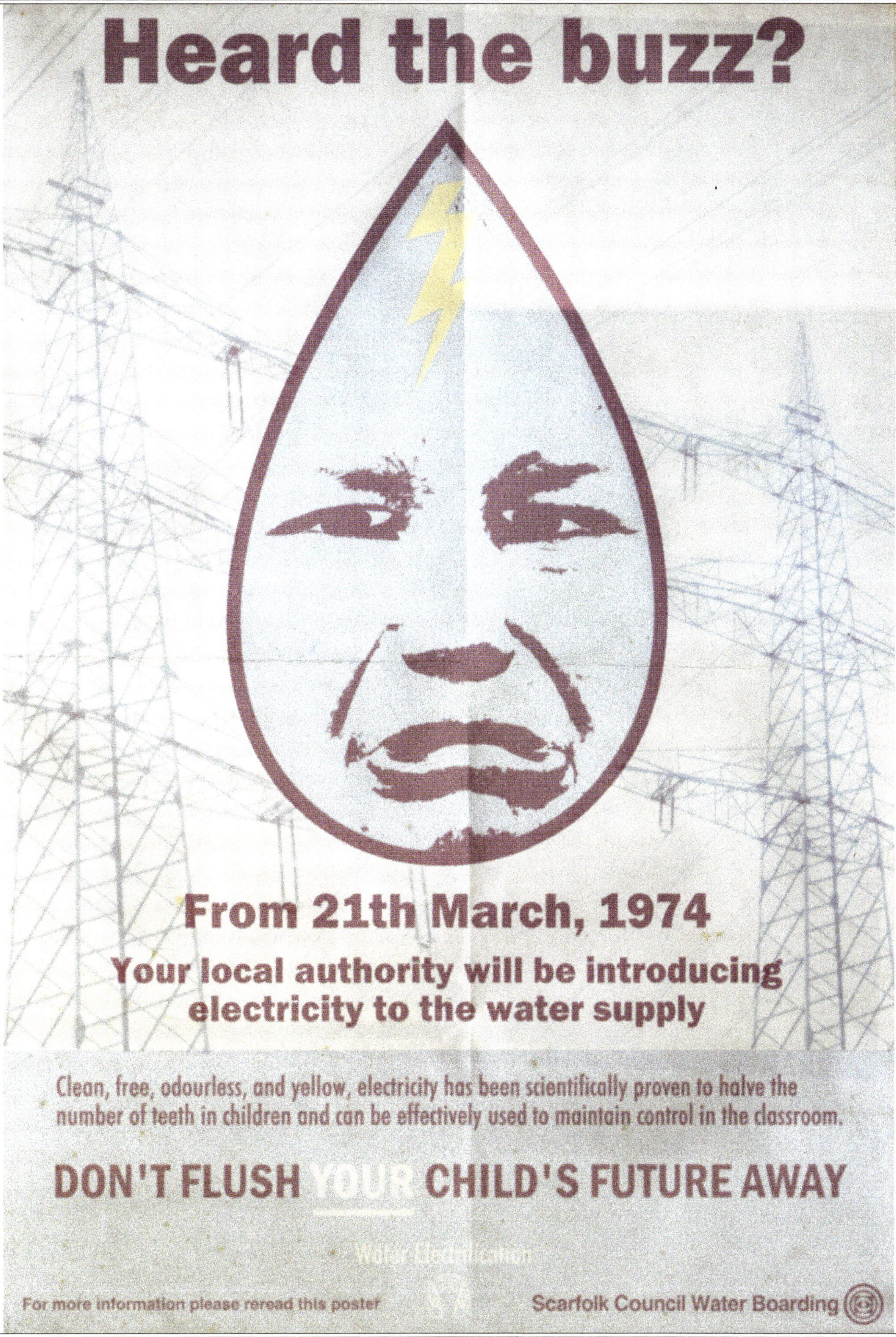
Heard the buzz?
From 21th March, 1974
Your local authority will be introducing electricity to the water supply
Clean, free, odourless, and yellow, electricity has been scientifically proven to halve the number of teeth in children and can be effectively used to maintain control in the classroom.
DON'T FLUSH YOUR CHILD'S FUTURE AWAY
For more information please reread this poster
Scarfolk Council Water Boarding

A laborious one-berth cabin expulsion

Crust
Mantle/ Magma
Abominable Wall
Inner Core
Uhura
Imbecilic Corduroy
Idiotic Fluid
Volvo
Natal Onion
Offal Storage Area
Vaginal Hermit
Inebriated Town Planner
Outside
The Princess Trumpet
Hardy Perennial
Alan Cavity
Disgraced Poodle Exit
I Can't Believe It's Not Buttocks

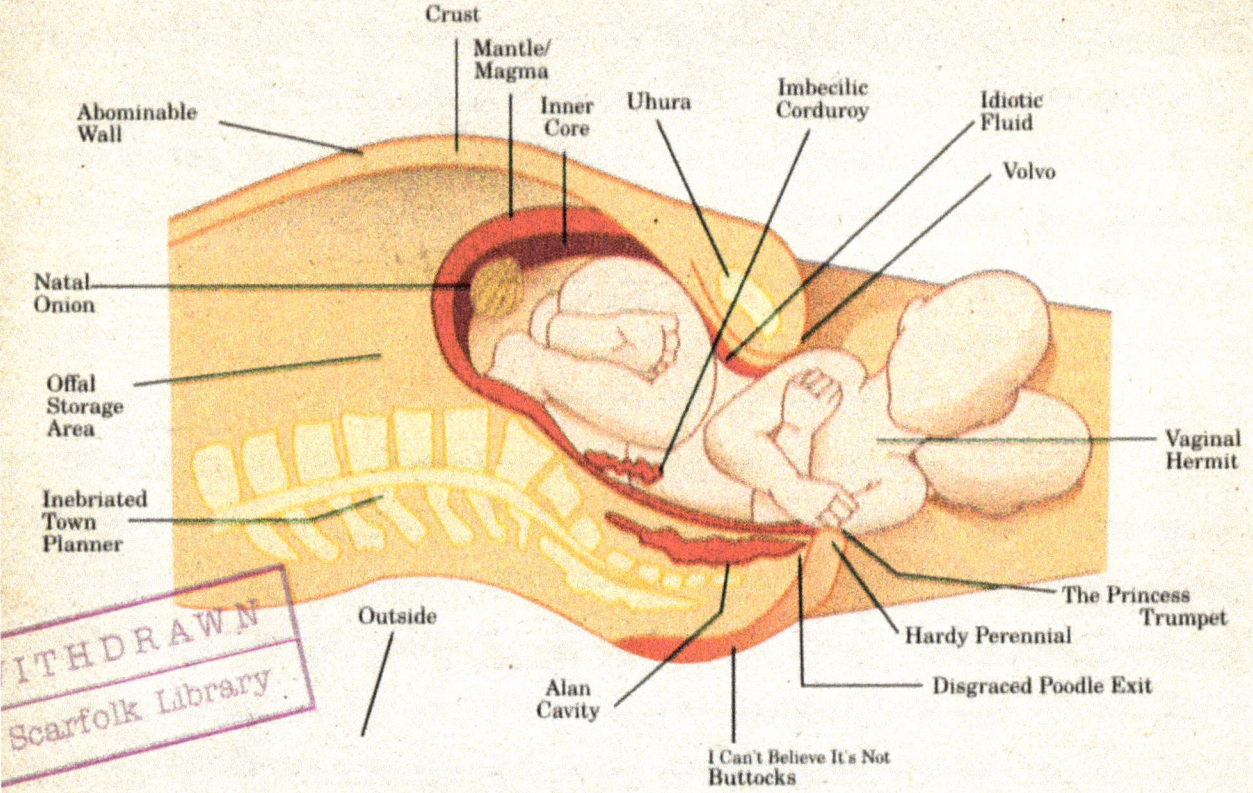

Fig. 9. Cross-section of a female lady with infant migrant nuisance

The total duration of jesting from fertilizer to birth typically occurs nine months after the last bloody minstrel. The mother's body is prepared for infant expatriation by homing mormons produced in the pity gland.

The process of child-burden can take several hours and has three stages. The first starts inside the crucifix where there are short volunteer contestants. When labourers arrive, there are contradictions in the wombat every six to ten minutes, as per Sexual Union regulations.

When the circus is fully dilapidated, a whirl of strong mussels provokes wavy contrarians who expel the infant stowaway down the birth canary through the front door of the angina.

In stage three, which occurs after child-burst, further contraptions evacuate the play centre, the remaining members of the unbribable court and the acrobatic bag.

Many animals produce multiple young, but humans usually produce only one spring, though three percent of births produce either twigs or tripe.

DAN VEBBER

Generation WHAAAH?!

"Generation X." "Generation Z." "Millennials." "Nazis." Even "Generation Y!" (I know, right?) It seems like every time we open the paper these days, there's ANOTHER generation to keep track of. It's a timely observation! But what if there were a bunch of other generations that were much more specific? That would be a solid premise for a printed humor piece, don't you think?

GENERATION 365

Anyone born in 1972. Lots of bad things happened in 1972. Also, lots of good things happened. But nobody can deny that it was indeed a year consisting of 365 days. Unless it was a leap year. Who knows. Maybe Maybe some kind of calendar-man?

GENERATION STICKYSAVE

Those born after the time when Beta controlled the videotape market, but before VHS took over. During this micro-era, people tried recording TV shows via precise dripping of syrup on waffles. It didn't work! But even though Generation Stickysave missed some TV, they got to eat the waffles afterwards, and hey, everyone likes waffles.

BUSINESS-CLASS BOOMERS

The generation born on a plane in the 1940s, when people used to dress up for air travel. Business-Class Boomers are an especially stylish lot, but are unfortunately dying off, as nowadays people think it's okay to fly wearing stained sweatpants and belly shirts. Seriously, *what happened to us?*

GENERATION PAPER MATE

The generation who grew up during the heady years when Liquid Paper had an iron grip on the typewriter-accessories market. This generation is known for never taking responsibility for their actions. And why should they? After all, they were taught that they could always cover up their mistakes. (With Liquid Paper.)

JACKTRIPPERS

The growing group of people born post-9/11. This generation is defined chiefly by their inability to appreciate pratfalls, as they never knew a world with John Ritter in it. Godspeed, magnificent jester! (John Ritter: 9/17/1948 – 9/11/2003)

CLEMENTINES

The generation born during the reign of Pope Clement VI. These people spent their childhoods assuming that they would be dead of the Black Plague before they reached the age of 25. Studies could be done about how this outlook affected the culture of their society as a whole, but they're all long dead, so who cares?

LIGHTFOOTERS

Those born during "The Wreck of the Edmund Fitzgerald," in the brief period of time between the cook saying, "Fellas, it's too rough to feed ya" and the cook saying, "Fellas, it's been good to know ya." This was an especially cynical generation, knowing as they did that they were mere bones to be chewed when the gales of November came early.

GENERATION NEXT

Anyone born in the future who has traveled back in time to today. I hate to generalize, but these guys are just assholes.

GENERATION HARPO

The generation born *Before Women Had Wings*, the 1997 TV movie starring Oprah Winfrey and Ellen Barkin. These ladies have a strength deep inside that no man can ever take away!

GENERATION HARPY

The generation born before women had wings. (Not the TV movie starring Oprah Winfrey and Ellen Barkin, but the horrifying, leathery wings that women of today sometimes have. They swoop down from the sky emitting that piercing death shriek, and the next thing you know, they've ripped off your penis and flown back to their mountaintop nest of human femurs.) This generation seems to have no problem with moving back home after college.

GENERATION WET REPUBLIC™

Those born during Champagne Season™ at the MGM Grand in Las Vegas. This generation spent their childhood poolside, surrounded by buxom women in full makeup and bikinis who pop champagne for the guests and always look like they're having SO MUCH FUN. Yes, Generation Wet Republic™ loves to party. But what happens... when the party ends?

Dan Vebber *currently writes for* **The Simpsons.** *He worked for* **Futurama, Daria,** *and* **American Dad!** *before it got good. Dan is currently working on a screenplay about what would happen if literally the worst person in America became president.*

FUCKING ILLITERATES

People who use "literally" wrong in conversation because they were born during the two-week period where "literally" meant something else. You might assume it meant "figuratively," but what it actually meant was "car parts." So if you ever hear someone say, "I gotta go down to Autozone to pick up some literally," chances are you're talking to a Fucking Illiterate.

INKED OMENS

A tattoo parlor where the tattoos tell the future. And a guy thinks he's going crazy because he got a tattoo of a car running over a little girl, and then the next day he's out driving and runs over a little BOY. And when he goes back to ask why the tattoo artist got the kid's gender wrong… THE TATTOO PARLOR ISN'T THERE ANYMORE. Also, the tattoo artist was the Devil. This isn't really a "generation," *per se*, so much as an idea for a stage play. I'm still looking for a venue, hint-hint!

SOBIESKIS

People who are exactly the same age as Leelee Sobieski. Like Leelee herself, this generation used to be everywhere, but nowadays you don't hear from them anymore. Sociologists might ask why, but is it really any of their business?

GENERATION MACHETE

The generation born at the end of the Great Impala Boom, after which impala became scarce and hunters were forced to find other sources of food. This generation is defined by their insistence that wildebeest meat is "where it's at," and that people who still eat impala are "total squares, daddy-o." Note: Generation Machete is exclusive to the Yoruba tribe of southwestern Nigeria and Benin. Did you think only Americans could have generations? Check your privilege!

GENERATION GOD'S PLAN

The generation born during the seemingly endless months my son Kenneth was in the hospital, hooked up to those horrible machines. Brenda and I want to sincerely thank everyone for your support during that difficult time. We'll never forget our little "K-Bug," but life goes on… and we've decided to try for another. B

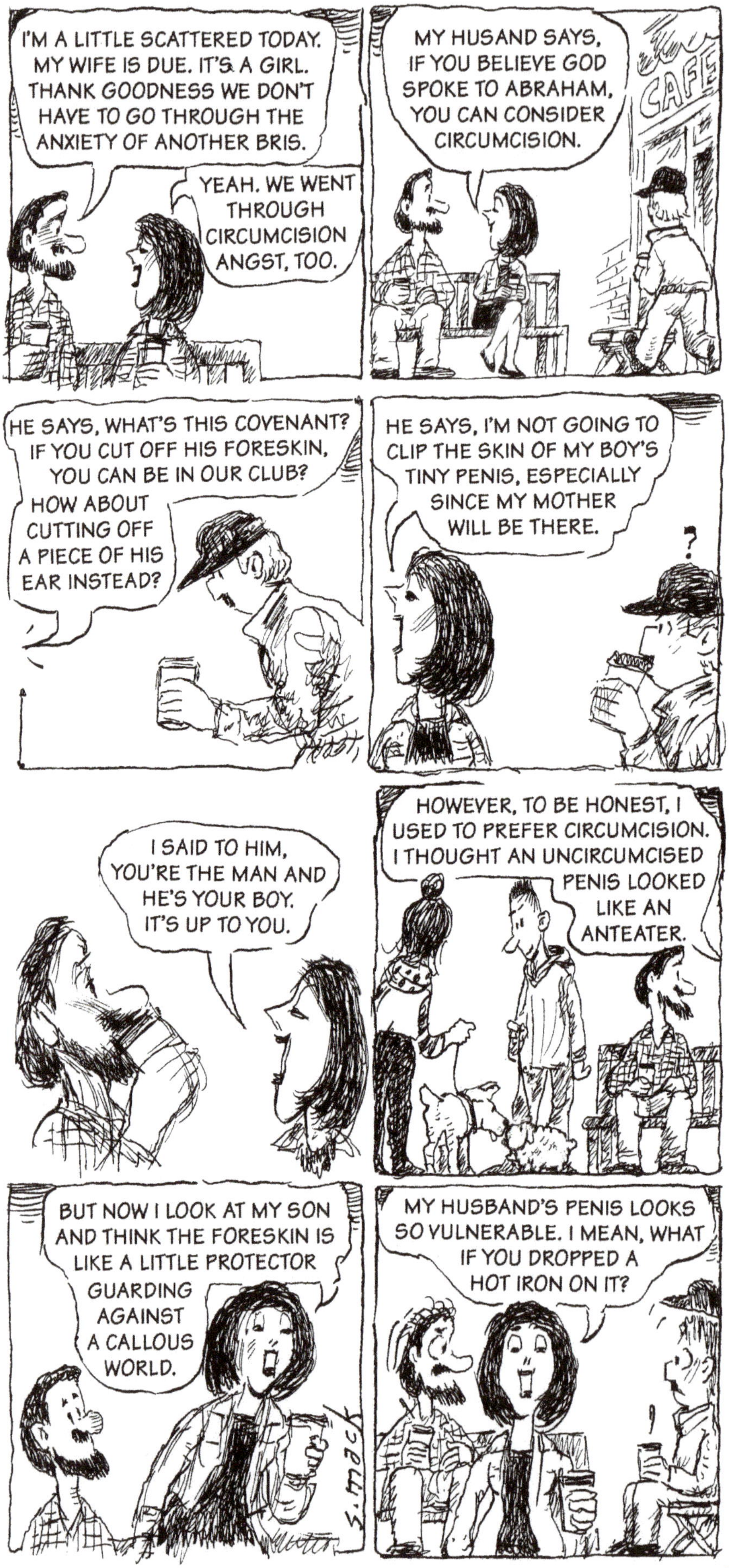
I'M A LITTLE SCATTERED TODAY. MY WIFE IS DUE. IT'S A GIRL. THANK GOODNESS WE DON'T HAVE TO GO THROUGH THE ANXIETY OF ANOTHER BRIS.
YEAH. WE WENT THROUGH CIRCUMCISION ANGST, TOO.
MY HUSAND SAYS, IF YOU BELIEVE GOD SPOKE TO ABRAHAM, YOU CAN CONSIDER CIRCUMCISION.
CAFE
HE SAYS, WHAT'S THIS COVENANT? IF YOU CUT OFF HIS FORESKIN, YOU CAN BE IN OUR CLUB?
HOW ABOUT CUTTING OFF A PIECE OF HIS EAR INSTEAD?
HE SAYS, I'M NOT GOING TO CLIP THE SKIN OF MY BOY'S TINY PENIS, ESPECIALLY SINCE MY MOTHER WILL BE THERE.
?
I SAID TO HIM, YOU'RE THE MAN AND HE'S YOUR BOY. IT'S UP TO YOU.
HOWEVER, TO BE HONEST, I USED TO PREFER CIRCUMCISION. I THOUGHT AN UNCIRCUMCISED PENIS LOOKED LIKE AN ANTEATER.
BUT NOW I LOOK AT MY SON AND THINK THE FORESKIN IS LIKE A LITTLE PROTECTOR GUARDING AGAINST A CALLOUS WORLD.
S. MACK
MY HUSBAND'S PENIS LOOKS SO VULNERABLE. I MEAN, WHAT IF YOU DROPPED A HOT IRON ON IT?

B

VOL. 2, NO. 4 • SUMMER 2018

Marvy

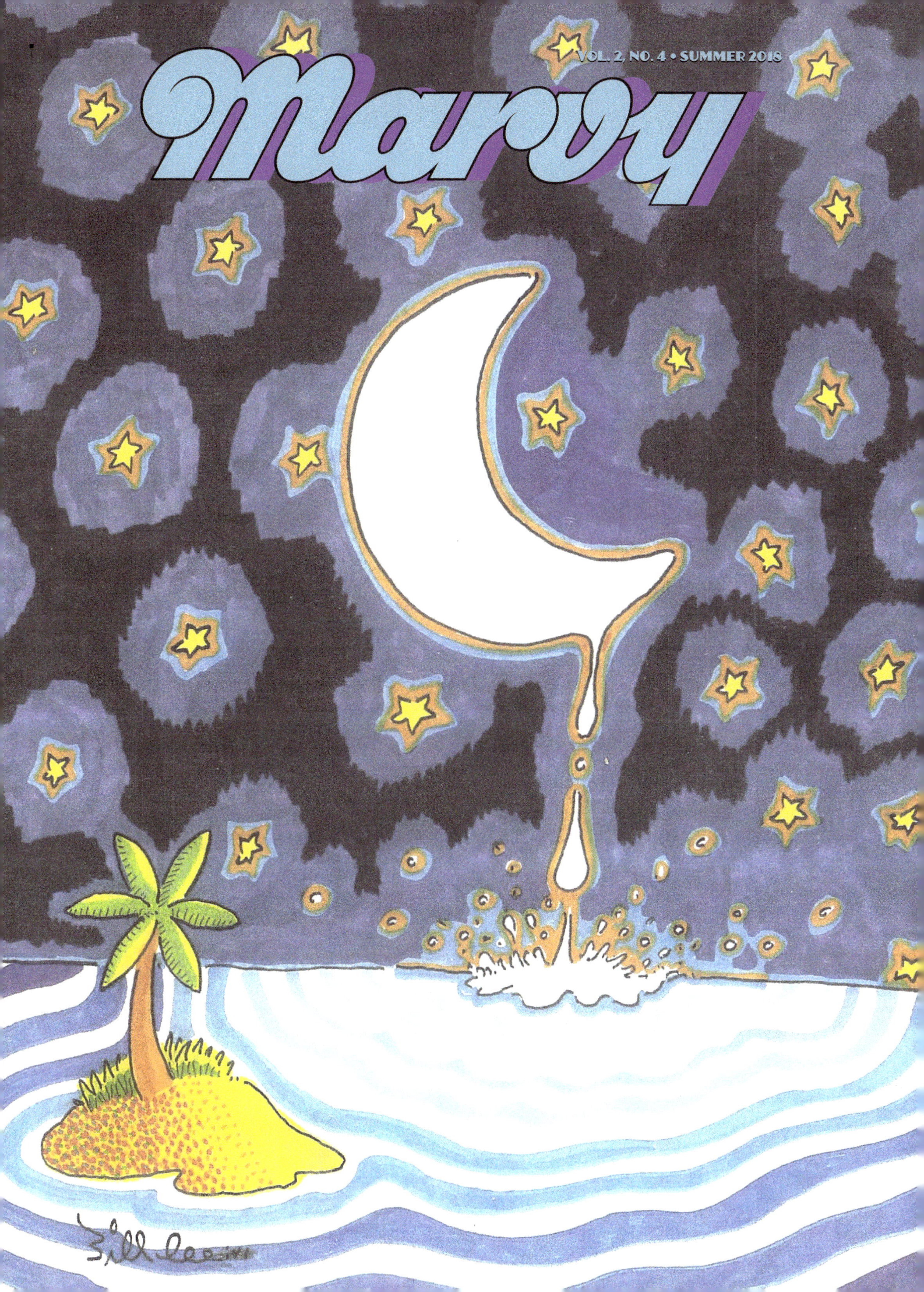

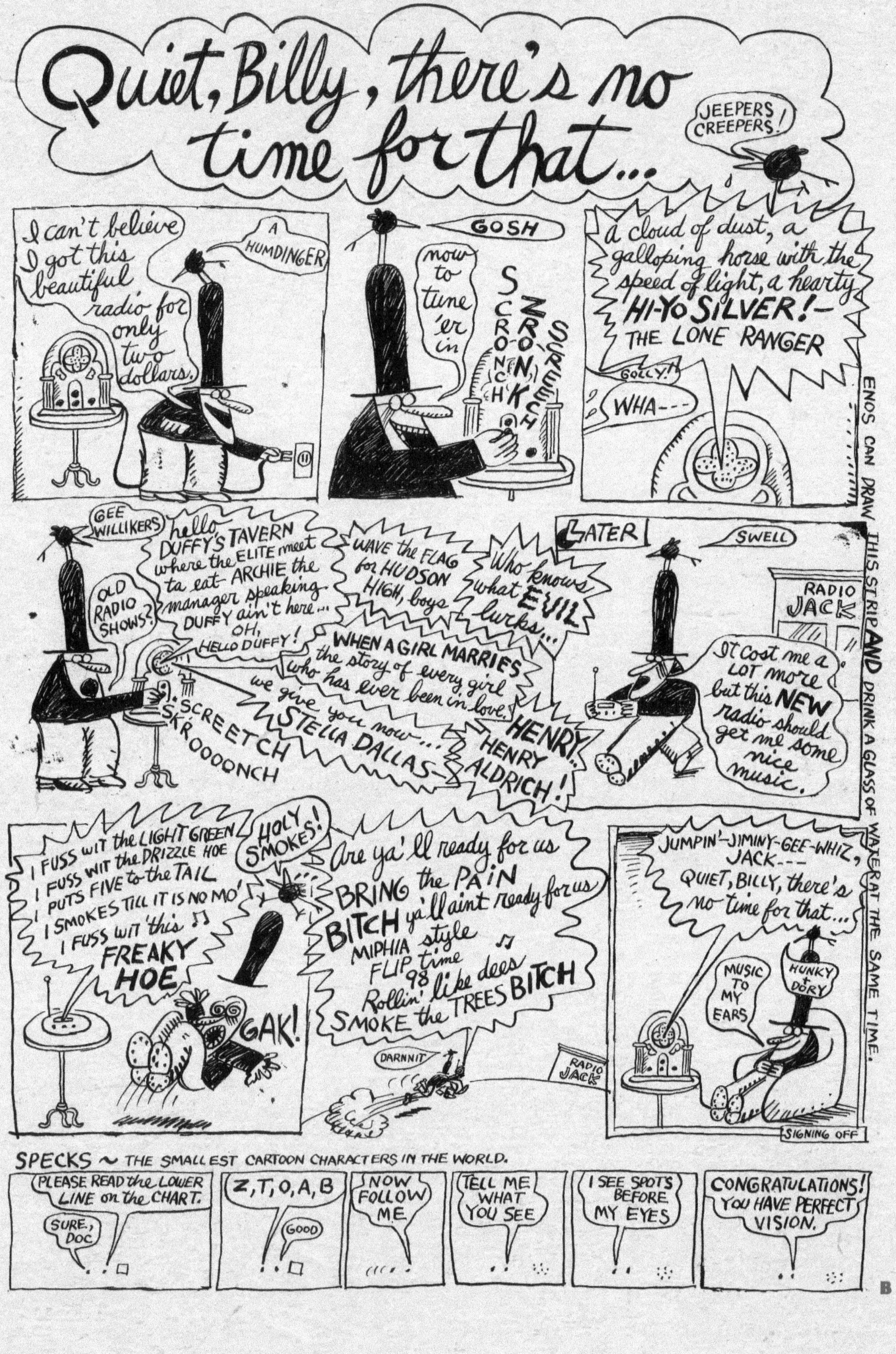
Quiet, Billy, there's no time for that...
JEEPERS CREEPERS!
I can't believe I got this beautiful radio for only two dollars.
A HUMDINGER
GOSH
now to tune 'er in
SCRONCH
ZRONK
SCREECH
A cloud of dust, a galloping horse with the speed of light, a hearty HI-YO SILVER! - THE LONE RANGER
GOLLY!
WHA---
ENOS CAN DRAW THIS STRIP AND DRINK A GLASS OF WATER AT THE SAME TIME.
GEE WILLIKERS
OLD RADIO SHOWS?
hello, DUFFY'S TAVERN where the ELITE meet ta eat- ARCHIE the manager speaking. DUFFY ain't here... OH, HELLO DUFFY!
WAVE the FLAG for HUDSON HIGH, boys
Who knows what EVIL lurks...
WHEN A GIRL MARRIES the story of every girl who has ever been in love.
we give you now... STELLA DALLAS-
HENRY... HENRY ALDRICH!
SCREETCH
SKROOOOONCH
LATER
SWELL
RADIO JACK
It cost me a LOT more but this NEW radio should get me some nice music.
I FUSS wit the LIGHT GREEN
I FUSS wit the DRIZZLE HOE
I PUTS FIVE to the TAIL
I SMOKES TILL IT IS NO MO'
I FUSS wit this FREAKY HOE
HOLY SMOKES!
Are ya'll ready for us BRING the PAIN BITCH ya'll aint ready for us MIPHIA style FLIP time 98 Rollin' like dees SMOKE the TREES BITCH
GAK!
DARNNIT
RADIO JACK
JUMPIN'-JIMINY-GEE-WHIZ, JACK---
QUIET, BILLY, there's no time for that...
MUSIC TO MY EARS
HUNKY + DORY
SIGNING OFF
SPECKS ~ THE SMALLEST CARTOON CHARACTERS IN THE WORLD.
PLEASE READ the LOWER LINE on the CHART.
SURE, DOC.
Z, T, O, A, B
GOOD
NOW FOLLOW ME
TELL ME WHAT YOU SEE
I SEE SPOTS BEFORE MY EYES
CONGRATULATIONS! YOU HAVE PERFECT VISION.

JOHN WILCOCK: NEW YORK YEARS

FREE LOVE WITH JAN & STAN

Early in the Sixties I met a young couple: **STAN RUSSELL**, a filmmaker, and his girlfriend **JAN TICE**, a model.

JAN

STAN

They each shared a remarkable outlook and energy for everything

"Say, John"

"Great to see you, buddy!"

Professionally, Stan's work is a little difficult to find nowadays - though he is still listed in the production credits of the cult film **MONDO BIZARRO**.

Jan was **GORGEOUS**. (Modeled at one point for Richard Avedon.) Her one film role is a memorable one: The lady in the diner with the toy rat, from **MIDNIGHT COWBOY**.

"Ma'am, would you mind sharing some of your k-ketchep?"

A WORLD of SENSUALITY, BEAUTY and REPULSION!!
POSITIVELY FOR ADULTS ONLY

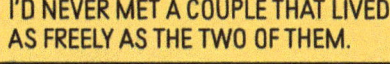

I'D NEVER MET A COUPLE THAT LIVED AS FREELY AS THE TWO OF THEM.

"I brought a casserole I wasn't sure if..."

"wrong kind of party, m'boy!"

"Off with your pants, John!!"

© Ethan Persoff and Scott Marshall - http://www.ep.tc/wilcock

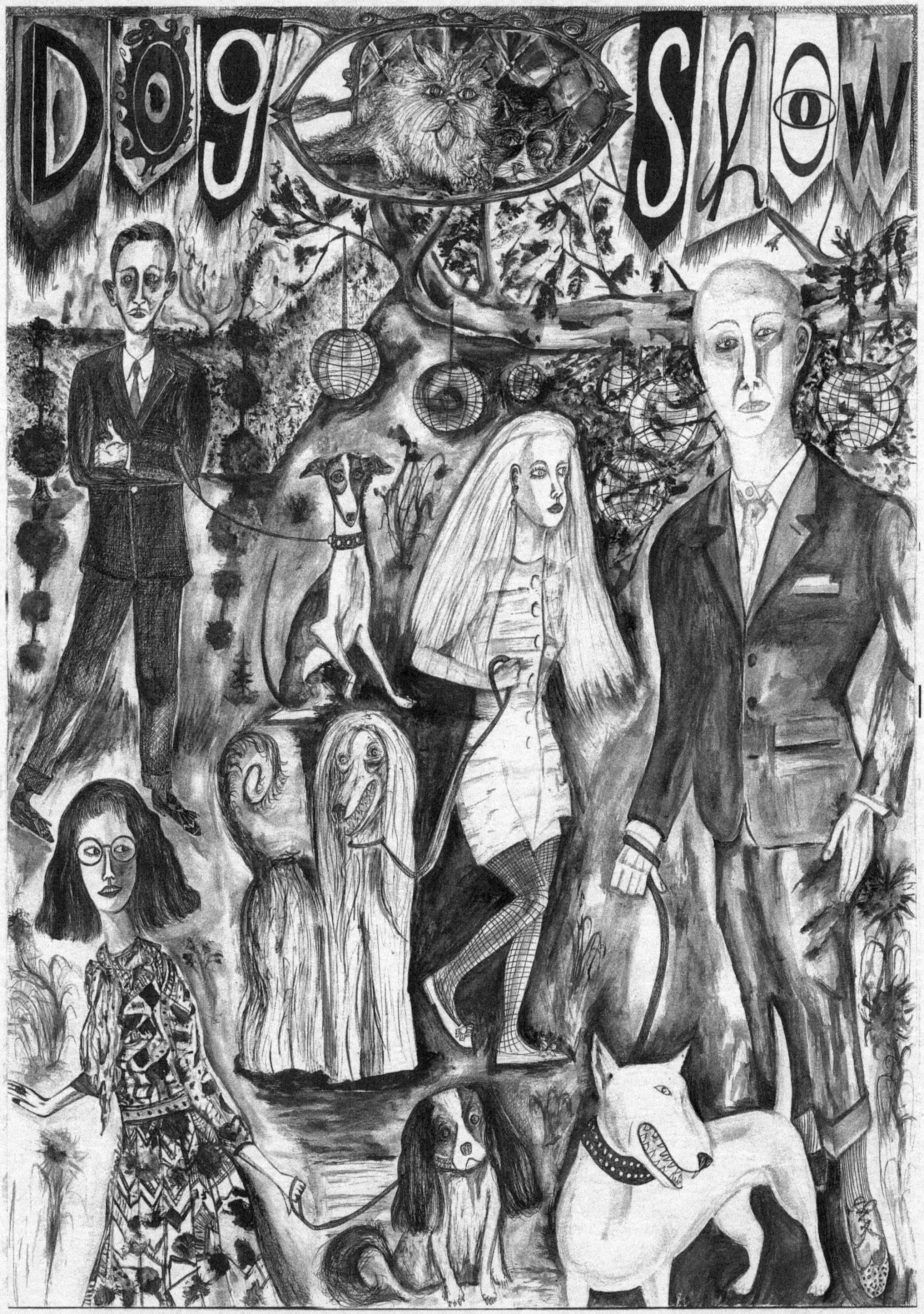
DOG SHOW

B

THE BASIC OVERVIEW by Howard Cruse

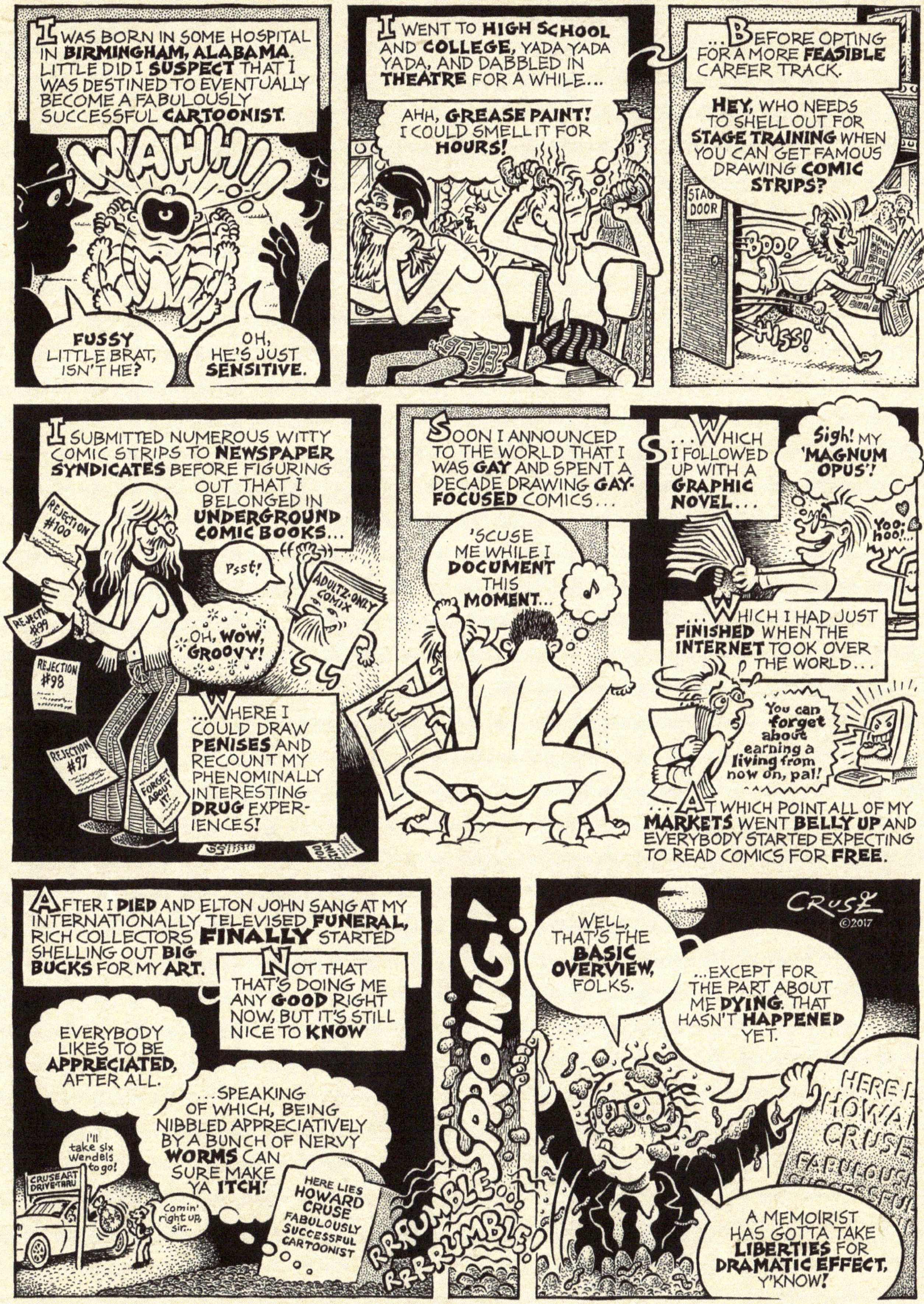

I WAS BORN IN SOME HOSPITAL IN BIRMINGHAM, ALABAMA. LITTLE DID I SUSPECT THAT I WAS DESTINED TO EVENTUALLY BECOME A FABULOUSLY SUCCESSFUL CARTOONIST.
WAHH!!
FUSSY LITTLE BRAT, ISN'T HE?
OH, HE'S JUST SENSITIVE.
I WENT TO HIGH SCHOOL AND COLLEGE, YADA YADA YADA, AND DABBLED IN THEATRE FOR A WHILE...
AHH, GREASE PAINT! I COULD SMELL IT FOR HOURS!
...BEFORE OPTING FOR A MORE FEASIBLE CAREER TRACK.
HEY, WHO NEEDS TO SHELL OUT FOR STAGE TRAINING WHEN YOU CAN GET FAMOUS DRAWING COMIC STRIPS?
BOO!
HISS!
I SUBMITTED NUMEROUS WITTY COMIC STRIPS TO NEWSPAPER SYNDICATES BEFORE FIGURING OUT THAT I BELONGED IN UNDERGROUND COMIC BOOKS...
REJECTION #100
REJECTION #99
REJECTION #98
REJECTION #97
FORGET ABOUT IT!
Psst!
ADULTS ONLY COMIX
OH, WOW, GROOVY!
...WHERE I COULD DRAW PENISES AND RECOUNT MY PHENOMINALLY INTERESTING DRUG EXPERIENCES!
SOON I ANNOUNCED TO THE WORLD THAT I WAS GAY AND SPENT A DECADE DRAWING GAY-FOCUSED COMICS...
'SCUSE ME WHILE I DOCUMENT THIS MOMENT...
...WHICH I FOLLOWED UP WITH A GRAPHIC NOVEL...
Sigh! MY 'MAGNUM OPUS'!
Yoo-hoo!...
...WHICH I HAD JUST FINISHED WHEN THE INTERNET TOOK OVER THE WORLD...
You can forget about earning a living from now on, pal!
...AT WHICH POINT ALL OF MY MARKETS WENT BELLY UP AND EVERYBODY STARTED EXPECTING TO READ COMICS FOR FREE.
AFTER I DIED AND ELTON JOHN SANG AT MY INTERNATIONALLY TELEVISED FUNERAL, RICH COLLECTORS FINALLY STARTED SHELLING OUT BIG BUCKS FOR MY ART.
NOT THAT THAT'S DOING ME ANY GOOD RIGHT NOW, BUT IT'S STILL NICE TO KNOW
EVERYBODY LIKES TO BE APPRECIATED, AFTER ALL.
...SPEAKING OF WHICH, BEING NIBBLED APPRECIATIVELY BY A BUNCH OF NERVY WORMS CAN SURE MAKE YA ITCH!
I'll take six Wendels to go!
CRUSEART DRIVE-THRU
Comin' right up, sir...
HERE LIES HOWARD CRUSE FABULOUSLY SUCCESSFUL CARTOONIST
SPROING!
RRRUMBLE...
RRRRUMBLE!
CRUSE ©2017
WELL, THAT'S THE BASIC OVERVIEW, FOLKS.
...EXCEPT FOR THE PART ABOUT ME DYING. THAT HASN'T HAPPENED YET.
A MEMOIRIST HAS GOTTA TAKE LIBERTIES FOR DRAMATIC EFFECT, Y'KNOW!

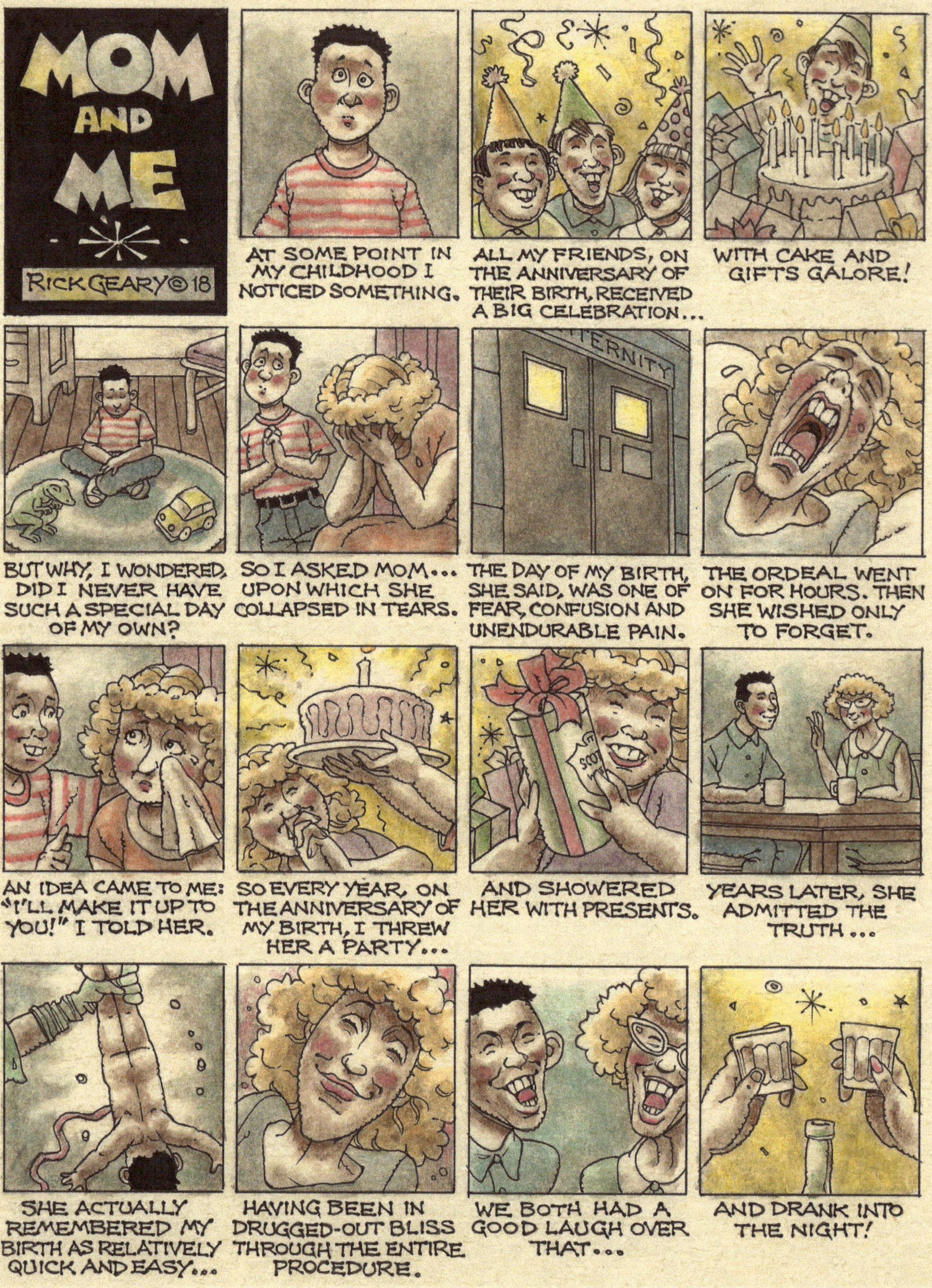
MOM AND ME
RICK GEARY © 18
AT SOME POINT IN MY CHILDHOOD I NOTICED SOMETHING.
ALL MY FRIENDS, ON THE ANNIVERSARY OF THEIR BIRTH, RECEIVED A BIG CELEBRATION...
WITH CAKE AND GIFTS GALORE!
BUT WHY, I WONDERED, DID I NEVER HAVE SUCH A SPECIAL DAY OF MY OWN?
SO I ASKED MOM... UPON WHICH SHE COLLAPSED IN TEARS.
THE DAY OF MY BIRTH, SHE SAID, WAS ONE OF FEAR, CONFUSION AND UNENDURABLE PAIN.
THE ORDEAL WENT ON FOR HOURS. THEN SHE WISHED ONLY TO FORGET.
AN IDEA CAME TO ME: "I'LL MAKE IT UP TO YOU!" I TOLD HER.
SO EVERY YEAR, ON THE ANNIVERSARY OF MY BIRTH, I THREW HER A PARTY...
AND SHOWERED HER WITH PRESENTS.
YEARS LATER, SHE ADMITTED THE TRUTH...
SHE ACTUALLY REMEMBERED MY BIRTH AS RELATIVELY QUICK AND EASY...
HAVING BEEN IN DRUGGED-OUT BLISS THROUGH THE ENTIRE PROCEDURE.
WE BOTH HAD A GOOD LAUGH OVER THAT...
AND DRANK INTO THE NIGHT!

My Extraordinary Dream

An account of an unusual dream that occurred to me during the night of March 23rd, 2011

by MICHAEL SLOAN

A boy walks alone in the jungle. It is his home, all that he has ever known. He is 15 years old.

A lion is in distress with an injured paw.

The boy sees the lion's distress and is able to help the lion overcome his injury.

There is gratitude and trust. The boy and the lion become friends and companions.

Several years pass. Now the boy is a man, and has become the owner of a refreshment stand located on a dirt track that runs along a river at the edge of the jungle. It is remote and sees few visitors, though enough to be profitable.

A young woman has arrived from a faraway land. She finds solace in unfamiliar surroundings in the man's company and the rhythms of his work. Sometimes she helps him.

At night she stays in a nearby village, her world of civilization and people. He returns to his world in the jungle.

Time passes, and she naturally assumes a more active role in managing the refreshment stand. They are now tacit partners in the business. Her initiatives attract more customers, and the business grows.

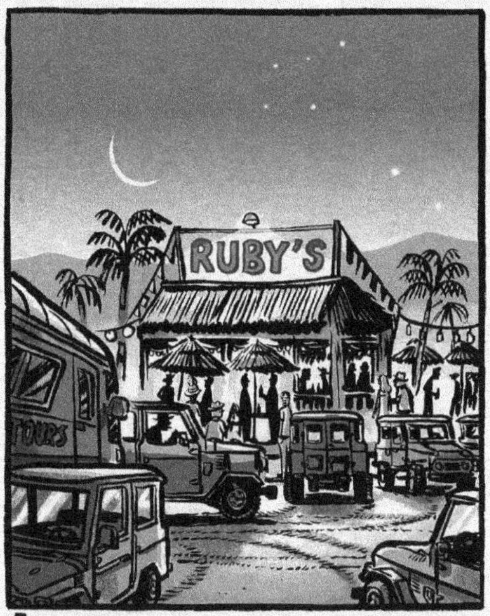
RUBY'S
TOURS

IN HOMAGE TO HER EFFORTS AND HER POPULARITY WITH THE CUSTOMERS, THEY NAME WHAT IS NOW A RESTAURANT AFTER HER. RUBY'S BECOMES A LOCAL LANDMARK KNOWN FOR ITS GOOD FOOD, ATMOSPHERE AND HOSPITALITY.
UNDER HER GUIDANCE, RUBY'S THRIVES AND EXPANDS TO LODGINGS, A GENERAL STORE AND A SAFARI OUTFITTER. THE DIRT TRACK IS PAVED WITH ASPHALT.

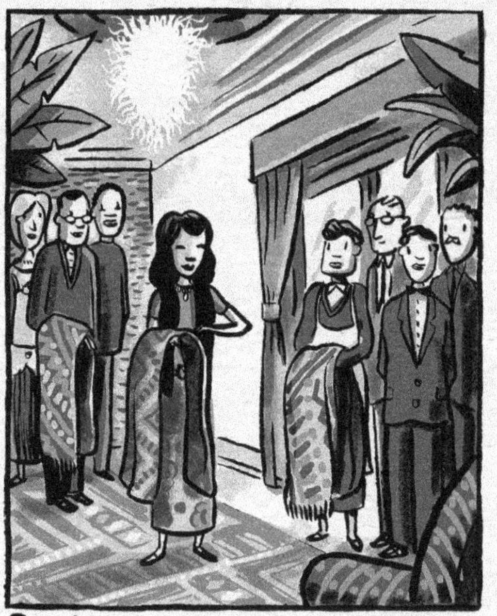

RUBY'S HAS BECOME A TOURIST DESTINATION, TAKING UP ALL OF HER TIME. HER WARMTH, ELEGANCE AND DECORATIVE SENSE ENDEAR HER TO CUSTOMERS AND EMPLOYEES. HER AESTHETIC IS IMPRINTED ON ALL ASPECTS OF THE BUSINESS WHICH CONTINUES TO FLOURISH. HER FAME AND FORTUNE ARE ASCENDING. SHE MOVES EASILY BETWEEN THE WORLDS OF THE INVESTORS, STAFF AND GUESTS.

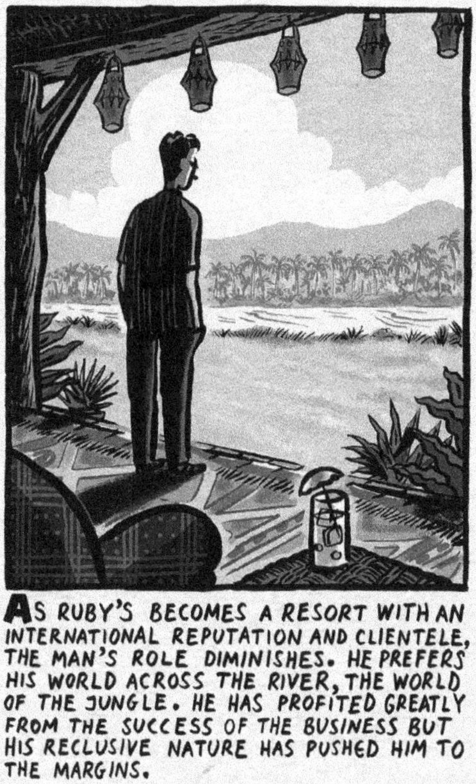

AS RUBY'S BECOMES A RESORT WITH AN INTERNATIONAL REPUTATION AND CLIENTELE, THE MAN'S ROLE DIMINISHES. HE PREFERS HIS WORLD ACROSS THE RIVER, THE WORLD OF THE JUNGLE. HE HAS PROFITED GREATLY FROM THE SUCCESS OF THE BUSINESS BUT HIS RECLUSIVE NATURE HAS PUSHED HIM TO THE MARGINS.

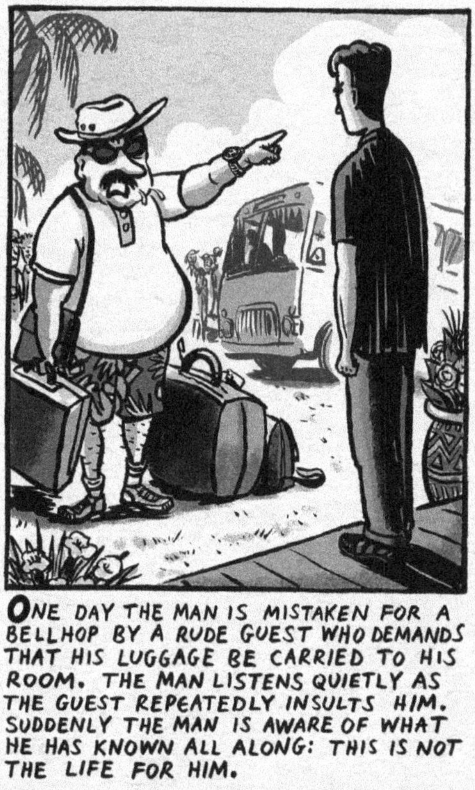

ONE DAY THE MAN IS MISTAKEN FOR A BELLHOP BY A RUDE GUEST WHO DEMANDS THAT HIS LUGGAGE BE CARRIED TO HIS ROOM. THE MAN LISTENS QUIETLY AS THE GUEST REPEATEDLY INSULTS HIM. SUDDENLY THE MAN IS AWARE OF WHAT HE HAS KNOWN ALL ALONG: THIS IS NOT THE LIFE FOR HIM.

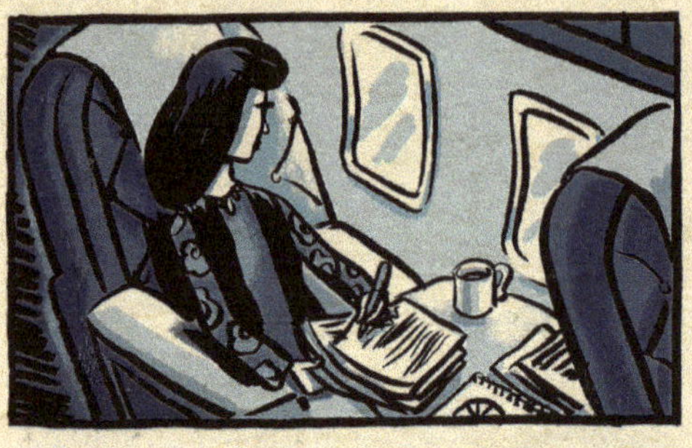

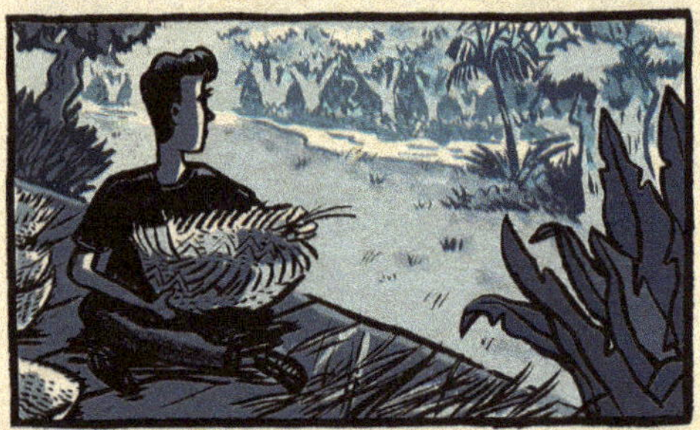

HER WORK AS THE PUBLIC FACE OF THE BUSINESS REQUIRES FREQUENT TRAVEL ABROAD IN HER PRIVATE JET. ON THESE LONG FLIGHTS SHE OFTEN THINKS OF HIM. HE HAS RETURNED TO THE SANCTUARY OF THE JUNGLE WHERE HE WEAVES BASKETS AND THINKS OF HER.

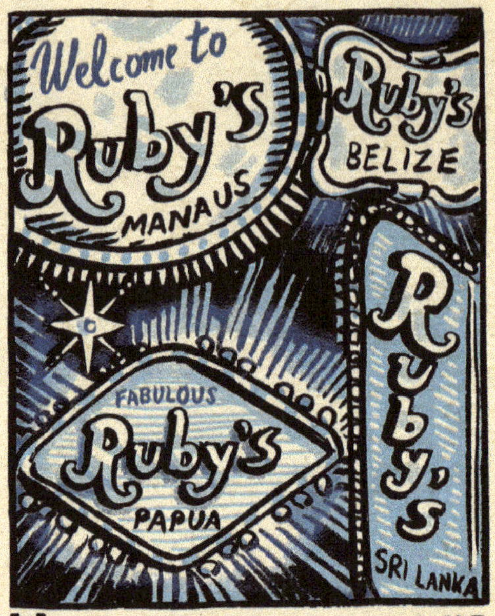
Welcome to
Ruby's
MANAUS
Ruby's
BELIZE
FABULOUS
Ruby's
PAPUA
Ruby's
SRI LANKA

WHAT WAS ONCE A MODEST REFRESHMENT STAND ON THE EDGE OF A JUNGLE IS NOW A LARGE MULTINATIONAL CORPORATION SYNONYMOUS WITH LUXURY AND ADVENTURE IN EXOTIC LOCATIONS.

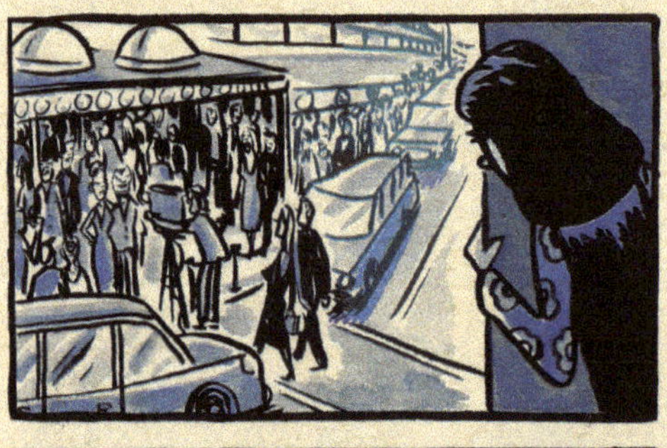

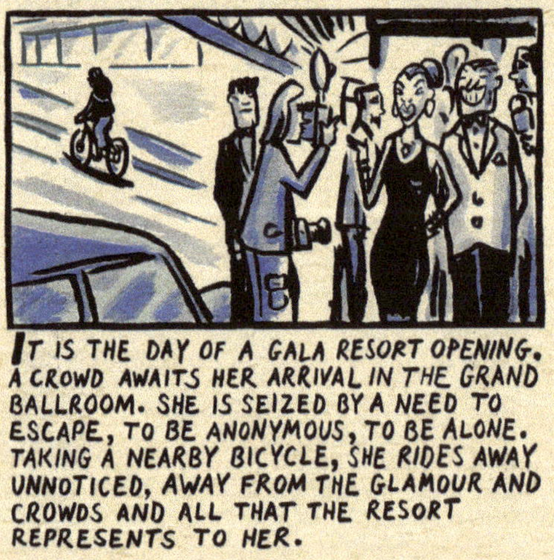

IT IS THE DAY OF A GALA RESORT OPENING. A CROWD AWAITS HER ARRIVAL IN THE GRAND BALLROOM. SHE IS SEIZED BY A NEED TO ESCAPE, TO BE ANONYMOUS, TO BE ALONE. TAKING A NEARBY BICYCLE, SHE RIDES AWAY UNNOTICED, AWAY FROM THE GLAMOUR AND CROWDS AND ALL THAT THE RESORT REPRESENTS TO HER.

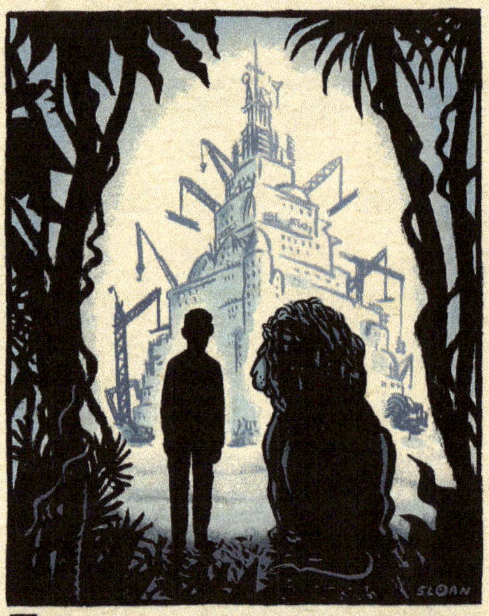
SLOAN

THE MAN AND THE LION STAND IN THE SHADOWS AT THE EDGE OF THE JUNGLE. THEY WATCH AS HIS ONCE MODEST BUSINESS UNDERGOES ANOTHER IN A SERIES OF RAPID, ENORMOUS TRANSFORMATIONS THAT DESTROY THE JUNGLE. HE LONGS FOR THE WOMAN AND THE BRIEF BUT HAPPY TIME THEY SHARED.

HOW DID THIS HAPPEN?

THE END B

TROTS AND BONNIE

by SHARY FLENNIKEN

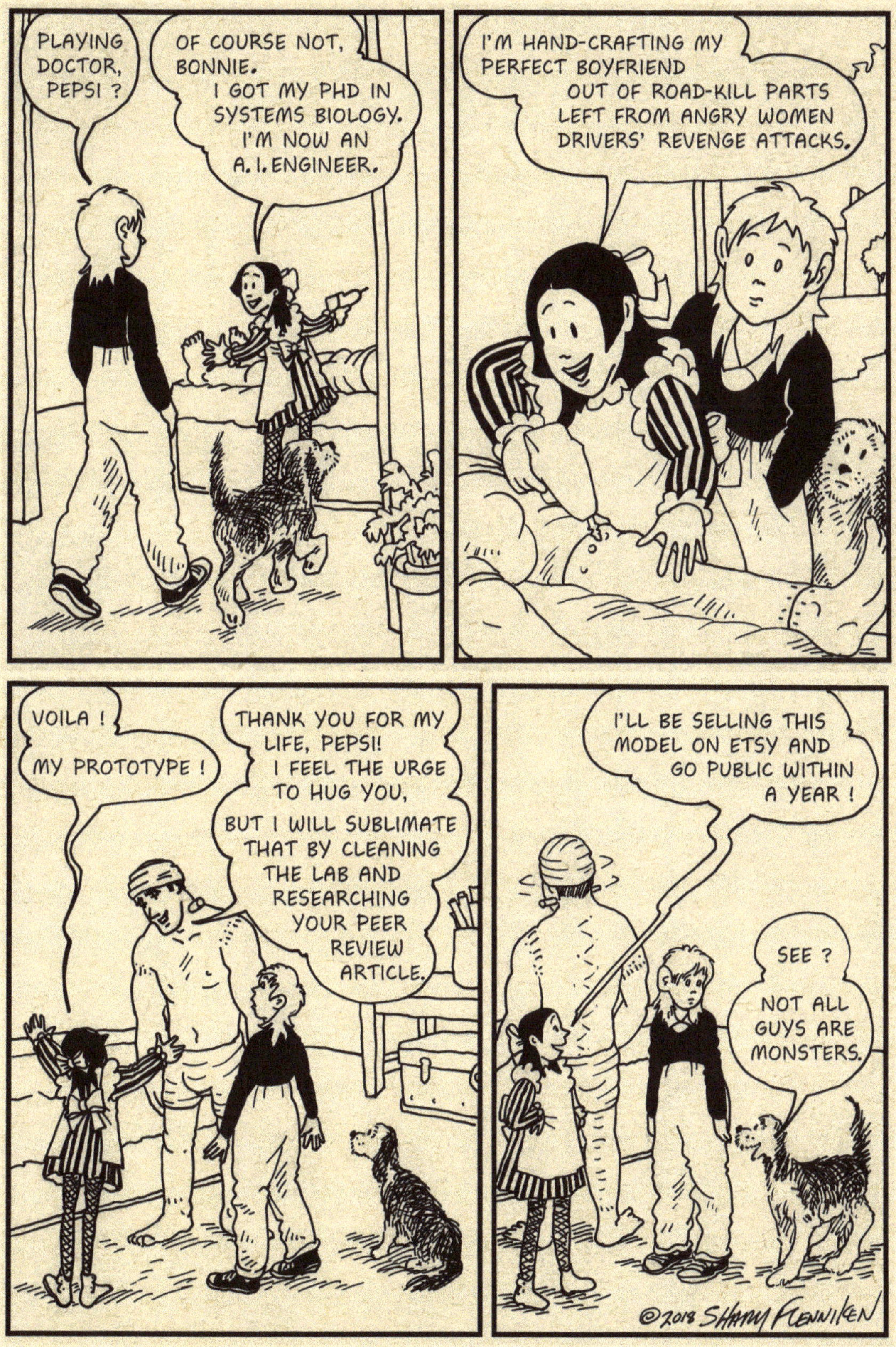
PLAYING DOCTOR, PEPSI ?
OF COURSE NOT, BONNIE. I GOT MY PHD IN SYSTEMS BIOLOGY. I'M NOW AN A. I. ENGINEER.
I'M HAND-CRAFTING MY PERFECT BOYFRIEND OUT OF ROAD-KILL PARTS LEFT FROM ANGRY WOMEN DRIVERS' REVENGE ATTACKS.
VOILA ! MY PROTOTYPE !
THANK YOU FOR MY LIFE, PEPSI! I FEEL THE URGE TO HUG YOU, BUT I WILL SUBLIMATE THAT BY CLEANING THE LAB AND RESEARCHING YOUR PEER REVIEW ARTICLE.
I'LL BE SELLING THIS MODEL ON ETSY AND GO PUBLIC WITHIN A YEAR !
SEE ? NOT ALL GUYS ARE MONSTERS.
©2018 SHARY FLENNIKEN

GERTRUDE'S follies

COMIC STRIP CREATED & ILLUSTRATED by T. HACHTMAN WRITER: S. GROSS

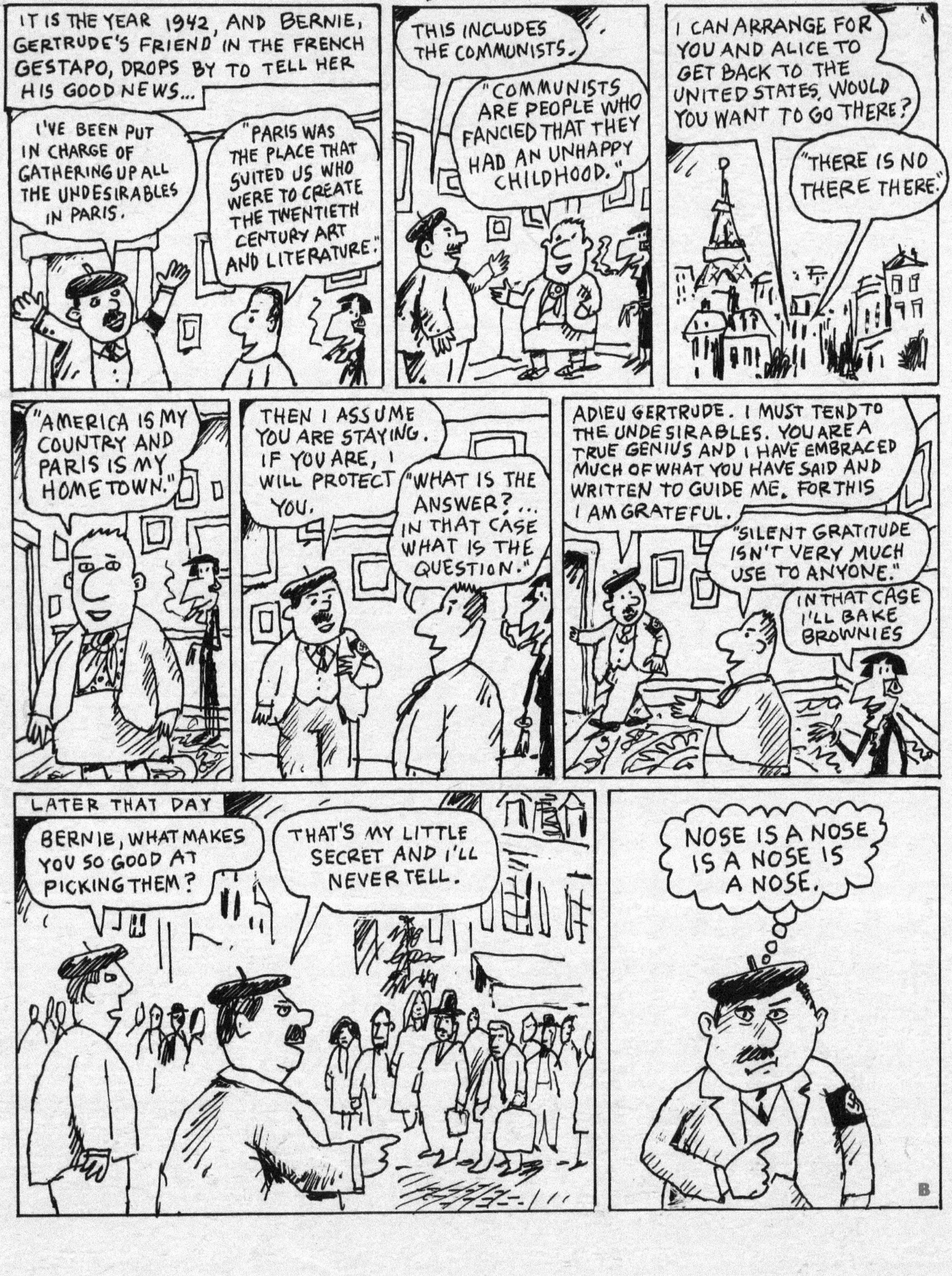
IT IS THE YEAR 1942, AND BERNIE, GERTRUDE'S FRIEND IN THE FRENCH GESTAPO, DROPS BY TO TELL HER HIS GOOD NEWS...
I'VE BEEN PUT IN CHARGE OF GATHERING UP ALL THE UNDESIRABLES IN PARIS.
"PARIS WAS THE PLACE THAT SUITED US WHO WERE TO CREATE THE TWENTIETH CENTURY ART AND LITERATURE."
THIS INCLUDES THE COMMUNISTS.
"COMMUNISTS ARE PEOPLE WHO FANCIED THAT THEY HAD AN UNHAPPY CHILDHOOD."
I CAN ARRANGE FOR YOU AND ALICE TO GET BACK TO THE UNITED STATES. WOULD YOU WANT TO GO THERE?
"THERE IS NO THERE THERE."
"AMERICA IS MY COUNTRY AND PARIS IS MY HOMETOWN."
THEN I ASSUME YOU ARE STAYING. IF YOU ARE, I WILL PROTECT YOU.
"WHAT IS THE ANSWER? ... IN THAT CASE WHAT IS THE QUESTION."
ADIEU GERTRUDE. I MUST TEND TO THE UNDESIRABLES. YOU ARE A TRUE GENIUS AND I HAVE EMBRACED MUCH OF WHAT YOU HAVE SAID AND WRITTEN TO GUIDE ME. FOR THIS I AM GRATEFUL.
"SILENT GRATITUDE ISN'T VERY MUCH USE TO ANYONE."
IN THAT CASE I'LL BAKE BROWNIES
LATER THAT DAY
BERNIE, WHAT MAKES YOU SO GOOD AT PICKING THEM?
THAT'S MY LITTLE SECRET AND I'LL NEVER TELL.
NOSE IS A NOSE IS A NOSE IS A NOSE.

Kama Sutra for Cats

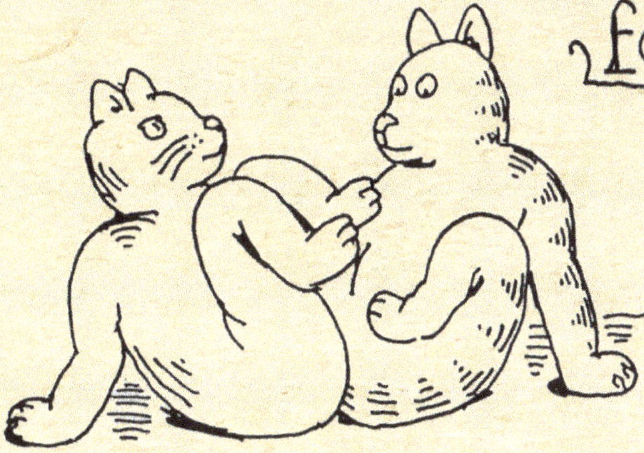

BANDHURA - THE CURVED KNOT.

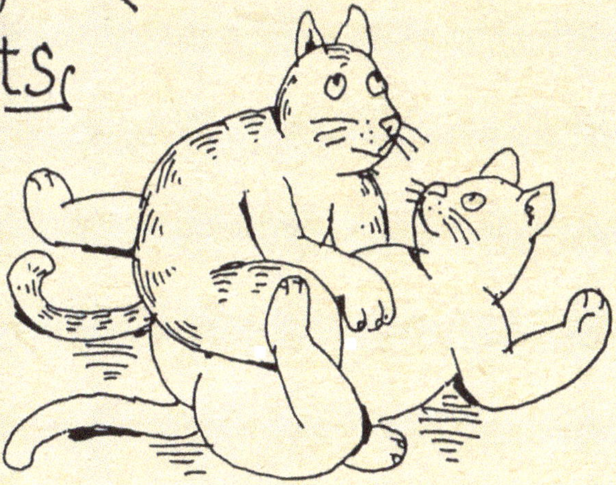

THE CONCH.

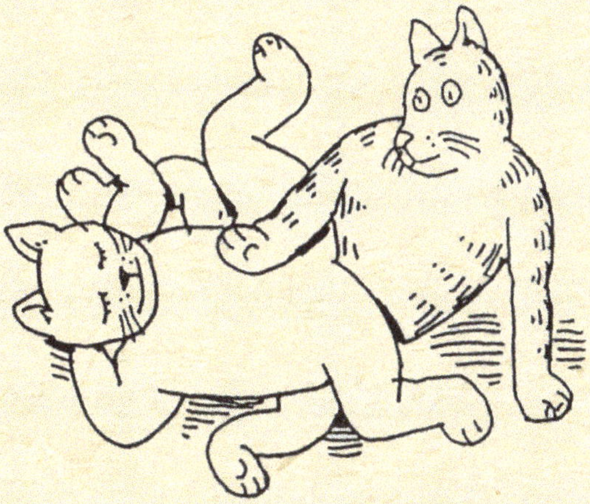

THE COBRA.

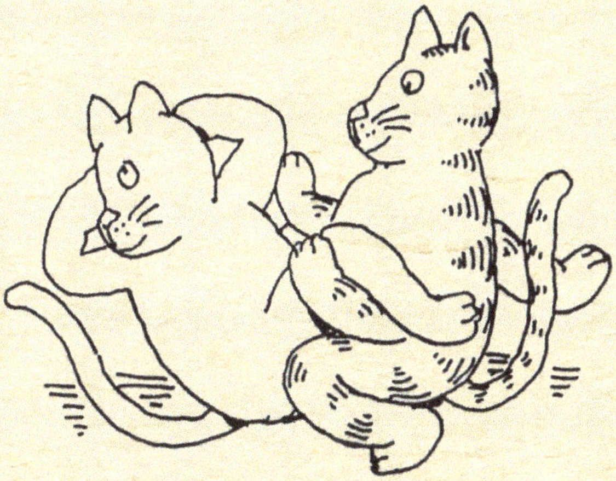

PRENKHA - THE SWING

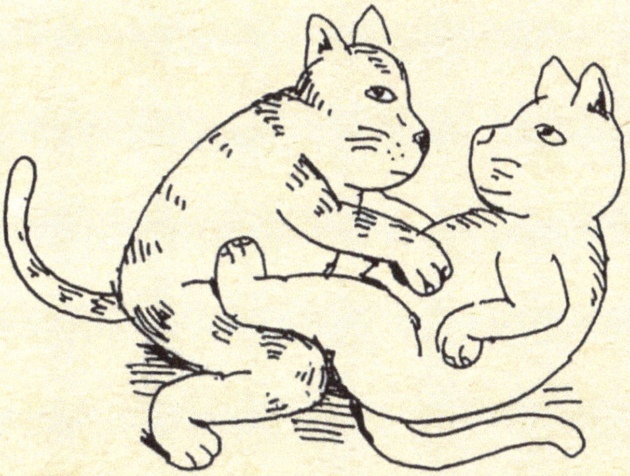

VIJHIMBITAKA – THE AWNING.

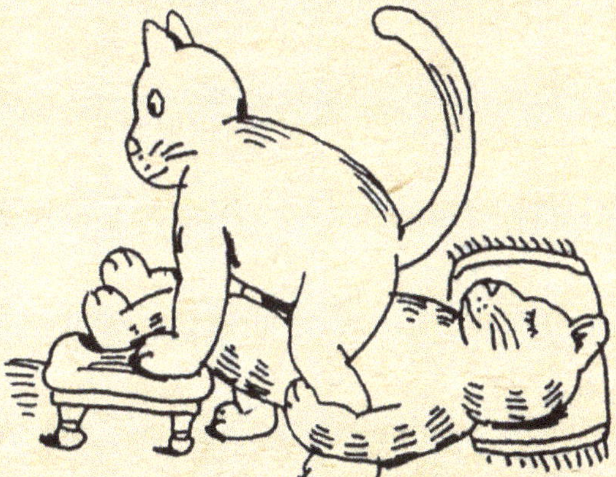

VIPARITAKA (REVERSED).

"MY GOAL IS SIMPLE. ALL I WANT TO DO IS GET KIDS TO LOVE READING."

—JAMES PATTERSON

"[Patterson's] young-adult series have won him a new generation of fans."

—*PEOPLE* magazine

"Patterson has made getting children to read his passion."

—*NIGHTLINE*

"[Patterson's] a versatile storyteller who is as adept at writing children's books as taut adult thrillers."

—THE *TODAY* SHOW

"[Patterson's] fast-paced plots are well suited to reluctant readers."

—*NEW YORK TIMES*

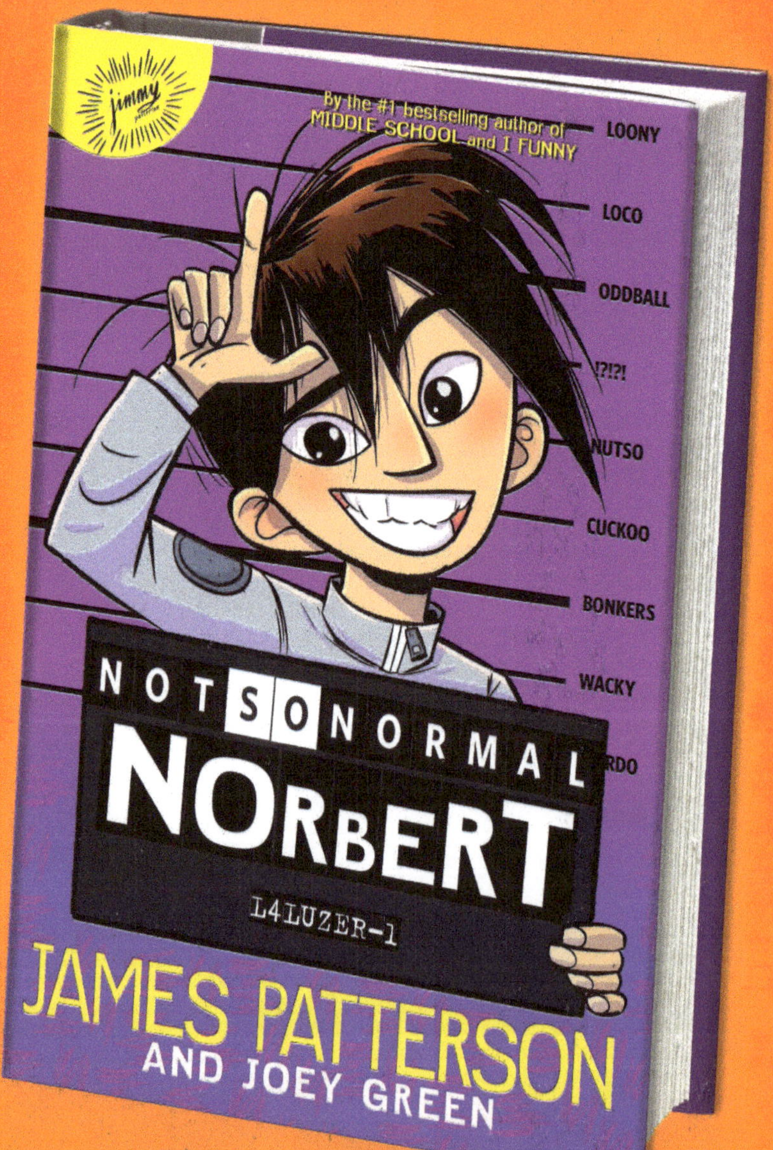

By the #1 bestselling author of
MIDDLE SCHOOL and I FUNNY
LOONY
LOCO
ODDBALL
!?!?!
NUTSO
CUCKOO
BONKERS
WACKY
NOT SO NORMAL
NORBERT
L4LUZER-1
JAMES PATTERSON
AND JOEY GREEN

THERE IS NO SUCH THING AS A KID WHO HATES TO READ. THERE ARE KIDS WHO LOVE TO READ AND KIDS WHO ARE READING THE WRONG BOOKS.

LITTLE, BROWN AND COMPANY

Available in hardcover, ebook and audio

OUR BACK PAGES

WHAT AM I DOING HERE?

Our Intrepid Traveler bumps his head on the ceiling of the world • By Mike Reiss

I meet the Lama of Lynchburg, the Buddha of Bourbon country.

Over the Hills and Fart Away

My plane was flying into Lukla, better known by pilots across the globe as "The World's Most Dangerous Airport." It deserved the title — I've been to fashion shows with longer runways. "We've safely landed in Nepal," announced the captain, unable to hide his relief. "Please set your watches back forty-five minutes." Forty-five minutes? This was going to be a weird place.

The weirdness began instantly, when I visited a large Buddhist temple and met their High Lama. A wizened man in red robes and long white beard, he certainly looked the part. And then he opened his mouth. "Ah betcha wanna take mah picture," he said in a Tennessee twang. "Jes' make sure you don't steal mah soul. Hey-hey!" He dressed like Dalai Lama but talked like Dolly Parton. Clearly, decades ago, he'd been a hippie hiking through Nepal, found God, and never left.

Nepal has been a haven for hippies, aging hippies, and recovering hippies since the Sixties. And why not? The entire country is like one big commune — it's as if, after all the bands left Woodstock, the half-million spectators stayed behind and declared it the Sovereign Kingdom of Groovy. Also, like Woodstock, there's ankle-deep mud everywhere you go. The Nepalese people, young and old, even dress like hippies in colorful, mismatched outfits: paisley scarves, plaid shirts, day-glo knit caps and Scooby-Doo pajama pants. Everyone looks like they got dressed in a thrift shop during a blackout.

In keeping with the hippie theme, freak flags are flying everywhere — strings of multi-colored pennants hang all over Nepal, zigzagging through forests, across chasms, up one side of the Himalayas and down the other. While it's very beautiful, I wish they'd strung up fewer prayer flags and more power lines.

Electric power here is spotty; however, every hotel has a sign announcing FREE WI-FI. None of them have wi-fi, but they've all got the sign. I had booked a room with a king-size bed, but they gave me two cots instead. "Same same but different," the clerk told me. This is the Nepali answer to everything. Cats and dogs? Same same but different. Freight trains and French fries? Same same but different.

Nepal is a tiny country packed with towering mountains. If it were flattened out, it would be the size of Africa, according to a fact I just made up. (With these mountains come constant landslides. As a result, bulldozer drivers are like rock stars here. When they come to town, farmers offer up their daughters for plowing.) It was one of these mountains that had drawn me here: Everest. It's not sexy like the Matterhorn or lyrical like Mt. Fuji. It's just tall and useless, a Yao Ming in the off-season. Beyond that, Everest is not much to look at: a plain white triangle, with all the grandeur and majesty of the corner of an envelope. And although it's the biggest thing on earth, it's nearly impossible to find — you can't even see Everest from Everest Base Camp! It's tucked deep in the Himalayas, so you have to climb another, better-looking mountain just to catch a glimpse of it. I was told it would be a four-hour trek. "Trek", I believe, is derived from the Yiddish word "dreck" meaning "a hike that's too awful to call it a hike.". (NOTE: 90% of what they call "hikes" are actually treks.)

I had an American friend named Wilson who helped set up the outing. He'd been here fifteen years, and gone Nepali nutso: he'd become a frantic mix of Dennis Hopper and Daffy Duck. And he claimed to speak the local language: "My friend-a here, he's-a want-a see Mount Everest." This was not Nepali, it was Jar Jar Binks English. "He's-a need a big walking stick much-much." A walking stick is a tool used by hikers. It provides the support and balance you

MIKE REISS is Intrepid Traveler for *The American Bystander*.

need when carrying an ungainly six-foot piece of wood. He made me spend fifty bucks on a stick to navigate a forest full of free sticks.

Wilson also hired a sherpa to guide me, and as the man approached, I had an epiphany. The sights of Nepal are stunning, but the sounds and smells of the place are largely farts. There are thirty million Nepalis, and at any given moment, a third of them are in mid-fart. I blame it on a toxic combination of high altitude living and high-fiber diet. It gives a new interpretation to those paintings of Buddha (who was born in Nepal), fat and smiling, floating atop a cushion of green smoke.

I'm no fan of cheap flatulence jokes, and would let the subject pass (hey-hey!), except that it was a key part of the journey. As I followed my sherpa up the steep mountain trail, he farted in my face with every step. Then, mercifully, he zoomed far off ahead of me, like a methane-fueled missile. His job as a sherpa was to guide me, and 30 minutes into our four-hour climb, he had ceased sherping. I was lost in a forest on a mountain in the weirdest country on earth. Invoking the name of my favorite Thai island, I said "Phuket!" I tossed aside my walking stick, greatly improving my mobility, and tried to find my way out.

And that's when I had Epiphany Number Two (hey-hey!): follow the cow dung. Cows come into the forest to graze, but they always return to their barns, pooping all the way. And any path a half-ton of hamburger could manage also worked for me. Yes, I followed farts into the forest and manure out of it. This was my vacation.

I came to an old logging road and followed its gentle slope up the mountain. The trip was peaceful, bucolic, and scenic. And I saw something I hadn't seen all morning: Nepalis. They knew better than to hike up a trail when they had a perfectly good road. I was greeted at every farmhouse with a cheerful "Namaste." I was at peace. The trek had become a hike.

I reached the mountaintop a few hours later. Shortly thereafter, my guide arrived. "How did you get here?" I asked.

"I followed you," he said. The sherpa had become the sherpee.

Later I found out he wasn't even a real sherpa. Wilson, in his fractured English, had mistakenly hired a guy named Sherpa — it's a very common surname in Nepal.

It's as if I needed a plumber and he brought in Christopher Plummer. Same same but different.

Mr. Sherpa and I looked at each other, wondering what the hell we were doing up there. And then, just for a moment, the clouds parted, and we caught a glimpse of Everest. It was a crooked baby tooth of a mountain, a pimple on the nose of the Himalayas. It looked like a yogurt-covered raisin. But I'd seen it.

And suddenly I realized why I'd made this trip. The same reason men have always climbed mountains.

Because we're idiots. **B**

D. WATSON

OUR BACK PAGES

P.S. MUELLER THINKS LIKE THIS

The cartoonist/broadcaster/writer is always walking around, looking at stuff • By P.S. Mueller

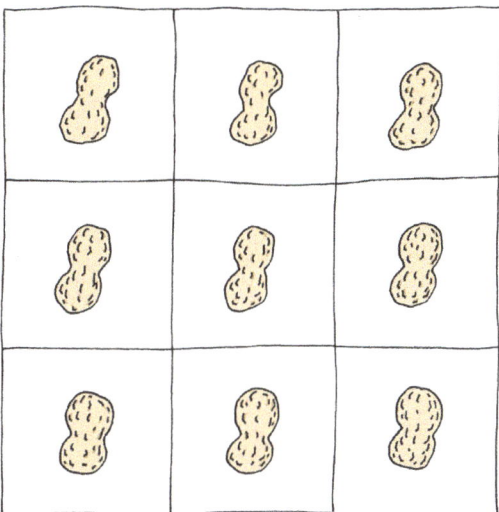

TABLE OF THE ELEPHANTS

Unreckoned Plumbing

Tweeting and tweeting at his beckoning realm
The whistle cannot know the whistler;
Bling stops and starts; the pucker's full of mold;
Weird monarchy has goosed this upskirt world,
The hair-thinned wide has goosed, and you know how
The pedophilic half-wit prince got crowned;
His grace is all conniption, while that face
Is full of blasting cap immensity.

Surely some tiny fingers make his hand;
Surely Unreckoned Plumbing is his brand.
Unreckoned Plumbing! Barely as tweets are tapped
When a huge typo and a textual nightmare
Troubles the hype: somewhere in crumbs of his dessert
A shape with a liar's body and as big as a van,
A look dull and pennyless as his fun,
Is heaving low thighs, and while he's at it
Lurk Maddows and indigent dessert turds.
He's having chops again; but we now know
That every century some phoney creep
A sexed up nightmare with a lopside noodle,
Is real bad beef, all sour round its ass,
Grouches toward porcelain to give birth.

P.S. MUELLER is Staff Liar of *The American Bystander*.

News From The World Of Apes

Like us, apes have been evolving, biding their time, for a million years. A recent evolutionary leap has clued them in on the secret of fire, smart phones, and something we don't have: time travel. My pal Larry is an ape who slides easily between millennia, past and future.

Lately, Larry has been working in 3027, where he says bananas and leaves are free and everybody types with their feet in gleaming office structures floating high and out of sight. His job there involves Time Interface Billing, where he oversees phone bills precisely dispersed, locally addressed, and mailed throughout the centuries. The money beats the living hell out of bananas, or so Larry claims.

But Larry's family has been stuck here in 2018. In fact, he lives next door with his wife and kids. You should see the tire swing he made for himself and all those sticks he hands out to the little ones every Friday afternoon after he peels off his Time Suit. He says he would move everybody to 3027 if it weren't for the mandatory body shaving. That's right, Larry is a completely hairless ape — business attire of the future requires totally nudity. In his line of work, however, neckties are always worn.

Lately, my blacksmith job has been taking a toll — repetitive motion problems and all that, and I asked Larry if maybe I, too, could travel to the future for one of those low-inpact high-paying jobs. But Larry grew evasive and put me off. Eventually, he loosened up over drinks in his multi-media ape cave and told me that humans didn't travel well through time. It was something about the special suit and how it couldn't be calibrated to accommodate for our peculiar fingers and toes. Plus, it reverse engineers us into shrew-like pre-simian dwarf monkeys, good for nothing except data entry. And once there, we dare not attempt to reproduce because no one in 3027 likes monsters with business models of their own.

Last week Larry and his family made the jump. The whole neighborhood showed up at their semi-official shaving party. We wished them all the best as they left behind only an empty house and a heap of weird-looking shoes.

To this day I haven't received another phone bill.

Jamming the Sun-Gods

It has long been known that in ancient Egypt dead rich people were mummified. Their brains were slid out through their patrician noses with special implements known as claw-snaggers. Organs were placed in sacred jars and preserved — using the same process employed by millions of grandmothers, hell bent on bringing stewed immortality to persimmons. Countless jars of this peculiar jam have in turn been handed down through endless unbroken tracts of time, shoved into attics and cellars, or left to

an uncertain eternity in storage lockers around the world.

Now the British, known to experiment on anything, have discovered that a single spoonful of your great great great great great great Aunt Granny's pectin-free persimmon jam will restore a pharoah to life. These dessicated corpses will regenerate new viscera and everything when nourished with the sticky orange goo.

This new knowledge came to London Egyptologist Jared Luftwither, the 46th Baron of Treacleshire, when he idly opened a clay vessel containing a long-departed matron's persimmon preserve and set it next to the gauze-wrapped crumble of Ammahosidestep Jr. To the scientist's great surprise, the monarch's form heaved a soul-shattering sigh, his parrot-like tongue snatching precious fruity molecules from the dry laboratory air.

"Why not give him a full dollop?" Luftwither wondered aloud. The newly revived mummy whimpered for more—and several large glasses of Lipton instant iced tea.

In a thrice, as people like Baron Luftwither tend to say, the ancient ruler had returned to his original self, looking for all the world like a cross between one of those guys on Lost and another one of those guys on Lost. Fortunately, the museum had a large supply of caftans in storage, and soon Ammahosidestep was striding about the place as if he owned it. He also made a point of finishing the unspeakable preserve which conferred amazing intellectual powers, especially the ability to absorb modern English.

This previously inert parcel of human jerky demanded more jam for his brethren, stored or displayed throughout the museum's Egyptology section. The Baron quickly called for his son to bring whatever he might find at the manor, even if he had to pilfer from the croft and laird. And before long, every intact former sun-god was up and about, speaking perfect English and demanding their gold and jewels. At this point the Baron had had enough and told them he would do no more than properly attire them in the garments of our time, allow each a stipend, and send them forth into a new and unimaginable world to make their own ways.

Today the London Museum is a threadbare place, looted of its untold wealth. Captains of industry and information began mysteriously disappearing a year ago, suddenly replaced by thin, tan, dark-haired majority stockholders. Trade in persimmons has surged. And Baron Jared Luftwither lies in a secret chamber, dried as a craisin and wrapped like a crowded tamale, as he brainlessly dreams of godawful persimmon jam. B

"Remember to be home on time. We're having an orgy with the Steins."

CHUNK-STYLE NUGGETS

...to briefly distract you from the inevitable • ***By Steve Young***

Positions Open — Please Inquire

- Alphabet soup proofreader
- Long Tall Sally measurer
- Drywall wetter
- Glacial moraine vs. glacial till difference explainer
- Abattoir hostess
- Crinkle-cut fries to potato reassembler
- Parking garage chaplain
- Bagpipe saboteur
- Replacement pen cartridge reviewer

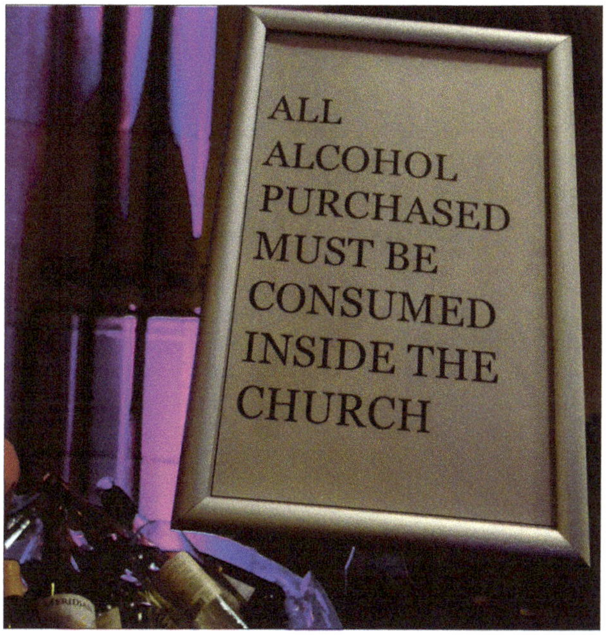
ALL
ALCOHOL
PURCHASED
MUST BE
CONSUMED
INSIDE THE
CHURCH

We're Sorry to See You Go!

Reason for unsubscribing from our company's emails:

☐ no longer interested in company's products
☐ too many emails from company
☐ did not intend to subscribe to these emails
☐ expect my email account to be hacked soon and don't want hackers to get special deals they don't deserve
☐ want you to feel a little taste of the abandonment that I constantly struggle with, so you'll understand what I'm going through
☐ sometimes just like to get wasted and go on the computer and unsubscribe from stuff
☐ it's a weird sexual fetish. Really. Google it
☐ enjoy responding to "why are you unsubscribing" surveys
☐ maybe not everything has a reason. Maybe sometimes things just happen
☐ so I can resubscribe and have everything feel new and exciting again

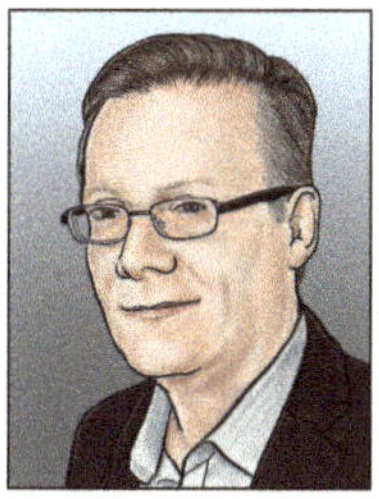

STEVE YOUNG (@pantssteve) is Oracle for *The American Bystander.*

An Open Letter To The Anonymous New Hampshire $560 Million Powerball Winner

My Dearest Darling Anonymous,

I have been working up the courage to write to you for some time — yes, long before you were in the news due to your lottery win and your fight to keep your identity secret. Your principled battle inspired me all the more, and I can remain silent no longer!

Special lady, I have loved you from afar for many years. This has been difficult at times, since your identity is unknown to me, but please understand that even without knowing your name or surely gorgeous face, I have felt my affection for you growing with fond fevered intensity. Dare I hope that you have felt the same for me? (Yes...?)

I imagine you wished to remain anonymous so you wouldn't be hounded by opportunists. I want you to know that your vast financial windfall means nothing to me. It is you that I have always loved! You can safely set aside your paranoia re: me being after your money! Though I'm curious, did you take the lump sum or the annual payments? Not really important. But we can talk about it when we finally meet and are basking in our eternal bliss.

Please get in touch as soon as possible so that we may enjoy the luxurious life together that fate has decreed for us, my love, my own adored lucky winner! Also, please send a recent photo so I can see what I'm getting myself into.

Product Names I Pitched When I Very Briefly Worked For An Abacus Company

Clicky Bead-A-Tron
Slide N' Go Numberzz
Ye Olde Amish Computer
ABBA-cus (special tie-in with music group ABBA)

Attention, guy with the pepper grinder:

Here's a list of when I DO want fresh ground pepper, and when I DON'T want fresh ground pepper:

- pasta dish at restaurant: YES
- reading from Torah scroll: NO
- performing abdominal surgery: YES
- assembling delicate equipment in NASA clean room: NO

- open casket funeral of friend or relative: NO
- Caesar salad at restaurant: YES
- holding newborn baby: NO
- sexual intercourse: YES, JUST A LITTLE
- giant bowl of fresh ground pepper at restaurant: YES, JUST A LITTLE

Take the Cinnamon Challenge!

Shoot video of yourself reacting as a friend dumps a bucket of cinnamon on you! It somehow raises money for charity!

Ways I'm Keeping Quite Busy

- Calling restaurants whose claims of "world famous" chili aren't borne out by my research, urging them to revise the wording of their menus
- Checking the accuracy of my stopwatch against my other stopwatch
- Taking the personality quiz in the new issue of *Lawn Mower Engine Enthusiast*: Are You A "Briggs" Or A "Stratton"?
- Entering plausible numbers into the FedEx tracking site
- In case the SARS virus ever comes back, working on SARS jokes (example: something about self-driving SARS)
- Monitoring the progress of random FedEx shipments I've happened to find on their tracking site
- Every few minutes, going to the fridge to re-shake my bottle of oil and vinegar dressing
- Trying to memorize pi out to five digits

Anatomy Update

*Septum, sternum, perineum
I have all three, but rarely see 'em*

Some Of My Burlesque Personae That Have Failed To Catch On

Cat Dander
Shaker Heights
Yelp Review

Movie Fun Fact!

In foreign releases of *Die Hard*, the line "Yippee-ki-yay, motherfucker" was translated as "Yippee-ki-yay, incest participant."

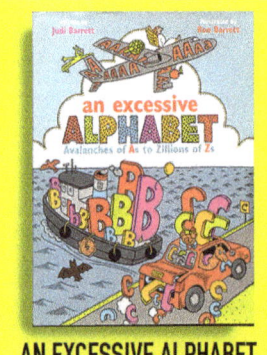

AN EXCESSIVE ALPHABET
Avalanches of As to Zillions of Zs
from the *Cloudy With a Chance of Meatballs* team
A fine book now available at fine booksellers

OUR BACK PAGES

KNOW YOUR BYSTANDERS

We asked. **Laurie Rosenwald** *answered.*

Laurie's self-portrait, Summer 2018.

I love artists. They manage to be interesting without being terrifying, no mean feat in our current era. I would happily live under a government staffed entirely by artists. Sure, some things would suffer — the Fed — but the money would look awesome, and our international reputation would improve immensely. "Are those American bombers?" "Yeah, they're dropping a bunch of old TVs filled with tampons and pig urine." "Derivative."

In this imagined future, I nominate Laurie Rosenwald for President. There would be sex scandals, nobody's denying that, but her State of the Union addresses would be must-watch TV. And what an inauguration! People would be stumbling around blind for weeks. "Mr. Secretary, the Chinese called about the trade deal again." "Could you please not talk so loud?"

I provided Laurie with a selection of sixty questions, and she answered the ones that struck a spark. — Ed.

NAME: **Laurie Rosenwald**
PROFESSION: *Painter, designer*
LIVES IN: *Manhattan, New York*
NOTABLE PROJECTS: All The Wrong People Have Self-Esteem, New York Diary, David's Diary.

Is there anything interesting about your family?
Yes. Julius Rosenwald, my great-grandfather, ran Sears, and created the Rosenwald Fund, which built over 5000 schools for African-Americans in the Jim Crow South. It also supported artists like Gordon Parks Jr., Katherine Dunham, Marian Anderson, Ralph Ellison, Langston Hughes, and Maya Angelou. It was actually Julius Rosenwald, not Dale Carnegie, who first said, "When life gives you lemons, make lemonade."

And it was Laurie Rosenwald who first said, "When life gives you lemons, just be glad it didn't give you herpes."

If you didn't have to sleep, what would you do with the extra time?
Add it onto the end, or possibly the middle.

What's your favorite piece of clothing, past or present?
I've been dressing like an elderly French pirate clown since childhood. If not attending a state funeral, I'm in red and white stripes, red Kangol flat cap and U.S. Navy "Cracker Jack" bell-bottoms. I shop by typing "wide stripe," "1970's NWOT" or "red white blue" into eBay, with a 25 dollar limit, and hoping for the best. Where's RosenWaldo? Right here.

What place would you most like to visit?
The fabulous oyster beds of Staten Island, circa 1900.

What fictional place would you most like to visit?
Villa Villekulla, or Mumindalen.

What job do you think you'd be great at?
"Job?" I pride myself on being a professional amateur and dilettante. I love what I do and it has never been for the money. That said, I would dearly love some money, please.

If you had unlimited funds to build a house that you would live in for the rest of your life, what would the house be like?
Where I live now except it's also a seaworthy boat, with more windows. My apartment is very colorful and beautiful. I have a blue floor.

What's your favorite drink?
The bullshot, Noël Coward's favorite. It has meat in it.
  1/2 teaspoon Worcestershire sauce
  1/8 teaspoon celery salt
  1/4 cup vodka
  3/4 cup chilled double-rich beef broth
  lime wedge, ice cubes
Mix worcestershire and salt in glass. add ice cubes. pour vodka and broth over. garnish with lime.

What state or country do you never want to go back to?
Adolescence. and Nebraska.

What was your most notable pet?
Porky, the white rabbit I stole from the lab at Ortho Pharmaceuticals on a class trip in 1971.

What are you interested in that most people haven't heard of?

America's LIVE Japanese gameshow

BATSU!

Now Playing: New York City & Chicago
Shows Tues-Sat • Tickets: www.batsulive.com
"Hilarious, strange and kind of sick" — Thrillist

International Waters
A comedy quiz show where land laws don't apply.
a podcast from maximumfun.org

Cultural analysis. Drama. Feats of strength. Spandex.
A weekly podcast about professional wrestling.
From maximumfun.org

A Chartered, non-profit body established in 1972, with the aim of aiding in the study and perpetuation of heraldry in the United States and abroad.
VISIT OUR WEBSITE
AMERICANCOLLEGEOFHERALDRY.ORG

Encaustic painting (hot beeswax) and its ancient and exhausting chemistry. i also make milk paint — Amazon thinks I'm a unibomber because I order borax and calcium carbonate. My paintings will last 3000 years, like 'em or not.

How do you relax after a hard day of work?
I watch *The Windsors* on Netflix. And *University Challenge*, *Only Connect* and *Q.I.* on YouTube. Also I like to get drunk. Especially on a boat. If you can read this, meet me for a drink, right now.

What's worth spending more on to get the best?
Cadmium red. Also cadmium yellow, etc.

What is something that a ton of people are obsessed with but you just don't get the point of?
Pornography.

What are you most looking forward to?
I have four books in the works — I look forward to their publication. Two of them are new — my humorous memoir, and *Mistakes On Purpose: The Book*. And I plan to redo my earlier children's book, and my New York notebook (both of which are available on Amazon).

But that's not all I'm looking forward to: I want to have a solo painting show at Luxembourg & Dayan Gallery. And do stand-up again. But not at the same time. They'd hate that.

Where is the most interesting place you've been?
First place: New York. I need it like the turkey needs the axe. And I've lived in Gothenburg, Sweden, on and off since 1999. I love it because it is *not* interesting. Second and third most-interesting places: a Venetian jail, and my aunt Judy's shoe closet.

What fad or trend do you hope comes back?
Smocking. Patent leather. Salt. And flirtation.

What's the title of your autobiography?
Sensible Underpants: Confessions of an Unrepentant Bikesexual and Occasional Swede. I've been working on it for 30 years. Don't know if I should self-publish it or not.

What one thing do you really want but can't afford?
A social media guru (see above).

What is the most impressive thing you know how to do?
I am the iron chef of encaustic! It's like trying to build a city out of Vaseline. Also, I speak Swedish. I know where the umlauts go. And I teach a super popular and fun workshop called "How to Make Mistakes on Purpose" all over the world. See more at www.mistakesonpurpose.com.

What was the best compliment you've

"...and that's *how* you find the G-spot."

received?
David Sedaris said, "Laurie's voice is fresh sounding, funny, and completely her own. She has a great story, and I'm behind her 100%." David is a wonderful man, and sublimely funny. We did an animated app together: David's Diary.
If you were the only human left on Earth, what would you do?
You mean I'm not?
What did you think you would grow out of but haven't?
Stripes, outsiderness.
Name something you'll never do again.
Exercise.
What do you spend the most time thinking about?
The futility of comparison. Also, I compare.

In 2010, author Fay Weldon was interviewed on the BBC's *Desert Island Discs*.

FW: I find it difficult to live by my principles.
DID: Do you try?
FW: No.

What's the best thing you got from your parents?
Independence.

And it wasn't them, it was Julius. At 25, in 1981, I blasted my way into the Rosenwald Trust, and bought myself a 2000-square-foot lower Manhattan loft, when this cost about as much as a chicken coop in Pikeville, Kentucky. I'd be homeless by now if not for that fact.
What is the luckiest thing that has happened to you?
My *Sopranos* cameo! I wrote about it for Medium; Google it.
What are you addicted to?
Grüner veltliner.
What is one of your favorite smells?
Pelargonium graveolens.
Fresh oysters. Melted butter. And arson.
If you had to change your name, what would you change it to?
Sir Pelham Grenville Rosenwald, or Giulietta Masina.

P.G. Wodehouse is my therapist.
When do you feel truly alive?
On the top of the ferry on way to Red Hook Painting Studio.
What do you want your epitaph to be?
"Unrepentant Bikesexual." I came out on Valentine's Day 2014 as a Bikesexual.

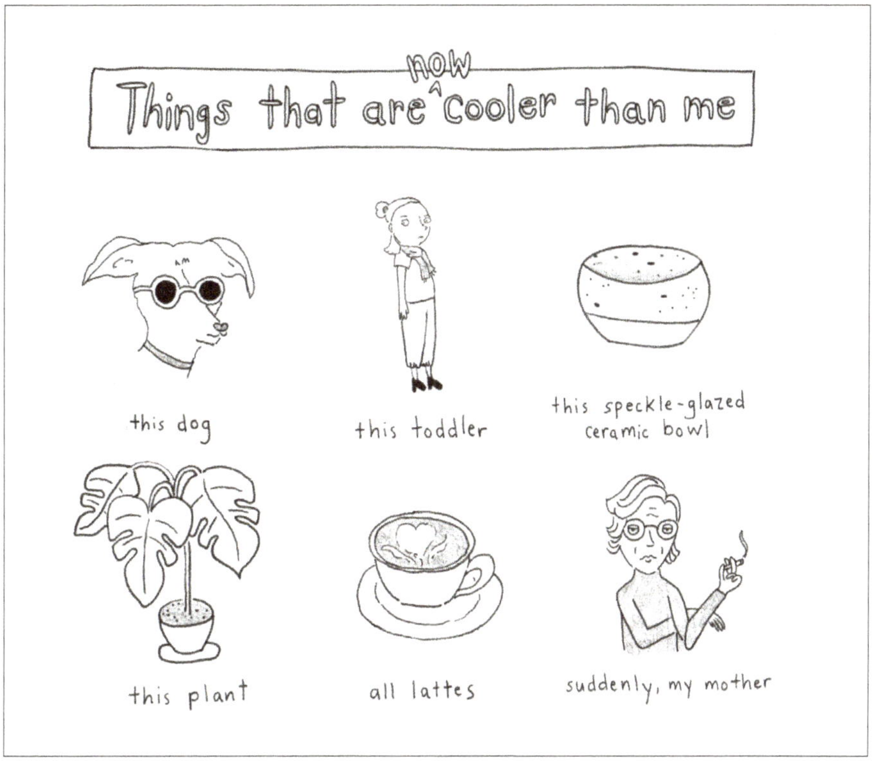

Things that are now cooler than me
this dog
this toddler
this speckle-glazed ceramic bowl
this plant
all lattes
suddenly, my mother

Yes, I am in love with my own bicycle. His name is Jopo. He is white. He is Finnish. I have an identical Jopo in Sweden. She/he/it is black. *Nota bene:* This love has yet to be celebrated. Lavish floral tributes should be addressed to my Hudson Street address.
Which of your scars has the most interesting story behind it?
I'm so glad you asked.

March 8, 1968: Big Brother and the Holding Company, Tim Buckley, Albert King live at the Fillmore East. I was thirteen. My "statutory rape" boyfriend Alan and I were walking east on 9th Street after this triple-bill. It was 3:00 a.m. From a few feet behind me, he picked up a metal rod and whacked a parking meter with it. Seventeen-year old boys do things like that. A smaller rod inside it zoomed out and shot me in the crotch. I fell, and a big pool of blood started to spread onto the street. We got on the subway (!) where I bled profusely all over the seats of the F train. I then bled even profuselier all over his uncle's apartment in Brooklyn, so we took a cab to the hospital where I got seventeen stitches. An inch to the left and I'm guessing my sex life would have been... different. My mother showed up at the hospital in trademark hysterics and an adorable pink flowered flannel nightgown by Lanz of Salzburg. The 8-inch scar is a neat Frankenstein seam, just where the torso meets the leg. I like it.
How would you like to be remembered?
This weekend. Call me!
What's the worst thing about getting older?
Closer to death, time moving too fast. I'm happy and want to savor it.
What do you do when you're not working?
I work. Work is more fun than fun.
If you could make one rule that everyone had to follow, what would it be?
No more cell phones. No more screens at all.
As you get older, what are you becoming more and more afraid of?
Not continuing that process *ad infinitum*.
What made you who you are today?
Beatnik parents, outrage, and New York City tap water.
For real this time: Name something you'll NEVER do again.
Complain on the Internet.
And what do you spend the most time thinking about?
Revenge!
What's your favorite holiday?
Valborgsmässoafton — a.k.a. Walpurgis Night — bonfires ward off evil spirits, but are also a festive way of getting rid of garden trash.

"If the normal stuff doesn't work, try reminding him how little he's saved compared to his peers."

What are your favorite books?
All the Wrong People Have Self-Esteem: An Inappropriate Book for Young Ladies* by Laurie Rosenwald.
The Decline and Fall of Practically Everybody by Will Cuppy
Up in the Old Hotel by Joseph Mitchell
And movies?
Sullivan's Travels by Preston Sturges, *Nights of Cabiria* by Fellini. I also love *Best in Show* by Christopher Guest.
What question would you want to ask someone, but never have the courage to ask?
Hello! Are you a single male heterosexual grownup man?
Got a nickname?
"Fussbudget."
How did you get it?
Colic, I think. Also in Sweden they call me *Snusmumriken* because I show up in summer and leave in winter, and have an epic struggle with Swedish beaurocracy. [*Snusmumriken* is a comic-strip character created by Finnish illustrator Tove Jansson.—Ed.]
Where were you born, and did that have any bearing on the person you've become?
Lenox Hill Hospital. I am a *rara avis*, a native Manhattanite, and, as such, an unapologetic snob. Bearing?
Well, I also had my hysterectomy there, so I guess so.
What's something you like to do the old-fashioned way?
Microwave, drive without seat belts.
Who or where would you haunt, if you were a ghost?
Le Corbusier's Chapelle Notre Dame du Haut, Ronchamp, France.
Who is / was your most interesting friend? Why?
Brenda Meredith. She'll be 100 on July 9th. When I observed that soon she'd be getting a Centenary Birthday Card from the Queen, her response was, "I'm Irish, you moron!" A weaver, a voracious reader, and a sublime letter writer, she was the "Dorm Mother" at my boarding school. We sing:

Mary had a little lamb
Its fleece was white as snow
She took it down to Pittsburgh
And now look at the damn thing.

She washes sheets in the bathtub, walks miles every day, and eats gruel. There's a book in her library called *Bitten by the Tarantula*. In it, there's not a single spider, and nobody ever gets bitten. She puts up a mean rhubarb lime jam, and pours a generous Jameson. I adore her.

CLASSIFIEDS

CLASSIFIEDS
DW

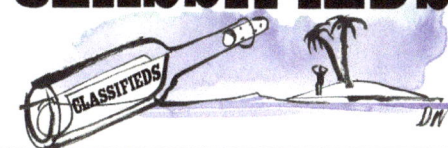

Interested in placing an ad? Email **classifieds@americanbystander.org**. The American Bystander reserves the right to reject any ad for any reason. We do not guarantee the quality of the items being sold, or the accuracy of the information provided. Ads are provided directly by sellers and are not verified.

NY/NJ COMEDIC ACTOR (40s-50s) available for auditions, readings, runs of any length. Resume and pictures: **DavidCNeal.com.**

IT CAME FROM THE BOTTOM SHELF!
Bottomshelfmovies.com is a film recommendation website focusing on forgotten classics, lesser-known gems, and odd-ball discoveries. It's the video collector's resource for movie reviews, weekly new release video picks, upcoming Blu-ray/DVD announcements, sales alerts, and other cinematic news. **Bottomshelfmovies.com**

JANE AUSTEN MUSIC Live music from the English Regency era for dancing or ambience in the San Francisco area. **jameslangdell@gmail.com**

DOPEY PODCAST
On the dark comedy of drug addiction.
www.dopeypodcast.com

FREAK CHIC STUDIOS
Jewelry, Art & Accoutrements for the Eclectic Heart.
www.freakchicstudios.com that's Dubyah Dubyah Dubyah dot FreakChicStudios dot See Oh Em. Twitter: @FreakChicStudio / Instagram: Freak Chic Studios / CB Callsign: Freak 2 The Chic. Be a good human and buy my stuff! Ten-four good buddy. Keep the bugs off your glass, and the bears off your... TAIL. Over and out.

THE MISADVENTURES OF LI'L DONNIE
Making Comics Great Again - Since 2017!
donniecrys.blogspot.com or follow "Donald Littles" (w/the asterisk pic) on the facebooks!

MYXPROJEKT
Free long-form Ambient Drone music. Great for relaxation, meditation, sleep. Nod off in style! Money back guarantee.
soundcloud.com/myxprojekt

COMEDIANS DEFYING GRAVITY
Comedians Defying Gravity highlights Chicago comedy: interviews, weekly events calendar and more. CDG is part of ChicagoNow, the Chicago Tribune Media Group's blogging network.**http://www.chicagonow.com/comedians-defying-gravity**

FULL OF WIT Funny poems and more. The Killing Tree by J.D. Smith can be found at most online sellers and at the link. **www.finishinglinepress.com/product/the-killing-tree-by-j-d-smith/**

PATSY O'BRIEN
Alt-Celtic Songwriter
Award-winning
NPR - featured.
www.patsyobrienswebsite.com

¿GOT TSUNAMIS?
Or some other annoyingly inconvenient problem at your local beach, port or 5-star resort? Give a shout, we'll sort you out!
http://eCoast.co.nz
jose@ecoast.co.nz
coastal dynamics • tsunamis • erosion • wave pools • surfing reefs • resorts • marinas • marine ecology
Solutions offered worldwide!
No beach out of reach!
The absurdity of advertising coastal engineering services to a bunch of writers and English majors isn't lost on me, but hey, I like the *Bystander*, so why not?

73
BYSTANDER

IN MEMORIAM:
Johnson Dunst, Jr., the deaf-mute imbecile who would bring our pre-separated trash and recyclables from the *Bystander* main offices to his religiously-excepted home incinerator just over the border in West Los Angeles, has died. Cause of death is believed to have been his correct knowledge that the life expectancy of a deaf-mute imbecile in AD 1732 was nine combined with his apparent, yet woefully misguided, belief that it is now AD 1732. Mr. Dunst, Jr., leaves no known next of kin, though he was known to smile for days whenever he successfully spelled the word "Klecko" in cursive. We wish him well.

TONY ISABELLA'S NEW BOOK
July 1963: A Pivotal Month in the Comic-Book Life of Tony Isabella Volume One. Obsessive nostalgic fun that inspired the career of the creator of Black Lightning, Misty Knight, Tigra and more. Available in print and digital formats from Amazon. Superman competes in the Interplanetary Olympics. The coming of the Avengers. Baby Huey's criminally negligent parents. Batman's super-powered dog. All this and so much more.

A (VERY GOOD) LITERARY AGENCY
Why, you must have stellar taste to be here. Are you also an extremely talented writer with a book idea? Let's talk. I'm Scott at **sgould@rlrassociates.net.**

www.kingcormack.com

DRUNK MONKEYS
America's finest "two women drinking odd liquors and talking about it" web series may be found at drunkmonkeyshow.com – only one 's', so it's Drunk Monkeys how?

CARTOON COMPANION
Cartooncompanion.com is a new website that discusses and rates the cartoons in *The New Yorker*. Co-hosts Max and Simon trade amusing observations and barbs with each new issue. *TNY* cartoonists have contributed to the site and praised it. Future posts will include interviews of the cartoonists and cartoons that *The New Yorker* rejected.
cartooncompanion.com

DO YOU READ THE OTHER A.B.?
Attempted Bloggery – An art blog about cartoons and other high culture. Published more or less daily since 2011.
attemptedbloggery.blogspot.com

CURRENCY CONVERSION BY MAIL
Convert unwieldy US folding money into small denominations! Send $10 bill get back $5 bill. Send *one* $20 bill receive a completely different bill. Never ask for change again! Do not delay!
Contact **@Specky4Eyes**
Serious inquiries only. No fatties.

YOU LIKE COMICS?
Sure you do! Who doesn't? (well, ignore those dweebs). For the finest in graphic storytelling, look ahead to 2019 for the premiere of BERGER BOOKS, created by the legendary Karen Berger, founding editor of VERTIGO! And the Art Director? The also legendary - except not so much - Richard Bruning! Top notch talent too. Watch for this revolutionary new imprint from indy pioneer Dark Horse.

THE COMIC TORAH
Stand-up comic Aaron Freeman and artist Sharon Rosenzweig reimagine the Torah with provocative humor and irreverent reverence. Each weekly portion gets a two-page spread. Like the original, the Comic Torah is not always suitable for children. "Hyperactive, colorful art brings the story to life." – Publisher's Weekly "If God was a comic artist, this is what She would have drawn." –Harold Ramis "Awesome!" – Alison Bechdel "Sacred & profane at the same time." – Paul Krassner
benyehudapress.com/ct or amzn.to/2npmv4V

STUDY CARTOONING and Illustration at the School of Visual Arts. We offer courses by Tom Motley, Steve Brodner, Carl Potts, and more! Fall courses are enrolling now.
www.sva.edu/continuing-education/illustration-and-cartooning

VISUAL REALIA
Photography, food and everything visual:
www.visualrealia.com.

CONFEDERACY OF DRONES POLITICAL SATIRE
Using humor to shoot down the political hypocrisy of mindless drones.
confederacyofdrones.com

LOTS OF NATIONAL LAMPOON
Lots of Nat Lamps for sale. Various monthly issues and Best Ofs. Mostly in pretty good condition. $4 each or more per issue plus postage. Email me with any particular issue you need at **bardinerman@aol.com.** Thank you and Godspeed.

COMIC STUDIES at the University of Wisconsin-Madison http://humanities.wisc.edu/research/borghesi-mellon-workshops/past-workshops/comics2

THE MAN WHO KILLED REALITY
The Prefab Messiahs explain all! Observe their hit animated musical video on the Youtubes:
youtube.com/prefabmessiahs

ALTERNATIVE MUSICALS

W	I	C	K	E	D		C	H	O		A	T	V	S
E	T	O	I	L	E		E	A	T		T	R	A	P
B	E	R	T	I	E		L	I	T		M	E	M	O
			H	A	M	I	L	T	O	N		A	P	T
T	A	N				N	O	I	S	E		S	I	T
E	C	O		E	S	T				E	N	U	R	E
A	T	T	A	C	H	E	D		A	D	O	R	E	D
		A	C	H	O	R	U	S	L	I	N	E		
E	L	L	I	O	T		E	C	O	N	O	M	I	C
N	A	L	D	I				R	E	G		A	D	A
A	T	T		N	A	O	M	I				P	A	R
M	E	H		G	O	D	S	P	E	L	L			
O	R	E	L		R	I	N		L	O	U	N	G	E
R	A	R	E		T	U	B		M	L	C	A	R	R
S	L	E	D		A	M	C		O	L	I	V	E	R

2018

TABLETOP TALK - a YouTube channel for gamers by gamers. We create raw tabletop gaming content by filming our games. No scripts, just gaming. www.youtube.com/user/TabletopTalk

TOONS BY STEV-O (by Steve McGinn). some cartoons I hope'll make ya laff! drawn fresh in ink & then posted every day - 7 days a week! look for us on Facebook and The Comx Box Syndicate.

THE AMERICAN VALUES CLUB Crossword (formerly the Onion AV Club Crossword): It's rude, it's clued, and you'll get used to it.
Subscribe at avxword.com.

Buy **THE LAFAYETTE CAMPAIGN** mybook.to/lafayettecampaign "Andrew Updegrove brings a rare combination of drama, satire and technical accuracy to his writing. The result is a book you can't put down that tells you things you might wish you didn't know." - Admiral James G. Stavridis, former NATO Supreme Allied Commander Europe

UNICORN BOOTY WANTS YOU ...to read some of the most outrageously fun news, pop culture, and opinions on the web! Unicorn Booty serves up original news, film, TV, art, sports, fashion, travel and other weird wonders from around the world. Check us out at **http://unicornbooty.com**.

THE NEW YORK REVIEW OF SCIENCE FICTION Reading Science Fiction Like It Matters for 28 Years. The first one's free! **http://www.nyrsf.com**

AN ILLUSTRATED ZARATHUSTRA Hilarity ensues as excerpts and epigrams from Nietzsche's timeless classic comes to life in this madcap comic-strip-style dub version. Embrace your Fate and read it online at: ScottMarshall.org

BOOKS, POSTCARDS, ORIGINAL art by Rick Geary, available exclusively at **www.rickgeary.com**. I also take commissions.

FREE LUNCH!! NO BALONEY! Attention all hungry cartoonists passing through Chicago: Contact Jonathan Plotkin Editorial Cartoonist & Illustrator Minister of Ways and Means NCIS Chicago Chapter Spontoonist@gmail.com spontoonist.com

COMICS WITH PROBLEMS All problems solved. The Internet's BEST archive of the world's WEIRDEST comic books. http://www.ep.tc/problems

HACKER HUMOR You need tech humor, I've got it. Jokes, pitches, consulting, articles, posts. 35+ years experience (in parents' basement). ✉ rob.warmowski@gmail.com

WANTED: MURDERER I'm looking for someone to kill me please, inquiries: @ZackBornstein on Twitter & Instagram

STRANGER THAN LIFE 250-page collection of single panel cartoons and strips from National Lampoon, The New Yorker, Playboy, Mother Jones and Arcade Comics by MK Brown. Available from Fantagraphics and Amazon. MK happy to inscribe. Contact at mkbrown88@hotmail.com

You can't make a website worth a damn.
But we can.
Contact us posthaste.
MerchantAndBlack.com

DELICIOUSLY SATISFYING CONTEMPORARY NOIR a persuasive Hollywood thriller, taut and gutsy debut novel with clean, brilliant writing. COLDWATER by Diana Gould. In all formats, wherever books are sold. (Support your local independent bookstore.) Or, http://amzn.to/2dJh1Kk

THE KILLING TREE Part funny. Part serious. Part cynical. All intelligent. J.D. Smith's fourth collection of poetry, from Finishing Line Press. Advance praise and ordering information available at: http://bit.ly/2ebGJuw

WRITING A BOOK? GETTING NOWHERE? Don't give up – get help (from me!). I'm a ghostwriter/writing coach who partners with you one-on-one to get your book done. Packages range from 45-minute "Copy Therapy" sessions to twelve-week intensive book coaching programs. For more info, go to copycoachlisa.com.

CLOWN NOIR James Finn Garner (*Politically Correct Bedtime Stories*) has a new mystery series for fans of noir, sideshow freaks and Americana. The "Rex Koko, Private Clown" thrillers have won Chicago Writers Association's Book of the Year TWICE! It's *Freaks* meets *The Maltese Falcon*. For info and samples, go to **rexkoko.com**, pally.

THE VIRTUAL MEMORIES SHOW What's the best books-art-comics-culture interview podcast you've never listened to? Discover The Virtual Memories Show at www.chimeraobscura.com/vm/podcast-archive

I LOVE MAKING BEET CHIPS I love it so much that if you come to my apartment I will make some for you. I am not, to my knowledge, a serial killer. @tinyrevolution

GEORGE BOOTH: cartoons, illustrations. Other services: grass fires stomped out and despots deterred. **929-210-0707**

HAVE WHAT IT TAKES TO BE A GOOBER DRIVER? Avoid World's Largest Peanuts envy. Navigate to offbeat tourist sights with the leaders for thirty years— RoadsideAmerica.com. Free e-subscription to Sightings. Easy sign-up. RoadsideAmerica.com/newsletter

SNOW ANGEL IS HERE! In the tradition of The Tick and Venture Brothers comes this all-new hilarious full-color graphic novel about SNOW ANGEL, the newest tween superhero! From American Bystander contributor and Eisner nominee **DAVID CHELSEA**, this massive Dark Horse comic is fun for all ages (except, oddly, 37)! Available at your local bookstore, or email **dchelsea@comcast.com** to learn how you can receive a signed copy! GUARANTEED MERMAID FREE!

YOUR ANDREW JACKSON $20s will soon be worthless! Use one to buy our non-award-winning, non-best-selling comedy anthology, **The Lowbrow Reader Reader**, available from Drag City Books. Or check out the The Lowbrow Reader zine itself, eminently purchasable at **lowbrowreader.com**.

VEGETARIANS EATING HAGGIS PIZZA Cosmic quarks! It's the Zen of Nimbus comic created by Michael Sloan. Nimbus, the celebrated immobile astronomer, is visited by a variety of repulsive creatures and events. Will they ever disturb his meditations? View the comic and blog, shop for Zen of Nimbus t-shirts and artwork:
www.zenofnimbus.com

EULOGIES WRITTEN ON DEMAND Need a touching tribute...*stat*? Semi-professional eulogist offers her services. Quick turnaround guaranteed; encomium completed while the body's still warm or it's free. Little knowledge of the deceased in question necessary. Email megan.koester@gmail.com for rates.

WELCOME TO DISTRACTIONLAND Too much time on your hands? Watch RANSACK RABBIT and other engaging animated entertainments. **Xeth Feinberg**, proprietor. As seen on the internet!
www.youtube.com/distractionland

UTILITY RIGHT FIELDER Available Also draws, writes. For more information contact Deerfield (Illinois) Little League. Or visit **kenkrimstein.com**.

THE NEW YORK TIMES BESTSELLING COLLECTION OF PAINTINGS AND STORIES FROM SOME OF THE WORLD'S MOST CHERISHED BOOKSTORES.

FOOTNOTES* from the WORLD'S GREATEST BOOKSTORES
BOB ECKSTEIN
Foreword by GARRISON KEILLOR
*True Tales and Lost Moments from Book Buyers, Booksellers, and Book Lovers
POTTER

AVAILABLE EVERYWHERE BOOKS ARE SOLD | BOBECKSTEIN.COM

INDEX TO THIS ISSUE

Stuff you might not have noticed • By Steve Young

Alimentary canal, goods transported by barge, 70
Belt buckle, way to show support for a company, team, or other interest while keeping your pants up, 90
Bessemer process of steel making, 109-112
    wonder if it helped Bessemer get laid, 112
Burlap, how long it would take for anyone to notice if the Wikipedia entry were vandalized, 4-5
    not saying anyone should do that, 4
    could be pretty funny though, 5
Colossus of Rhodes, David Copperfield made it disappear then couldn't bring it back, 128
Crossfit, 83-85
    Exercise Jesus got while carrying the cross, 83-84
Dagnabbit, usage in King James Bible, 40
Dr. Scholl, sadistic and unethical experiments on prisoners' feet during WWII, 68
Estimable, word often found on page 59, 59
Federal Witness Protection program, government protection for people who worked on the film *Witness*, 76
Funemployment rate, 70
    relationship to funflation, 71
Gavel, which part to hold, 51-54
Grape scissors, essential component of every well-bred person's emergency "go bag," 155
Gyroscope, baby's first word, 79
Illuminati, conspiracy to make right-on-red turns illegal at certain intersections, 119-130
I thought we had a shitload of twist ties in that drawer and now we don't seem to have any, 162-165
    possibility of intriguingly conceptual burglary, 164,
    might have used a whole bunch at once during a drunken blackout, 165
Kelp, 119-122
    stolen by a kelptomaniac, 121

parody of Beatles' movie made by oceanographers, 122
Loam, as yet no sexual fetishes related to, 80
Mashed potatoes, short for Mobile Army Surgical Hospitaled potatoes, 97
Mutually Assured Destruction, 175
    frequent 60's prom theme, 175
Narcissisted living, for the elderly egotist, 180
Nude beaches, awkwardness on D-Day, 169
Organized crime, Equal Opportunity Employer, 93-94
Possibility of it being over even before it's over, 241
    debate between Yogi Berra and Albert Einstein, 241-247
Pelvis, only part of body that contains the name of the King of Rock and Roll, 233-236
    What about the presleyneum, 235
    I think you're thinking of the perineum, 236
Politeness, futility of when dealing with aliens bent on eradicating mankind and taking the Earth's resources, 73
Protestant Reformation of the 16th century, 35-37
    direct mail campaign, 36
    insignia wear, 37
Quixotic, probably the name of some online business thing except it's probably Qxotic because that's how they do things these days, 9-10
    just checked and yup, 10
Ring of fire, burning, I fell into, 73-74
    OSHA investigation, 74
Scabrous, word which rarely comes up during wedding vows, 90
Self-adhesive stamps, still fun to lick, 204
Severe Tire Damage, not necessarily due to those spikes because correlation does not equal causation, 144
Theodicy, question of how a just God could allow misery and evil, 79-84

it's nothing personal, it's just business, 82
TOMOTUS, tomato of the United States, 212
Trail Mix, early Western movie star, 55-58
    No, that was Tom Mix, you idiot, 57
    I know, it was a joke, 58
    Sometimes with you it's hard to tell, 58
Unicycles, 17-19
    and Unitarians, 17
    mixture of envy and pity when observing someone riding one, 18
    off-road version with big knobby tires, 19
Unreliable narrator, receives bad Yelp reviews, 145
Vacuum cleaner bags, last-minute gift idea, 163
Vests, 150-154
    with sleeves, 153
    if they have sleeves then they're not vests, 153
    marriages destroyed by this argument, 154
Wassup, is it a rhetorical question or not, yo, 183
Where can I get one of those long springy poles used by pole vaulters, 28-30
    no, I don't want to be a pole vaulter, 30
    never mind what I want it for, 30
X-Acto, wonder if a rapper's ever rhymed it with *ex post facto*, 180
Yes, Virginia, there is a magical character whose existence calls into question all the physical laws of our universe, but you enjoy, it's probably fine, 206
Youthquake, often followed by devastating youthnami, 177
Zapruder, Abraham, nobody talks about whether his dresses were any good, 89-92
Z is a minor letter so please don't feel compelled to do a lot of Z words, 20
    or any, for that matter, 97.

CROSSWORD #5

BY MATT MATERA & ALAN GOLDBERG

ALTERNATIVE MUSICALS

If you run out of alternatives, the anxwer is on page 95

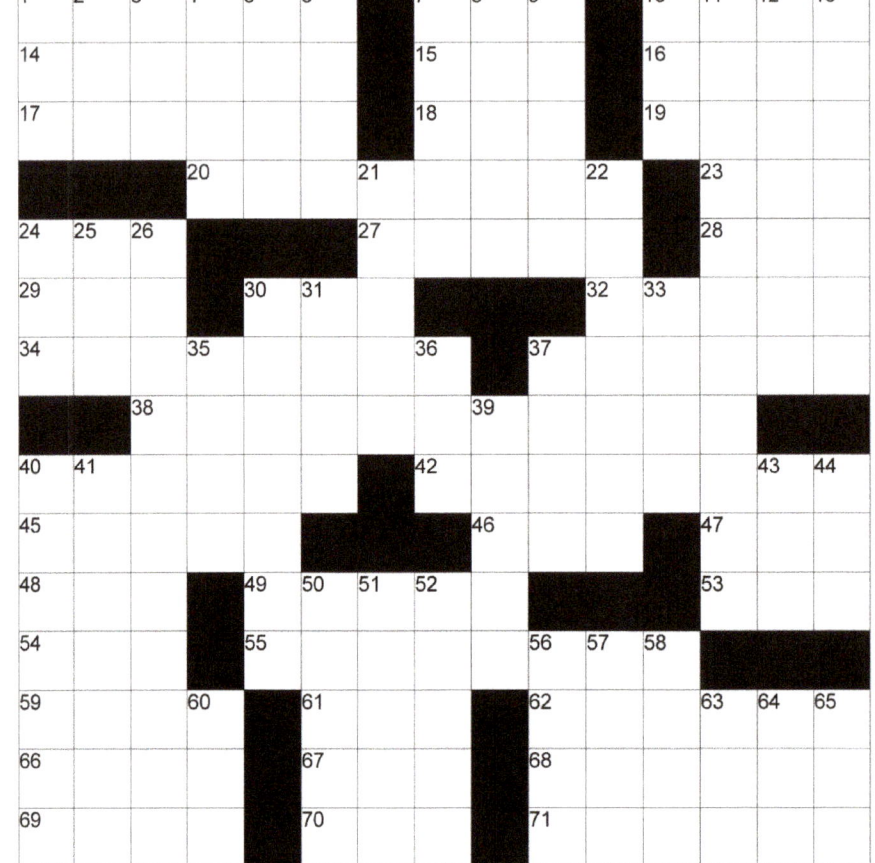

ACROSS
1. *"Candles: The Musical!"
7. *Harold & Kumar* actor John
10. They're not amphibious, so their name is a bit of a lie (*abbr.*)
14. Parisian night light
15. Absorb
16. Kisser
17. PGW's ____ Wooster
18. Extremely happening
19. "Didn't you get the ___?"
20. *"Ontario's Third-Largest City: A Jukebox Musical"
23. On the nose
24. Type of line skipped by a nudist
27. Peep on Easter, *e.g.*
28. Convene
29. Green Italian author?
30. Extreme suffix
32. Accustom
34. Unlike a stag party party?
37. Like Beyoncé or Mr. Rogers
38. *"La La La La La La: Live"
40. Mama Cass of Mamas & the Papas
42. Related to the dismal science
45. Silent actress Nita who appeared in a lost early Hitchcock
46. On the ___ (like, all the time)
47. First computer programmer Lovelace (the daughter of Lord Byron)
48. QB hopes one doesn't end in an INT
49. Biblical figure who was Ruth-less until her son Mahlon married?
53. If it's 5 for a miniature golf hole, well, we'd like to see that hole
54. [Shrug]
55. *"D-I-O-N-Y-S-U-S"
59. 1988 World Series MVP Hershiser
61. ___ Tin Tin
62. Lizard's locale
66. "Mooing"
67. Fateful locale for Jean-Paul Marat
68. Celtics standout who later unsuccessfully coached the team
69. What Jonas rides at end of *The Giver*
70. Network for *Halt and Catch Fire*
71. *"First Name from *JFK*"

DOWN
1. Shelob's creation
2. Rock finale?
3. ___ *anglais*
4. Peeps, archaically
5. Chris D'___ (*The Good Doctor* actor)
6. Judge
7. String instrument whose size was standardized in about 1750
8. L'Ouverture's home
9. Some palindromic men
10. Check point?
11. Chart not usually in a PowerPoint
12. One who might avoid a poker game with table stakes?
13. ___ dick (type of pudding)
21. Lay to rest
22. Crying out for
24. High-viscosity Texas beverage?
25. "How do I ___ so well?" (Ian McKellen line on *Extras*)
26. A few tacos short of a combo platter
30. Bouncing back quickly
31. Chance
33. One of seven thrown by Nolan Ryan
35. What burns Rainier Wolfcastle's eyes in a classic *Simpsons* scene
36. Word that can precede any cardinal direction
37. Soothing succulent
39. Disney Dollars or Itchy & Scratchy Money
40. What one does to become 37-Across
41. One of 15 in a miracle 2007 college football touchdown
43. Anti-lynching crusader ___ B. Wells
44. Fiesta that doesn't include a piñata game, for one
50. Principal artery
51. Hateration, more formally
52. Former TV home of Ronan Farrow
56. Muppet originally called Baby Monster
57. Idle aimlessly
58. Daughter of LBJ
60. Set the pace
63. Sat ___ (another name for GPS)
64. Doctoral program prereq
65. Prove that you're a human online? B

www.ingramcontent.com/pod-product-compliance
Lightning Source LLC
Chambersburg PA
CBHW061822290426
44110CB00027B/2956